AMAZING NORTHEAST

MANIPUR

AMAZING NORTHEAST

MANIPUR

Edited & Compiled by
Aribam Indubala Devi

Vij Books India Pvt. Ltd.
(Publishers, Dustributors & Importers)
4675-A, 21, Ansari Road, Darya Ganj,
New Delhi-110002

Published by
Vij Books India Pvt. Ltd.
(Publishers, Distributors & Importers)
4675-A, 21, Ansari Road, Darya Ganj,
New Delhi-110002
Phone: 91-11-65449971, 91-11-43596460
Fax: 91-11-47340674
E-mail: vijbooks@rediffmail.com

First Edition: 2010

ISBN: 978-93-80177-26-7

Contents

Preface

- -

In India, the Northeastern region is quite charming and interesting enough to be known about. Among the eight Northeastern States, Manipur is situated on the eastern frontier of India. It is bounded on east by Myanmar, on north by Naglaland, on west by Assam and on south by Mizoram and Myanmar. Manipur lies between 23.83N and 25.68N latitude and between 93.03 E and 94.78E longitude. It has an area of 22.327 sq km. Physically, Manipur comprises two parts — the hills and the valley. The valley is at the centre surrounded by hills on all sides. The hills cover about 9/10 of the total area of the State. Manipur Valley is about 790 metres above the sea level. The hill ranges are higher on north and gradually diminish in height as they reach southern part of Manipur. The valley itself slopes down towards south.

Manipur has a long and glorious history, since the beginning of the Christian era. The recorded history of kingship started from 33 AD, which marked the coronation of Pakhangba. After Pakhangba a series of kings ruled over the kingdom of Manipur. The independence and sovereignty of Manipur remained uninterrupted, until the Burmese invaded and occupied it for approximately seven years in the first quarter of 19th century (1819-1826). Then came the British parmaountcy in 1891. Manipur regained independence along with the rest of India in 1947. When the Constitution of India came into force on 26th January, 1950, Manipur became a Part C State under a Chief Commissioner in 1950 - 51, a Council of Advisors was introduced in 1957, which was replacedby a territorial Council of 30 elected and 2 nominated members. Later, in 1963 a Territorial Assembly of 30 elected and 3 nominated members was established under the Government of Union Territories Act, 1963. In December 1969 the Chief Commissioner was replaced by Lt. Governor. Manipur became a full-fledged State on 21st January, 1972, with a Legislative Assembly of 60 members of whom 19 are reserved for Scheduled Tribes and one for Scheduled Castes. The state is represented in Lok Sabha by two members and by one member in Rajya Sabha.

This small but comprehensive and compact book on this northeastern state, offers all information, within one cover. Hopefully, it would serve all those working on or interested in knowing about northeastern India, be they scholars, researchers, journalists, students or general readers. This is in fact, 'Knowledge in Nutshell'.

— Editor

Manipur

An Overview

Governor	:	Gurbachan Jagat
Chief Minister	:	O. Ibobi Singh
Speaker	:	Dr. Sapam Budhichandra Singh
Chief Secretary	:	D.S. Poonia
Capital	:	Imphal
High Court	:	Guwahati (Bench at Imphal)

Brief Description

Manipur, literally meaning the land of gems, is stretched between 23.80° to 25.68° North latitude and 93.03° to 94.78° East longitude, in the southeast corner of the Northeastern Region. Spread over an area of 22,327 sq km, Manipur comprises 8.52 per cent of the total area of the Northeastern Region and 0.67 per cent of Indian landmass. It is bounded on the north by Nagaland, on the east by Myanmar, on the south by the Chin Hills of Myanmar, and the Lushai Hills of Mizoram and Cachar Hills of Assam on the west. It shares a 352 km long international boundary with Myanmar.

After India's independence in 1947, the princely state of Manipur

Facts and Figures

- *Area :* 22,327 sq km (8.5% of area of North-East)

- *Geographical Location:* Situated between latitude 23.83°N to 25.68°N & longitude 93.03°E to 94.78°E

- *Capital:* Imphal

- *Population:* 22,93,896 (2001 Census) (6% of population of North-East)

- *Density of Population (per sq km):* 107 (National Figure: 324)

- *Population below Poverty Line:* 17.3% (National Figure: 27.5%)

- *Language: Manipuri*

Contd...

was merged with the Indian Union on October 15, 1949 and became a full-fledged state of India on 21 January 1972 after being upgraded from the status of a Union Territory. The state capital is located at Imphal.

Of the total area, about nine-tenths constitute the hills surrounding the remaining valley area. The state is divided into nine districts. Whereas the valley is divided into four districts, five districts constitute the hill area of the state. The forest cover accounts for 78.01 per cent of the state's geographical area.

According to Census 2001, Manipur with a total population of 23,88,634 constitutes 0.23 per cent of the population of India and 6.12 per cent of the population in the North-East. The state has a population density of 107 persons per sq km. Manipur is inhabited by three major ethnic groups — the Meiteis in the valley, and the Nagas and the Kuki-Chin tribes in the hills. The state is home to 33 recognised tribes. People are predominantly Mongoloid, and speak Tibeto-Burman languages. Manipuri language which is the mother-tongue of the Meitei people is the *lingua franca* of the state. The literacy rate in the state is 59.89 per cent.

In Manipur, agriculture contributes a major share to the State Domestic Product and provides employment to about 57.38 per cent of the total population. The state has a vast area of forests, covering as

- *Sex Ratio:* 978 females to 1,000 males (National figure: 933 females to 1,000 males)
- *Literacy Rate (%) (2007):* 76.5 (National Figure: 67.6%)
- *Birth Rate (2006):* 13.4 (National Figure: 23.1)
- *Death Rate (2006):* 4.5 (National Figure: 7.4)
- *Infant Mortality Rate (2007):* 12 (National Figure: 55)
- *Per Capita Income (in Rs.) (2006-07):* 22,495 (National Figure: Rs. 29,901)
- *Net State Domestic Product (NSDP) (Rs. in crore) (2007-08):* 5,044 (National Figure: 38,11,441)
- *Per Capita NSDP (2007-08):* Rs. 19,258 (National Figure: Rs. 33,283)
- *Per Capita GSDP (2004-05):* Rs. 16,299 (National Figure: Rs. 25,944)
- *No. of Villages:* 2,391 (as per 2001 Census)
- *No. of Towns:* 33 (as per 2001 Census)
- *State Bird:* Nongyeen
- *State Animal:* Sangai
- *State Flower:* Siroi Lily
- *State Tree:* Uningthou (Phoebe hainesiana)
- *State Fish:* Pengbe (Osteobrama Belangeri val.)
- *No. of Districts:* (09) Bishnupur, Chandel, Churachandpur, Imphal-East, Imphal-West, Senapati, Tamenglong, Thoubal, Ukhrul.

Contd...

much as 17.418 sq km, which forms about 78 per cent of the total geographical area of the State. The per capita Gross State Domestic Product (GSDP) in 2004-05 is rupees 16,299. The per capita Net State Domestic Product in 1999-2000 is rupees 11,370. The average annual growth rate between 1995-96 and 2004-05 has been 4.97 per cent. According to the Human Development Report 2001, Manipur ranks 9th in the human resource development index and 21st in the poverty index in India.

- *Major Towns:* Moreh, Churachandpur, Andra, Jiribam, Thoubal, Kakoching, Imphal, Ukhrul, Mao, Tamenglong
- *Major Crops:* Maize, Oil seeds, Pulses, Rice, Sugarcane, Wheat
- *Major Plantations:* Rubber, Coffee Major Fruits, vegetables & spices: Cabbage, Brinjal, Carrot, Cauliflower, Bean, Knolkhol, Potato, Pea, Radish, Tomato
- *Major Minerals:* Chromite, Limestone
- *Airport:* Tulihal (Imphal)

Underdevelopment, its alleged forcible merger with the Indian union and late grant of statehood has been seen as some of the reasons behind the rise of several insurgency movements in the state. Most of the tribes, inhabiting the hill areas of the state too have been represented by several outfits. In addition, the Naga insurgent outfits' demand for the inclusion of the hill districts of Manipur in the present day Nagaland has also impacted on the prospects of peace in Manipur.

Area, Population and Headquarters of Districts

S.No.	District	Area (sq km)	Population	Headquarters
1.	Senapati	3,271	2,83,621	Senapati
2.	Ukhrul	4,544	1,40,778	Ukhrul
3.	Chandel	3,313	1,18,327	Chandel
4.	Churachandpur	4,570	2,27,905	Churachandpur
5.	Tamenglong	4,391	1,11,499	Tamenglong
6.	Imphal (West)	519	4,44,382	Lamphel
7.	Imphal (East)	709	3,94,876	Porompat
8.	Thoubal	514	3,64,140	Thoubal
9.	Bishnupur	496	2,08,368	Bishnupur

[Based on Latest Official Data Available]

(*xii*)

Manipur

Outline Map

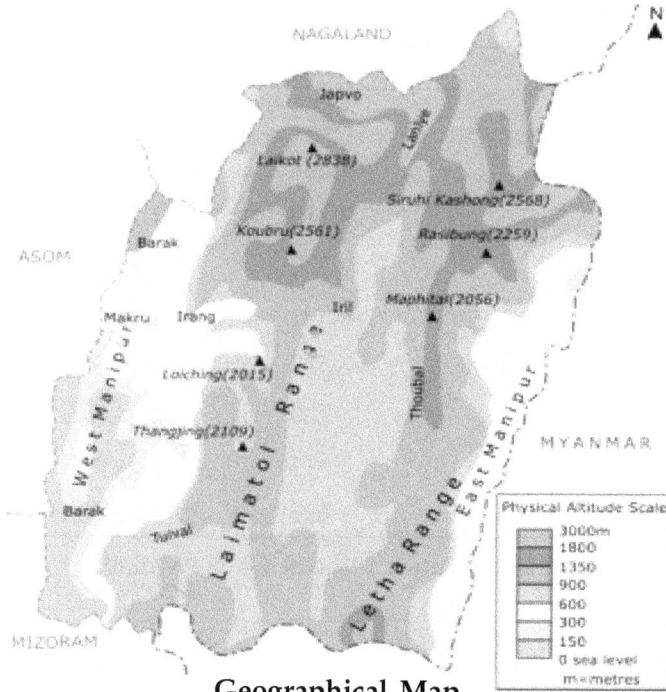

Geographical Map

Tourist Map

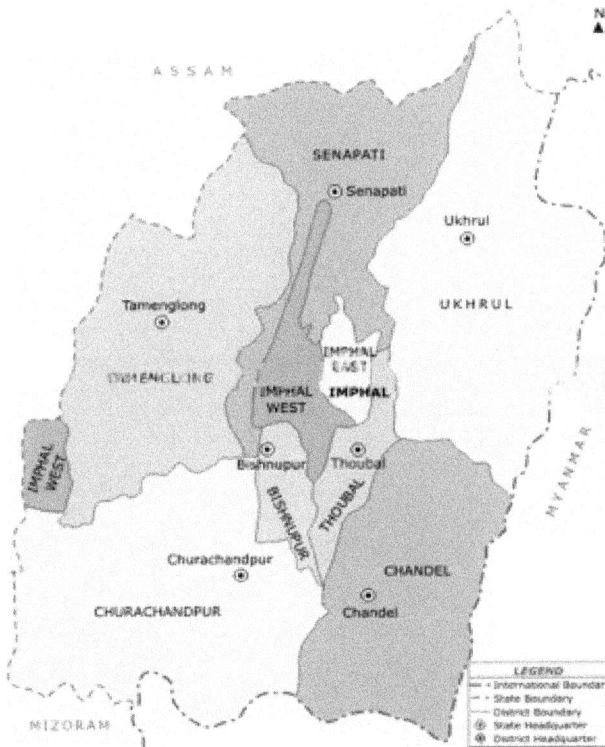

Districts of the State

$$\boxed{1}$$

Introduction

Manipur is a state in Northeastern India, making its capital in the city of Imphal. It is bounded by Nagaland to the north, Mizoram to the south and Assam to the west; it also borders Myanmar to the east with an area of 8,620 sq mi (22,327 sq km).

The Meiteis, who live primarily in the state's valley region, are one of the primary ethnic groups. Their language, Meiteilon (also known as *Manipuri*), is also the *lingua franca* in the state, and was recognised as one of India's national languages in 1992. The Kukis and Nagas live in the hills of the state. Manipur is considered a sensitive border state. Foreigners entering Manipur (including foreign citizens born in Manipur) must possess a Restricted Area Permit, which can be obtained from the Foreigners' Regional Registration Office in the "metros" (Delhi, Mumbai, Kolkata, Chennai) or certain other State Government offices. Permits are valid for only 10 days, and visitors must travel only on tours arranged by authorised travel agents, in groups of four. Furthermore, they may come to Imphal only by air and are not permitted to travel outside the capital.

Symbol of the State

The State symbol or emblem of Manipur is Kanglasha (Nongsaba), i.e., half lion and half dragon. Sangai or brown antlered deer is the state animal, while Nongin remained as the state bird. Iningthiu is regarded as the state tree and the world famous Shiroy Lily (Lilium) is the state flower. Friday, January 21 (1972) is the statehood day and Date of Manipur.

Historical Aspects

As per the royal chronicle, or Cheitharol Kumbaba, the region of Manipur, was established in the 1st century AD. It was a former kingdom, formed by the unification of ten clans under the Ningthouja clan. The region has historical significance as well — it had been the site of trade routes between India and Myanmar and also served as the arena for battle between the Japanese and the Allied forces, during World War II. A democratic form of government was established in accordance with the Manipur Constitution Act, 1947, and the Maharaja was appointed as the Executive Head. The area became independent India in 1949. The government in the state consisted of an elected legislature as well. In 1956, Manipur was conferred the status of a union territory of India, which continued till 1972. On January 21, 1972, it was given the status of a state.

Ancient Period

The earliest known occupation of Manipur can be traced back to Tang, the 14th generation ruler of Qi tribe that inhabited the central part of the present-day China, who later found Tang-Shang Dynasty. After him, his son (Tangja Leela Pakhangba) and grandson (Kangba) ruled over the area. The reign of Kangba, on Manipur region, stretched from 1405 BC to 1359 BC, after which his son Koikoi took over. He was one who introduced the dating of Meitei calendar (Cheraoba), known as Mari-Fam and the surnames like Koikoijam and Keirambam.

The records of Manipur show have obscure information on its history between the reign of Kokoi and that of Korou Nongdren Pakhangba, who ruled around 934 BC and after him, Chingkhong Poireiton, whose reign lasted from 34 BC to 18 BC. The information on what happened in-between these two rulers is again vague. Still, it is believed that for about 700 years during this period, there were no rulers in the Manipur area, which was then known as Tai-Pong-Pan.

Early Period (33-1149 AD)

In the early period history of Manipur, Nongda Lairen Pakhangba ruled over the region. He ascended the throne in 33 AD. After him, it is Meidingu Yanglou Keiphaba whose mention has been found in the historical records, with his reign lasting from 965 AD to 983 AD. The last major name of the early period is that of Meidingu Loitongba, who ruled from 1121 AD to 1149 AD. His son Atom Yoireba ascended the throne in 1149 AD, but by 1162 AD he was driven out by his brother Hemtou Iwang-Thaba.

Medieval Period (1467-1798 AD)

The medieval period in the history of Manipur brings forth the name of Medingu Senbi Kiyamba, who became King in 1476 AD, at the age of 24. He was a friend of the King of Pong (Shan Kingdom), who presented him with a stone, known as Pheiya (Almighty). It was after this that worship of God, in the form of a sacred stone, was started. From 1708 AD to 1747 AD, the region of Manipur was under the rule of Meidingu Pamheiba, who extended his kingdom from Kabow valley, in the east, to Nongnang (Cachar), Takhel (Tripura), in the west.

Ningthou Ching-Thang Khomba, the son of Samjai Khurai-Lakpa (the eldest son of Pamheiba), became the King in 1747 AD and ruled for the next 4 years, after which he was expelled by his brother Borotsai, in 1751 AD. After Borotsai, Gaurisiam became the ruler signed a treaty with the British, encouraging trade and commerce. Gaurisiam's death, in 1763 AD, again led to the reign of Ningthou Ching-Thang Khomba. It was during Khomba's rule that the name "Manipur" for "Meitrabak" or "Sanna-Leipak" came into existence.

Modern Period (1819 AD-Present)

The modern period started in 1819 AD, when King Marjeet ruled over Manipur. In the said year, Manipur was attacked and won over by the Burmese and Chahi-Taret Khuntakpa became the King. In 1825, Gambir Singh led Manipuris in an attack over the Burmese and declared himself as the King of Manipur. After his death, his son Maharaja Chandrakirti ascended the throne, at the age of two. Maharaja Surchand, the eldest son of Chandrakirti, ascended the throne after his father and ruled for 5 years (from 1886 AD to 1890 AD).

In 1890, Surchand's younger brothers, Zillangamba and Angousana revolted against him, along with Jubaraj Tikendrajit. Later, Kullachandra, the elder brother of Tikendrajit, became the King. British waged an open war against Manipur sometime later and conquered it on 27th April, 1891 AD. Thereafter, the region saw two Kings only — Maharaja Churachand Singh (1891-1941 AD) and Maharaja Budhachandra Singh (1941-49 AD). In 1949, Manipur was merged into independent India. On 21 January 1972, Manipur was granted statehood.

Geographical Aspects

Manipur is one of the eight states of North-East India, and one of the Seven Sister States. The state is bounded by Nagaland in the North, Mizoram in the South, Assam in the west, and by the borders Myanmar in the east as well as in the south. The state capital of Manipur is Imphal. The state lies at latitude of 23°83' N-25°68' N and longitude of 93°03' E-94°78' E. The total area covered by the state is 22,327 sq km. The capital lies in an oval shaped valley of approximately 700 sq mi surrounded by blue mountains and is at an elevation of 790 metres above the sea level. The slope of the valley is from north to south. The presence of the mountain ranges not only prevents the cold winds from the north from reaching the valley but also acts as a barrier to the cyclonic storms originating from the Bay of Bengal. Within the state of Manipur, there are two major river basins, viz., the Barak River Basin (Barak Valley) and the Manipur River Basin. The total water resources of the two basins have been estimated to be 18,487 cubic kilometres in the form of annual yield.

The Barak River, the largest river of Manipur, originates from the northern hills and is joined by a number of tributaries such as Irang, Maku, Tuivai, etc., and thereafter enters

Cachar District of Assam. The Manipur river basin has eight major rivers such as Imphal, Iril, Nambul, Sekmai, Chakpi, Thoubal and Khuga. All these rivers originate from the surrounding hills. Almost all the rivers in the valley area are in the mature stage and, therefore, deposit the load in the Loktak Lake.

The rivers draining the Manipur Hill Area are comparatively young due to the hilly terrain through which they flow. These rivers are corrosive in nature and assume turbulent form in rainy season. Important rivers draining the western area include Maku, Barak River, Jiri, Irang and Leimatak. Rivers draining the eastern part of the state include Chamu, Khunou and other short streams.

Physiographically, Manipur may be characterised in two distinct physical regions — an outlying area of rugged hills and narrow valleys and the inner area represents the features of flat plain topography with all associated land forms. These two areas are not only distinct in respect of physical features but are also conspicuous with regard to various floras and faunas. The valley region would have been a monotonous, featureless plain but for a number of hills and mounds rising above the flat surface. The Loktak Lake is an important geographic feature of the central plain area. The total area occupied by all the lakes is about 600 sq km. The altitude ranges from 40 m at Jiribam to as high as 2,994 m at Mt. Iso Peak near Mao.

The soil cover can be divided into two broad types, viz., the red ferruginous soil in the hill area and the alluvium in the valley. The soil generally contains small rock fragments, sand and sandy clay and are of varieties. The top soil on the steep slopes are very thin. In the plain areas, especially flood plains and deltas, the soil is of considerable thickness. Soil on the steep hill slopes is subjected to high erosion resulting into formation of sheets and gullies and barren rock slopes. The normal pH value ranges from 5.4 to 6.8.

Vegetation

The natural vegetation occupies an area of about 14,365 sq km which is nearly 64 per cent of the total geographical area of the state. The vegetation consists of a large variety of plants ranging from short and tall grasses, reeds and bamboos to trees of various species. Broadly, there are four types of forests:

- Tropical Semi-ever Green.
- Dry Temperate Forest.
- Subtropical Pine.
- Tropical Moist Deciduous.

Teak, Pine, Oak, Uningthou, Leihao, Bamboo, Cane, etc., are important forest resources growing in plenty. In addition, rubber, tea, coffee, orange, cardamom, etc., are also, grown in hill areas. Food and cash crops occupy the main vegetation cover in the valley.

Climate

The climate of Manipur is largely influenced by the topography of this hilly region which defines the geography of Manipur. Situated at an elevation of 790 metres above the sea level, the state of Manipur is wedged between hills from all sides. This Northeastern corner of India is blessed with a generally amiable climate though the winters can be a little chilly. The maximum temperature recorded in the summer months of Manipur is 32°C. In winter the mercury often falls to subzero temperature making it frosty in the wintertime. Snowfall sometimes occurs in some hilly regions due to the Western Disturbance. The coldest month in Manipur is January and July experiences the maximum summer temperature.

The ideal time for tourism in the state, in terms of the climate of Manipur, is from the months of October till February, when the weather remains bright and sunny without the scorch of the sun. The hilly state is drenched in rains from May and continues till the middle of October. It receives an average rainfall of 1,467.5 mm, annually. However, the rain distribution varies from 933 mm in Imphal to 2,593 mm in Tamenglong. The downpour ranges from light drizzles to heavy showers. The normal rainfall of Manipur enriches the soil and helps in agricultural processes and irrigation. The South-Westerly Monsoon picks up moisture from the Bay of Bengal and heads towards Manipur, hits the Eastern Himalaya ranges and produces a massive amount of rain in the state.

Flora and Fauna

Blessed with an amazing variety of flora and fauna, 67 per cent of the geographical area of Manipur is hill tract covered forests. Depending on the altitude of hill ranges, the climatic condition varies from tropical to subalpine. The wet forests and the pine forests occur between 900-2,700 m above sea level and they together sustain a host of rare and endemic plant and animal life. Coveted the world over as some of the most beautiful and precious blooms, orchids have an aura of exotic, mysteries about them.

In Manipur, they are abound in their natural habitat growing in soil or on trees and shrubs speaking their beauty and colour, stunning the eye that is not used to seeing them in such profusion. There are 500 varieties of orchids which grow here of which 472 have been identified.

In addition to 'Siroi Lily' which is the only terrestrial lily grown on the hill tops of Siroi hill, Ukhrul, the Hoolock Gibbon, the Sloe Loris, the Clauded Leopard, the Spotted Linshang, Mrs. Hume's Barbacked Pheasant, Blyths Tragopan, Burmese Pea-Fowl, four different species of Hornbills, etc., form only a part of the rich natural fauna of Manipur. However, the most unique is the Sangai the dancing deer. The floating mass of vegetation on the Loktak Lake sustains small herds of this endemic deer which unfortunately has the dubious distinction of being the most threatened Cervid (known as Phumdi) in the World. Other mentionable fauna is Salamander known as 'Lengwa' found at the foothill of Siroi in Ukhrul.

Rivers

Manipur has Major Rivers — Imphal, Iril, Nambul, Sekmai, Chakpi, Thoubal and Khuga.

Main rivers draining Imphal west plain are Imphal river, Nambul River and their tributaries. The Nambul River is made up of a number of small streams on its upper course. The course of the river is short and its outlet falls on Loktak Lake. This river passes through Imphal Municipality area dividing its area into almost two equal halves. This river serves as the main discharging drainage of Imphal Bazar area and its surroundings. During rainy season, swift flowing of water directed to it from its tributaries can't be contained in it. As a result, breaking of its river bunds causing waterlogging in the low-lying area is of regular feature.

Iril River: The Iril River is a river that runs through the eastern suburbs of the city of Imphal in the state of Manipur.

It starts from somewhere up front of Sagolmang area and flows through Lamlai, Top, Naharup, Pangong, and Irilbung before it joins with the Imphal River. It is fed with fresh water from the streams, very clear. The water supply plant located in Porompat is fed with its water.

Iril River still has a large population of endangered indigenous fish called *ngaton*, Meitei sareng. These fish are captured by local fishermen in the months of July and August.

Imphal River: Imphal River originates in the hill ranges of the Senapati District and flows south, forming the boundary line demarcating the Thoubal District on its north and the west. Though lean and dry in the summer, the river becomes violent and turbulent during the rainy season, causing wide spread damage to paddy fields and property. It was once a means of transport for valuable merchandise but the advent of cheap and faster means of road transport has made people less dependent on the river. Still the sand, pebbles and boulders obtained from the river provides for the livelihood of many people inhabiting its banks.

Nambul River: Nambul River is one of the major rivers draining the Imphal west plain. It is made up of a number of small streams on its upper course. The river traverses the Imphal Municipality area dividing its region into almost two equal halves before discharging to the Loktak Lake.

Thoubal River: The Thoubal river originates in the hill ranges of Ukhrul and is an important tributary of the Imphal river. On its course, it passes through Yairipok and Thoubal before joining the Imphal at Irong near Mayang Imphal. The Imphal River rises in the hills of Senapati District and flows south. It forms the boundary demarcating line of Thoubal District on its north and the west. During the dry seasons these rivers are lean and thin but, during the rainy monsoon periods these are very wild and frequent floods occur causing widespread damage to the paddy fields, property and life. These rivers were once good means of transport for valuable merchandise. Other rivers in the district are the Wangjing, the Arong and the Sekmai. These rivers originate in the hills of Ukhrul District. The Arong River flows through Khangabok and falls into Kharung Pat. The Wangjing River flows west via Heirok and Wangjing before joining the Loushi Pat. With the advent of cheap and faster means of road transport, these rivers no longer serve as routes of transportation of goods. Still they provide good building materials in the shape of sand, pebbles and boulders and a means of livelihood for a large number of people inhabiting along their courses.

Khuga River: Khuga River is one of the most important tributaries of the Imphal River. It originates in the hills of Singngat subdivision of Churachandpur District. It flows towards the west and joins the Imphal River at Ithai in Bishnupur District at the southern edge of Loktak Lake.

Hills

The hill ranges, connected by spurs and ridges, run generally north-south. These ranges include the Naga Hills to the north, the East Manipur Hills along the eastern Myanmar border, the Mizo and Chin hills to the south, and the West Manipur Hills to the west. Average elevations vary between 5,000 and 6,000 feet, although the hills in the north rise to more than 9,500 feet.

Lakes

In Manipur, lakes besides the rivers form the major part of wetlands. The lakes includes the Loktak Lake (a Ramsar site), Ikop, Waithou, Pumlen/Khoidum pat, Ushoipokpi pat, Loushipat, Utrapat, Sanapat, Tankha Pat, Karam Pat, Lamphel Pat, Zailad Lake and Jaimeng Lake. Out of these lakes only Loktak Lake has been identified under National Lake Conservation Programme (NLCP) by the Ministry of Environment and Forests, Govt. of India.

Social Aspects

The colourful kaleidoscope of Manipur society and culture has been a topic that aroused the inquisitiveness in the minds of erudite scholars and researchers all across the world. The social values of cultural legacy of the North-East Indian state are reflected in the lifestyle of the inhabitants.

Manipur is home of several tribal communities who live together in mutual harmony. The Meiteis and Tangkhuls are the principal tribes that reside in the hilly state. The people are simple, warm and hospitable and believe in egalitarian social practices. The people are industrious and diligent but also love adventure and like to participate in a variety of sports. In fact, Manipur has carved out a niche for itself and emerged as a forerunner in the world of polo. A unique feature of Manipur society is the position of women. Women are held in high esteem in the society. The senior citizens are also given due respect.

Manipur society does not follow the social stratification of the traditional Indian society. They follow a system of social classification where the society is divided between the Meiteis, the Bamons or the Brahmins, the Pangans or the Muslims and the lower caste Lois.

The Manipuri Dance and the colourful and finely woven handicrafts reflect the creativity and the cultural extravaganzas of the Manipur society. Another intrinsic feature of Manipur society and culture is reflected in the assorted cultural potpourri of state fairs and festivals.

Customs and Traditions

The religious customs and traditions of Manipur are unique. They are organised in such a manner that in temple institutions those reveal the real festivity and reflect the curious character of socioreligious life of the valley. It involves the ethics and aesthetics of Manipuris. Mass propagation of Hindu customs and traditions is the indicator of their reverence towards the Hindu deities and temples.

Birth

In Meiteis the rites and rituals are now on the Hindu pattern but certain traditional rituals are also combined. During pregnancy the mother is not restricted on any kind of food. Savasti Puja is conducted on the birth of the child. A day is fixed by the Brahmin. On the fixed day relatives from the child's mother side visit the house. They come in a procession. This procession is a unique one. The women wear saffron, fanek and white chader and woollen endi or white silk shawl. They carry presents in round baskets in which Muri Laddors, leaves, nuts, kalasa, fish and clothes for the child and the mother are placed. The procession is arranged in a single file, the women followed by the men. When they reach the house, they keep the gifts around the newly born child. Kirtans are arranged. Kirtan party and the mother and the child sit round the Tulsi plant.

Marriage

Marriages are performed in accordance with the customs. Before the marriage parents of the boy go to meet parents of the girl. This starting approach is termed 'Hainaba'. The horoscopes are tallied and if both the parents agree then the next date for the meeting is fixed. On the next meeting, called *Yathang Thanaga*, the consent is given by the girl's parents. The next stage is 'Waroipot puba' and the groom's family members bring food and the contract is finally sealed. Finally the engagement is declared amongst the friends and relatives, this is called *'Heijapot'*. Friends and relatives from the boy's side then go to the girl's parents with food, fruits and presents. The girl's parents also invite their friends and relatives. The marriage is fixed by the Brahmin. A Manipuri marriage party is of a great show but little is wasted for giving meals. A marriage in a Meitei house in Imphal will be attended by not less than thirty cars. A marriage attended by a procession of cars is considered a status symbol. The men dress in dhoti and kurta with a shawl wrapped around and women in pink 'fanek' and white chader. The reception is very formal. At the entrance of the gate a Meitei woman extends a Thali containing a banana leaf in which the betel nut, pan and tamul is arranged. The arrangement for sitting is made around the Tulsi rostrum. In each Meitei house the Tulsi plant is grown over a raised rostrum. All ceremonies are conducted around this plant.

The bridal dress is unique. It is obligatory for the bride to wear the Ras Lila skirt. The bridegroom's dress is white dhoti, kurta and turban. Kirtans and Shahnai music is started when the bride and the bridegroom make seven rounds round the Tulsi plant. The bride follows the steps in rhythmic styles with the Shahnai music. She has to perform the role of a gopi. There are many good points in Meitei marriages. There is no stress on huge expenditure. The laddoos and sweets are distributed after the marriage ceremony. The guests are given Dakshina. The dowry is not as a compulsion but voluntary. The parents of the girl provide essential items for her use such as utensils, sewing machine, implements, clothes, etc.

Food

In Manipur, eromba is a special fish delicacy. Vegetables and bamboo shoots are some of the other delicacies. Among the sweets, Kabok, made up of molasses and rice, is a famous name among the Manipuris. The drink called *shekmai*, made in a village with the same name, is a famous country wine of the state.

The principal food is rice, fish and vegetables. One of the favourite foods is the Ngri, which actually is a type of fermented fish. It carries a distinct smell but it is very popular for its taste.

Apart from Ngri, roasted fish and fried fish, they also love the Nga Aiyaba or the dried fish. Chicken is another popular dish of the people of Manipur. Some of the popular dishes and preparations are:

- Yongchaak singju.
- Monica gi chakum.
- Aloo mattar and smoked fish.
- Bora – a kind of pakora.
- Kanghau.
- Aloo angouba – fried potato.
- Pakoura mah.

- Nga atauba – fish fry.
- Nga athongba – curried fish.
- Khajing bora
- Khangau.

Along with the traditional Manipuri cuisines, the people have well adopted with the food from other regions like Chinese and North Indian.

Costumes

The costumes of Manipur carry their own unique characteristics. Stressed on its functionality, the traditional costumes are simple and easy to wear. A traditional Manipuri costume for women includes a shawl called *Innaphi*, a Phanek and a wrap around skirt called sarong. A man wears a dhoti, a jacket and a white Pagri or turban.

With the advancement of time and the spread of Christianity and Western education, people have become extremely fashion conscious. Jeans and jacket have emerged as a big hit with the youth. However, they still love to flaunt their traditional attires and have modified the old styled clothes with modernised variations. For instance, the Innaphis worn by women resembles the modern wrap around skirts. Innaphis are nowadays made with different materials from cotton to silk rather than the thick textured Innaphis of the yesteryears.

Different costumes are worn during the colourful Manipuri festivals. In fact, there are separate costumes for separate festivals. The Potlois and Kumins are the traditional costumes for the Rasa Leela festivals. Other traditional dresses worn during the festivals and festival related dances are the Koks, Phurits, etc. Some other dress forms used by different tribes in Manipur are Lmaphie, Saijounba, Ningthoupee and Phiranji.

Economic Aspects

Manipur Economy is based on agriculture, forest products, industries, mining, and tourism sectors. The gross domestic product of the state amounted to Rs. 8,210 million in 1990, this figure stood at Rs. 16,270 million in 1995, and in 2000 it increased to Rs. 29,200 million. The Economy of Manipur grew at the rate of 12.90 per cent from 1980 to 1997. The agricultural sector has been growing at the rate of 10.69 per cent per year and the manufacturing sector has been growing at the rate of 10.53 per cent per year.

The Economy in the state depends mainly on the agricultural sector for it is the biggest livelihood source for the rural people. The various kinds of crops grown are rice, maize, pulses, and wheat. The cultivation in the state is done using the Jhumming and terraced cultivation methods. Various kinds of fruits and vegetables such as pineapple, orange, mangoes, lemons, carrot, ladies' finger, cabbage, and pea are also grown. The agricultural sector contributes a great deal of revenue to the Economy.

The economy of the state also gets its revenue from the sector of forests products as the state has a huge forest cover. Various kinds of forest products are manufactured and sold all over the country and even exported to foreign countries. This has given a major boost to Manipur Economy. The economy in the state also depends to a certain extend on the industrial sector. Although this sector is not that well developed, the State Government is making efforts to make the state more industrialised. More than 7,700 small industrial units have been established in the state. Also industries related to cement, drugs and pharmaceuticals, plastic, and steel has been set up. This has contributed to the growth of the Economy.

The economy in the state also gets revenue from the mining sector. But the exploitation of this sector has not been extensive which has hampered the growth of the economy of the state. Due to geographical isolation the state gets very little revenue from the tourism sector. The major reasons behind the slow growth of the economy are that the infrastructure of the state is not well developed. The terrain of the state is also hilly which makes communication difficult.

Manipur Economy has showed slow growth. To boost the economy the State Government has taken efforts by setting up more industries and also developing the infrastructure.

Unique Handloom

Manipur enjoys a distinct place amongst the Handloom zones in India. Handloom industry is the largest cottage industry in the state. This industry has been flourishing since time immemorial. One of the special features of the industry is that women are the only weavers. According to the National handloom census reports 1988 there are about 2.71 lakh looms in Manipur.

It is believed that Chitnu Tamitnu, a goddess, discovered the cotton and she also produced the yarn. When the threads are ready for weaving she arranged the required equipments and constructed the 'Sinnaishang' (work shed). It is also believed that the goddess Panthoibee once saw a spider producing fine threads and making cowebs and from it she found the idea of weaving and thus started weaving.

Most of the weavers who are famous for their skill and intricate designing are from Wangkhei, Bamon Kampu, Kongba, Khongman, Utlou, etc., in respect of fine silk items. The rest of the villages of the state producing all varieties of fabrics. Tribal shawls are all varieties of fabrics. Tribal shawls with exotic designs and motifs are the products of five hill districts of the state. Fabrics and Shawls of Manipur are in great demand in the national and international market.

Today, major handloom production activities are undertaken by three Government organisations namely:

- Manipur Development Society (MDS).
- Manipur Handloom and Handicrafts Development Corporation (MHHDC).
- Manipur State Handloom Weavers Cooperative Society (MSHWCS).

Unique Handicrafts

Since cane and bamboo are abundantly available basketry has been a popular occupation of the people of Manipur. Different shapes and sizes with different designs are manufactured for domestic and ritualistic.

Heijing Kharai, Phiruk and Lukmai are exclusively meant for ceremonies such as wedding, birth and death. For domestic purposes baskets like Likhai, Sangbai, Chengbon, Meruk, Morah, etc., are made.

Again, there are fishing equipments made of cane and bamboo. They are Longup, Tungbol, etc. People of Maring tribe inhabiting the Chandel District are the main manufacturers of these types of basket. Other tribes and the Meiteis also contribute a lot to the production of baskets.

Pottery culture is very old in Manipur. Most of the pots are handmade and are of different colours (red, dark red and black). Pottery flourishes in Andro, Sekmai, Chairen, Thongjao, Nungbi and parts of Senapati District. Chakpa women are good potters and they make different types of pots for ritualistic and ceremonial purposes.

The Manipuris, especially the women, love to dress beautifully with colourful clothes and flowers.

Transportation

Tulihal Airport, the airport of Imphal, connects the state capital with Delhi, Calcutta and Guwahati. National Highway NH-39 links Manipur with the rest of the country through the railway stations at Dimapur in Nagaland at a distance of 215 km from Imphal. Highway NH-53 connects Manipur with another railway station at Silchar in Assam, which is 269 km away from Imphal. Road network of Manipur, having a length of 7,170 km, connects all the important towns and far off villages.

Political Aspects

Politics in Manipur is characterised by the presence of a large number of political parties, frequent splits, horse-trading and non-cohesive coalitions. Two new political parties, the Democratic People's Party (DPP) and the Manipur People's Conference (MPC), emerged taking the total number of political parties in the state to 16. Political instability has been a feature of the state since the 1984 polls, when the Congress (I) was forced to seek the help of independents to form the government despite winning half the seats in the 60-member Assembly. Defection is common, even though several legislators have been suspended for violating the anti-defection law.

The leaders of most parties have said that they are averse to pre-poll alliances and seat-sharing talks. They would rather wait until the results are declared before entering into any kind of alliance. This implies the inevitability of another coalition government. Such a coalition of convenience may not survive a full term, going by the track record of the various coalitions that have ruled Manipur.

After the 2000 elections, the MSCP, which won 29 seats, instigated defections. Nine MLAs from the Opposition, including the Manipur People's Party (MPP) and the Nationalist Congress Party (NCP), joined it. Thus Nipamacha formed a Ministry in coalition with the Federal Party of Manipur (FPM), which won six seats. But the government was wobbly from Day One.

The MSCP-FPM government did not last more than a year. Nipamacha resigned in February 2001, paving the way for a new coalition government headed by Samata Party leader Radhabinode Koijam. The Samata Party, which only won one seat in the last elections, had increased its strength to 12 after 10 of the 11 Congress (I) MLAs, under the leadership of Congress (I) Legislature Party leader Koijam, joined it. Koijam was supported by all Opposition MLAs except the lone Congress (I) legislator, Rishang Keishing. Although the Bharatiya Janata Party and the Samata Party are partners in the National Democratic Alliance (NDA) government at the Centre, the BJP with six MLAs did not join the Koijam government. Instead, it supported the government from the outside.

The political process is the structure and working of a political system within the parameters of a State. The concept of one nation, one State as the basis of a nation-state has undergone a change and it does not exist in its puritanical forms. Manipur was a nation-state but it had an ethnic diversity in her population. This diversity has been sharpened by ethnic identity formation and assertion amongst the tribal people of Manipur.

The Second World War and post-World War II relief compensations had made possible the inflow of government money and led to the emergence of contractors and businessmen. These elites made the state a centre of power, a resource base and a distributor of resources to harmonise the various interests in the plural State of Manipur. There was an ethnic competition for access to the power and resources of the state. They participated in the political process.

The new Constitution of Manipur to be enforced at the departure of the British in August 1947. The Manipur State Constitution Act, 1947 provided a Constitutional monarchy with a 53 member Legislative Assembly, basic human rights with universal adult franchise. The relation between Manipur and the Dominion of India was guided by the Instrument of Accession and the Stand Still Agreement signed by Maharaja of Manipur. Manipur was an autonomous State with complete internal independence though it accepted Indian currency, post and telegraph, foreign affairs and defence.

In such a political scene, there was a potential danger of the dominant group making the state an instrument of domination leading to despotism of one ethnic or cultural group. The success or otherwise of a multiethnic structure and plural society depends on the values and ethos of the dominant group and the readiness of the non-dominant groups to accept their leadership without losing their identity and fully protecting their interests. In this, the ethnic diversity is reflected in the management of power and governance of the state.

In the post-independence period, the representatives of the hill tribes were appointed as Ministers of the state which had never occurred in the history of Manipur. In the election of 1948, 18 seats were reserved for the hills but not on the basis of tribes, the remaining seats were for the valley including Muhammadan. Democracy had provided the opportunity for participation in the governance of the state either as Ministers or members of the Assembly. Every community was represented except the Mao as there was no election due to political agitation.

The election of 1948 was the endorsement of the state by the people of Manipur in a democratic way. There were 8 Naga MLAs, 5 Tangkhuls, 2 Zeliangrong and one Monshang, the other 9 were Kuki-Chins including Kom and Paite.

In this short-lived experiment in constitutional monarchy, the tribal people accepted the primal position of the Maharaja as the head of the kingdom and leadership of the Meiteis in the democratic setup as the Chief Minister was a Prince appointed by the Maharaja. The hill people accepted the Maharaja as the symbol of unity of the kingdom. The state was merged in India in October 1949. There was a strong and popular demand by the urban based Congress party for the abolition of the monarchy and integration into India.

During the two decades after the merger and adoption of the Indian Constitution, Manipur witnessed the assertion of the various ethnic groups. In 1951, the government grouped officially the tribes of Manipur into three categories as the Scheduled tribes, Any Naga Tribe, Any Kuki Tribe and Any Lushai Tribe. This was the official acceptance of the Naga and Kuki identity of the various tribes. But the tribes themselves did not like these nomenclatures and submitted to the Backward Classes Commission for individual tribes to be recognised as Scheduled tribes.

As per recommendation of the Commission, 29 tribes were recognised as Scheduled Tribes in the President's order of 1956. The ethnic principle was also applied by the Government of India in the Constitution of the Advisory Council of Manipur under the Chairmanship of the Chief Commissioner. The ethnic groups including the Nagas and Kukis participated in the first Indian Election to the Parliament and Electoral College of 1952, the subsequent elections in 1957, 1962, 1967, and 1971 before the attainment of

Statehood in 1972. Ethnicity at the tribe and clan level became a factor in the voting pattern in these elections.

Government

The Chief Minister is aided in the governance of the state by the council of ministers, which spearhead the separate departments of the government.

The government of Manipur has incorporated several plans and launched pilot projects to facilitate the government in the governance of the state. The NIC Manipur aids the government in developing the portals and lists the records for the use of the various departments of the government. The Community Information Centre in Manipur is an instrument developed by the government to utilise the information technology to make selective data available to the people of the state. The government has developed the infrastructure to support the development of the programme. Various sectors of the society has facilitated from the presence of the information on the websites developed at the Community Information Centre in Manipur.

The forest region of the state is maintained by the Forest Department of Manipur that was established in the year 1931 by the British Government. Prior to the establishment of this department, the revenue of the forested region of Manipur was shared between the state and the Cachar Forest division.

The Imphal Municipal Council is responsible for the administration of the two districts of Imphal East and Imphal West. The democratic body works effectively for the socio-economic progress of the Class I city of Imphal.

The various departments of the Manipur Government works to ensure the progress of the state retaining the rich cultural heritage of state.

Capital of the State: Imphal

Imphal is the capital of the Indian state of Manipur. In the heart of the town and surrounded by a moat, are ruins of the old Palace of Kangla. Until 2003, the grounds used to be occupied by the Assam Rifles, a paramilitary force. Another place of historical interest is the polo ground which is the oldest existing polo ground in the world. Near the polo ground is the Manipur State Museum, which has a good collection of old artifacts and nice pictures depicting the history of Manipur. 'Ima Keithel' at Khwairamband Bazar is the only market in the world where, as the name suggests, all the stalls are run by women.

In 1944, during World War II the Battle of Imphal, along with the simultaneous Battle of Kohima, was the turning point in the Burma Campaign. For the first time in the South East Asian Theatre of World War II the Japanese lost the initiative to the Allies, which they retained until the end of the war.

The state is also famous for the brow-antlered deer called the Sangai. This species of the deer is endemic to Manipur and is on the verge of extinction. Last count of Sangai deer revealed only 162 left in the Keibul Lamjao National Park.

On 18 June, 1997, the Imphal District was split into Imphal East and Imphal West.

On 21 October, 2008, Imphal was struck by a large-scale terror attack allegedly carried out by Myanmar based insurgents.

Geography

Imphal is the capital of Manipur, located at 24°49' N 93°57' E. It has an average elevation of 786 metres (2,580 feet). It is located in the extreme east of India.

The Imphal Valley is drained by several small rivers originating from the hills surrounding it. These include the Imphal, Iril, Sekmai, Thoubal, and Khuga rivers. One of the important places is Wangkhei village where one can see the Temple of Govindaji with nature's beauty and also Wangkhei village is famous for Handloom Products and Hand Made Products.

Main Tourist Attractions

Shree Govindaji Temple: This place was considered to be the highest place for any cultural activity during the times of the Maharajas. Located at a place near the Royal palace of past Maharajas, it has two domes and a raise congregation hall to keep the sacred deities in their place, aloof and high.

War Cemeteries: The cemeteries are the seats of remembrance for the British and Indian soldiers who fought and died in the Second World War. When people visit these cemeteries, the peace and the cleanliness of the place will entice them. If the tourists are not satisfied with the serenity then they can go through the various written messages on the stone markers and bronze plaques of the graves.

Women's Market or Ima Keithel: Cacophony, bargain of products and a spread of a beautiful and colourful cloth is what one would most notice when one visits this market place. But, this is the charm of the place, if a person wants to know how the trade goes in Manipur, this is the first place to buy. The bazar consist of two main sections — one where the vegetables, fruits and necessary items are sold and the other where the handloom products of the state is sold. The peculiarity of the market is that around 3,000 'Imas' or mothers run the stalls.

Manipur Zoological Gardens: The brow-antlered deer, which is a rare species, can be seen in the Manipur Zoological Gardens. Located at a distance of 6 km from the capital, the zoo is very modest to the core with its surrounding, a large expanse of open grounds.

Manipur State Museum: The museum, which is the representation of the tangible information of history, shows a display of the tribal heritage and the collection of the artifacts of the former Ningthourels of Manipur. Costumes of the common people and warriors, arms and weapons of the varied communities and relics and historical documents can be seen here. The priceless artifacts, documents and cultural heritage of a mentioned civilization can be first accessed through a Museum.

Demographics

As of 2001 India census, Imphal had a population of 2,17,275. Males constitute 50 per cent of the population and females 50 per cent. Imphal has an average literacy rate of 79 per cent, higher than the national average of 64.84 per cent: male literacy is 84 per cent, and female literacy is 74 per cent. In Imphal, 10 per cent of the population is under 6 years of age.

Area, Population and Headquarters of Districtsc

S.No.	District	Area (sq km)	Population	Headquarters
1.	Senapati	3,271	2,83,621	Senapati
2.	Ukhrul	4,544	1,40,778	Ukhrul
3.	Chandel	3,313	1,18,327	Chandel
4.	Churachandpur	4,570	2,27,905	Churachandpur
5.	Tamenglong	4,391	1,11,499	Tamenglong
6.	Imphal (West)	519	4,44,382	Lamphel
7.	Imphal (East)	709	3,94,876	Porompat
8.	Thoubal	514	3,64,140	Thoubal
9.	Bishnupur	496	2,08,368	Bishnupur

2

Salient Features

- -

Historical and Geographical Features

Not much of recorded history of Manipur is available though it has been in existence since time immemorial. According to the historians, Pakhangba ascended the throne of one of the seven main principalities in 33 AD and founded a long dynasty which ruled Manipur till 1891. Manipur came under the British Rule in 1891 and later on it was merged in the Indian Union as part 'C' State on 15 October 1949. This was replaced by a Territorial Council of 30 elected and two nominated members.

Later in 1963, a Legislative Assembly of 30 elected and two nominated members was established under the Union Territories Act, 1962. The status of the Administrator was raised from Chief Commissioner to the status of the Lt. Governor with effect from 19 December 1969. Manipur attained full-fledged statehood on 21 January 1972. With this a Legislative Assembly consisting of 60 elected members was established.

Geographically the state is divided into two tracts: the hills comprising of five districts and the plains with four districts. It is bounded by Myanmar on the east, Nagaland on the north, Assam and Mizoram on the west and Myanmar and Mizoram on the south.

Not much of recorded history of Manipur is available. It is commonly known that an adventurer named Pakhangba ascended the throne of the seven main principalities and founded a dynasty which ruled Manipur till 1949. A King named Loi Yamba in 1074 AD consolidated the kingdom to a great extent. In the later years, Kabaws (who lived at Indo-Burma border) tried to annex the south eastern part of Manipur Valley which was foiled by the King Khumomba. By 1470 Kabaw valley was annexed to Manipur. By 1542 Manipur dominions were further extended. There was a battle with the Chinese in which the Manipuris singly defeated them.

In the next 200 years, Manipur saw a steady prosperous time. In 1762, the Manipur King concluded a treaty with the British to ward off the growing menace of the Burmese. It is well-known that Burmese successes in Manipur, Assam and other places led to war between the Burmese and the British lasting seven years. The treaty of Yandabo in 1826 ended the war but failed to solve the problem for Manipuris. The British Government kept Manipur as a native state after much deliberations. After integration with the Indian Union in 1949, the problem of Manipur did not end as it was made a Part 'C' state. Central leadership was against its merger in Assam as was considered by the Reorganisation Commission.

Hence, it became a Union Territory under the State Reorganisation Act, 1956. At the growing dissent of the people, Manipur was made a full-fledged state of the Union in 1972. Geographically the state is divided into tracts — the hills comprising five districts and the plains with four districts. Manipur is bounded by upper Burma on east, the Chin Hills of Burma on southeast, Nagaland on north, Assam on west and Mizoram on south and southwest.

Religious Features

The people of Manipur follow several faiths and religions which can be traced down to its unique historical past. Manipur preserved an ancient indigenous religion rich in mythology and colourful in ritual, known today as the Sanamahi. Sanamahi worshipped is concentrated around Sidaba Mapu, the one God. The Manipuri copper plates dates Saka year 721 issued by King Khomtekcha, ruler of Manipur from 763 AD to 773 AD, mention worship of Sanamahi.

Early Manipuris were the devotees of a Supreme deity "Lainingthou Soralel" following the footprint of their Godly ancestors. That particular kind of ancestor worship and animism, with the central focus of worship on Umang Lai — that is, local governing deities worshipped in sacred groves. Some of the local gods (*Lais*) they worship are Atiya Sidaba, Pakhangba, Sanamahi, Leimaren, Oknarel, Panganba, Thangjing, Marjing, Wangbaren, Koubru.

The religious life of the people, even when they adopted mainstream Hinduism, retained many characteristics inherited from their pre-historic ancestors. The essentials of this religion remain recognisable to the present day. Hinduism has a long tradition in Manipur, however Vaishnavism penetrated Manipur during the reign of King Kyamba and King Khagemba in the 15th century. Towards the end of the 17th century and at the advent of the 18th century, a great force of Gaudiya Vaishnavism came and spread in Manipur. Over the last couple of decades, there has been a revival of Sanamahi religion and this is evident in the significant growth of the 'other' religion category in the 2001 census. Around 10 per cent of the population identified themselves under this category.

Sanamahi religion is the original religion of the Meitei people living in Manipur. Due to the changing demographic profile of the state, Sanamahi will now be included in the next Government of India population census in 2011.

Other Religions

Christianity: Christianity in the hill tracts of Northeastern Region spread as a result of the British religious policy in the area. At present, almost all of the hill tribal population is Christian. All groups of Nagas and Kukis of Manipur have adopted Christianity. The Bible is available in Tangkhul, Thadou, Lushai and Meitei dialects. Christianity is the second largest religion in the state accounting for 35 per cent of the population.

Islam: Most of the Muslims in Manipur are descendants of Bengali immigrants and are commonly referred to as Pangans. Muslims form about 8 per cent of the population.

Educational Features

Manipur has an overall literacy rate of 76.5 per cent. The Manipur University came into existence on June 5, 1980 and is located in the historic Canchipur with the ruins of the old palace of Manipur in the background. The university, which has jurisdiction all over the state of Manipur, has affiliated colleges and 3 permitted colleges situated at different parts of the state. Training facilities have also been created to enable the young men and woman to acquire technological capability and provide industries with ready-made trained manpower. A centre for electronic design and technology and the central institute of plastic Engineering and Technology have been set up at Imphal.

Education in Manipur today is at par with the rest of the country. Earlier, education in the state was meant for the elites of the Manipuri society. The tribes and the poor were not allowed in many places to take higher education. However, with the advancement of time, the modern outlook of the people and the efforts of the State Government have changed this outlook.

The arrival of the British missionaries in Manipur brought a change in the educational scenario of the state. Reverend Pattigrew became the first Inspector of Schools of the state in 1903 and brought many reforms strengthening the educational structure of the state. The introduction of a separate education department in 1950 was a step forward towards improved educational conditions in Manipur.

Today top of the line schools, colleges, technical institutions, universities and training establishments have made Manipur one of the leading educational hubs of the North-East.

Schools

There are a number of schools in Manipur and all of them operate with the sole intention of enlightening the young minds. There are different kinds of schools which include:

- Montessori Schools,
- Day Schools,
- Residential Schools,
- Convent or Anglo Schools,
- Government Schools,
- Public Schools.

Most of the secondary level schools follow the curriculum of the CBSE and also abide by the textbook lists provided by them. Besides providing textual education, the schools in Manipur provide physical education and aim towards the all round development of the students.

Colleges and Institutes

The educational needs of the people are catered to by the colleges and institutes in Manipur. There are several colleges and institutes that specialise in providing the students with technical knowledge in the streams of arts, commerce and science.

The courses offered by the colleges and institutes are approved by the All-India Council for Technical Education. Most of the educational institute and colleges are affiliated to the Manipur University that has its campus situated in the centre of the city of Imphal. Classes on law and computer applications are provided within the campus of the university. Other than the colleges that function under the Manipur University, there are other autonomous colleges and institutes that format their own syllabus and conduct their own examination. While some of the academic institutes are private institutes, some of the colleges in the state are set up by the government.

Most of the medical institutes and engineering colleges of the state are located in the capital city of Imphal, which is the hub of education in the state.

Manipur University

Established in 1980, the Manipur University is the ultimate governing board for most of the colleges and Manipur Institute of College — MIT. The university has a sprawling campus covering an area of 287 acres in Canchipur near Imphal.

IT Features

Recognising the vast potential of IT industry in the state, the Government of Manipur accords high priority to the Electronics and Information Technology sector as a major thrust area of development. A special package of incentives is provided to facilitate competitive growth of the sector.

Manipur has vibrant manpower potential ideally suited for electronics and IT-based industries in view of the unpolluted and eco-friendly environment conditions and ever-growing qualitative workforce.

The Manipur Industrial Development Corporation Ltd. has been established as a public sector undertaking to fill up the gaps for development of electronics including information technology based industries in the state.

The Centre for Electronics Design and Technology of India (CEDTI) at Imphal caters to the entire North-East India. This Centre has been imparting training to all the prospective youth and officials of the State Government and other organisations from the Region.

The Government College of Technology at Imphal provides computer education up to the graduation level. A Masters course in computer applications is also imparted in the Manipur University. There are also a number of private institutions in the state providing IT education, like NIIT, APTECH, LCC, etc. Computer education has been introduced in the school and college curriculums.

Community Information Centres with computers connected to the Internet via VSAT systems are being set up in every Block of the state. Such centres not only act as a point from where the local public can avail of any kind of information, but also as training centres in the use of computers and the Internet. Work is underway to increase utility of these centres by incorporating Government to Citizen interfaces and Web content of local relevance.

The State Government is at the final stage to adopt an IT Policy. Some of the objectives are:

- To set up the institutional framework to implement and monitor the policy.
- To use *e*-Governance to upgrade the standard and quality of administration and to provide citizen-oriented, efficient and cost-effective government.
- To promote investments and growth in IT industry, and encourage private sector initiative in IT related infrastructure and services, so as to increase the contribution of IT in the economic growth of the state:
  — To provide adequate infrastructure so that the IT sector can flourish.
  — To encourage percolation of IT literacy and education in the state.
  — To generate IT related employment opportunities for the educated youth.

Some IT areas where private participation is encouraged:

- Setting up of an IT Park.
- Setting up of IT Enable Service Centres such as Call Centres, etc.
- Development of a backbone network "Manipur State Wide Area Network" (MANNET) for voice, data and video transmission and dissemination.

- Issue of multifunction Electronic SMART cards to citizens.
- IT literacy programme in schools and colleges.

Cultural Features

The culture of Manipur is a fine blend of colourful festivals, rich history, vibrant customs, wonderful architecture, delicious cuisines, enchanting music, exciting dance forms and much more. The fun loving mentality of the people of the state is reflected in their different festivals and fairs.

These festivals are enlivened by enchanting folk music and exciting dances. Dances like the Thabal Chongba are performed by tribal men and women during the festival. The feet tapping rhythm of the dances will instantly make you fall in love with the music and dances. Two of the many music forms of Manipur are Lai Haraoba Ishei and Pena Ishei.

The Manipuri people have their own traditional dresses and colourful costumes. The craftsmen are excellent in weaving wonderful garments and other handicrafts made with bamboo, stone, etc.

The favourite pastime or sports of the people is archery. The expert archers take part in the archery competitions held during the festivals. The bamboo bows and arrows are extremely well made and elegantly decorated.

The Bengali architectural style has influenced the wonderful architecture of Manipur. The ancestral houses and ancient buildings bear the architectural brilliance of the region.

Museums

Manipur State Museum: This museum, located near the Imphal Polo Ground has a fairly good display of the state's heritage and a collection of portraits of Manipur's former rulers. Items of special interests are costumes, arms and weapons, relics and historical documents. It opens at 10 am and closes at 4:30 pm.

Sekta Archaeological Living Museum: Sekta Mound locally known as "Sekta Kei" is a protected archaeological site. The historical hotspot is located at Sekta village, about 16 km from Imphal on the Imphal-Ukhrul Road. It is a place where evidence of the practice of secondary burial was discovered. The site was jointly excavated by the Archaeological Survey of India and the State Archaeologists.

Festivals

Manipur is a land of festivities. Merriments and mirth-making go on round the year. A year in Manipur represents a cycle of festivals. Hardly a month passes by without a festival which, to the Manipuris, is a symbol of their cultural, social and religious aspirations.

It removes the monotony of life by providing physical diversions, mental recreation and emotional outlet, helps one to lead a more relaxed and fuller life.

Lai-Haraoba: Celebrated in hour of the sylvan deities known as Umang Lai, the festival represents the worship of traditional deities and ancestors. A number of dances by both men and women are performed before the ancient divinities. The Lai Haraoba of God-Thangjing, the ruling deity of Moirang, is the most famous one and attracts huge gatherings. It is held in the month of May.

Yaoshang (Dol Jatra): Celebrated for five days commencing from the full-moon day of Phalgun (February/March), Yaoshang is the premier festival of Manipur. The Thabal Chongba, a kind of Manipuri folk dance in which boys and girls hold hands and dance away their blues in festive tube-lit ambience is an inseparable part of the festival. Young and old folks collect donation from house to house and the money so collected is spent in parties and feasts. However, of late, time and energy earlier spent in this festival has been utilised in locally organised games and sports meets. Athletes got a shot in the arm, ever since.

Ratha Jatra: One the greatest festivals of the Hindus of Manipur, the festival is celebrated for about 10 days in the month of Ingen (June/July). Lord Jaganath leaves his temple in a Rath locally known as Kang pulled by pilgrims who vie with one another for this honour.

Ramadan Eid (The Premier Festival of Manipur Muslims): Ramadan Eid is the most popular festival of the Manipuri Muslims (Meitei Pangal) and is observed in the usual spirits of joy and festivities as in other Muslim world. Ramadan is the ninth month of Hijri year since the time of Prophet Muhammad and during this month the Muslims practice self denial by avoiding any food, drink and smoke from predawn till sunset. The month is spent on prayers. After the month on the second day of shawl, when the new moon is visible they break fast and this fast breaking day is called *Eid-ul-Fitr*. On this day, they go to the mosques to offer prayers and take delicious dishes, exchange greetings and call on the friends and relatives.

KUT (Festival of Kuki-Chin-Mizo): It is an autumn festival of the different tribes of Kuki-Chin-Mizo groups of Manipur. The festival has been variously described at different places amongst different tribes as Chavang-Kut or Khodou, etc. It is a happy occasion for the villagers whose food stock is bountiful after a year of hard labour. The festival is a thanks giving feasts with songs and dances in merriment and joviality for all, in honour of the giver of an abundant harvest, it is observed on the 1st of November every year.

Gang-Ngai (Festival of Kabui Nagas): Celebrated for five days in the month of Wakching (December/January) Gang-Ngai is an important festival of the Kabui Nagas. The festival opens with the omen taking ceremony on the first day and the rest of the days are associated with common feast, dances of old men and women and of boys and girls, presentation of farewell gifts, etc.

Chumpha (Festival of Tangkhul Nagas): Celebrated for seven days in the month of December, the Chumpha festival is a great festival of the Tangkhul Nagas. The festival is held after harvest. The last three days are devoted to social gatherings and rejoicing. Unlike other festivals women play a special role in the festival. The concluding part of the festival ends with a procession within the village.

Christmas (Festival of Christians): The Christmas is the greatest festival of all the Christians of Manipur, observed for two days on December 24 and 25. Prayers, reading of Gospels, eating, singing of hymns, lectures on Christ, sports, etc., form the major part of the festival. In some villages where the inhabitants are well-off, the celebration continues till January 1 on which the New Year's day is also observed.

Cheiraoba (The Manipur New Year): During the festival, people clean and decorate their houses and prepare special festive dishes which are first offered to various deities. Celebrated during the month of April, a part of the ritual entails villagers climbing the nearest hill tops in belief that it will enable them to rise to greater heights in their worldly life. The Pangals (Manipuri Muslims) also observe it.

Heikru Hidongba: Celebrated in the month of September, a festival of joy, with little religious significance along a 16 metre wide boat. Long narrow boats are used to accommodate a large number of rowers. Idol of Shri Vishnu is installed before the commencement of the race.

Ningol Chakouba (The Social Festival of Manipuris): It is a remarkable social festival of the Meiteis. Married women of the family who were married to distant places come to the parental house along with their children and enjoy sumptuous feast. It is a form of family rejoinder to revive familial affection. The festival is also observed by the Pangals (Manipuri Muslims) to a certain extent nowadays. It is observed on the second day of the new moon in the Manipuri month of Hiyangei (November).

Lui-Ngai-Ni: It is a collective festival of the Nagas observed on the 15th day of February every year. This is a seed-sowing festival after which tribes belonging to the Naga group begin their cultivation. Social gathering, songs, dances and rejoicing highlight the festivity. The annual festival also plays a great role in boosting the morale and strengthening the bond of Naga solidarity.

Kwak Jatra: Goddess Durga is propitiated with pomp and ceremony in this festival. It is celebrated in the month of October and represents the victory of righteousness over evil.

High Seats of Learning

- Central Agricultural University, Iroisemba, Imphal.
- Manipur University, Canchuipur, Imphal.

Religious Backdrop

The small territory in the southeast corner of India, now a part of the Indian Union and known as Manipur, comprises nearly 8.5 thousand square miles of which only about 650 square miles are covered by the valley and the rest by hills. It did not, however, bear that name in ancient times. It was called 'Suvamabhu' (land of gold) and was outside the political pale of Aryavarta and Bharatvarsa of later ages.

This is evident from the references to it as 'Kritadesa' in the Hindu Puranas. Subsequently, 'Suvamabhu' became Manipur (Jewel-land) and Aryan culture penetrated by slow degrees into the Meithei community, the hybrid race formed by the integration of seven of the many streams (Mongolian and Aryan) settling in the valley, while the tribals in the hill areas–mainly Kukis and Nagas remained comparatively unaffected.

The impact of the Aryan culture is supposed to have started much earlier than the age of the Mahabharata which relates the story of Arjuna and Chitrangada (Manipur in that story, according to some scholars, was on the sea coast of Kalinga or Ganjam or somewhere else, and not the land now called Manipur). Politically however the territory remained outside India practically till its annexation by the British after the 1891 Manipur war.

Culture has its roots in religion which enshrines the highest aspirations and the noblest ideals of people. But very little is known about the history of Manipur till the eighteenth century and, as such, about the religion and culture of the people, though the picture is a bit clearer up to the eighth century than from the eighth to the eighteenth century. During the first of these periods, the religion of the people was more or less tribal in character and consisted mainly of the worship of many gods and goddesses.

Later on, it was swamped by Hinduism which, however, could not totally wipe it out. The primitive religion still survives in a stray from by adjusting itself with the more powerful current of Hinduism. This is evidenced by the existence of temples of Thanjing at Moirang and Senameihi at Imphal.

Primitive Base of Religion

Traces of primitive religion, however, are clearly visible even now in some aspects of Manipuri culture for instance, in dances and dramas representing the story of Khamba and Thoibi. The second period, that is, from the eighth to the eighteenth century, is shrouded in darkness. Since the beginning of the rule of Gharib Niwaj Pamheiba in or about 1714 AD the way was paved for quick integration of the culture of Manipur with that of the rest of India through the rapid spread of Brahmanical Vaishnavism under royal patronage. Vaishnavism, of course, has been in vogue in Manipur from very ancient times and Chitrangada and her son Vabrubahan are said to have professed this religion. But it changed successively from one to another and Gharib Niwaj tried to introduce the

Ramanadi form. The present Vaishnavism of Manipur is largely Gauriya Vaishnavism of Shri Chaitanya Mahaprabhu and it came to be a popular religion since the time of Jai Singh.

This general background of the religion of the Manipuri people is necessary to understand their culture evolution because religion is the main source of cultural inspiration. Vaishnavism has powerfully influenced the outlook of the people by its tenets of universal love, habitual tolerance and perfect equality of all men. This outlook is reflected as much in the social customs as in the cultural patterns of the people. The culture of the Manipuris, as of any other people, finds expression through religious rites and festivals, literature, dance, craft and art; besides, one particular form of sport-polo, is a remarkable feature of it.

The Manipuris perform with due ceremony all the rites and festivals connected with Vaishnavism. The most important among them is 'Yaoshamg' (Doljatra). Other Hindu festivals like Durga Puja, Dewali, etc. are also observed by them. In addition to these annual festivals, the worship of 'Radha Govinda' is daily performed by the many in their family temples. There are also some festivals connected with the old faith like 'Lal Haraoba', 'Chairaoba', etc. which are celebrated along with other festivals. Visits to places of Vaishnava pilgrimage, too, are considered as meritorious acts and part of their cultural life.

Influenced by Bengali Culture

In literature, Bengali has had a noticeable influence on Manipur mainly through Gauriya Vaishnavism. Though she had her own script, language and literature, in olden times, these have now undergone tremendous changes almost beyond recognition. Drama is the particular branch of literature in which the Manipuris have made remarkable progress. The Manipuri people have a special knack for histrionically art and their dramatic performances have earned appreciation everywhere they have been held. Starting with translations of Bengali dramas, Manipur has not developed indigenous dramas though they even now bear the unmistakable stamp of the original model. Besides dramas, religious literature is making steady progress in the land.

The most important and widely known aspect of Manipuri culture, however, is reflected in dance which has gained wide popularity not only in every part of India but outside, too, principally through the efforts of Rabindranath Tagore who took a special interest in it because of its intrinsic qualities and introduced Manipuri dance in Santiniketan. These dances may be divided into two categories-classical and folk.

Of the classical group 'Rasa Nritya' is the most celebrated while the folk dance has a number of varieties. Both the categories have exquisite artistic features and are full of rare grace. 'Rasa' dance is an operatic and choreographic enactment of the original `divine play' of Krishna and Radha with her retinue. So it is purely devotional in form and nature but the sentiments and emotions are expressed so wonderfully through supply movements of the musical sound of 'mridangas', 'kartals', 'mandiras' and bamboo flutes, that even those unfamiliar with the subject matter become spellbound by its magic. It requires special training which the boys and girls receive from their 'gurus'. Besides these, there are other dances like 'Thabal Chongba', 'Laiharaoba', 'Khamba and Thoibi' dances associated with old faith and tradition. Dance is a living art in Manipur. Boys and girls start dancing at an early age and it has come down by tradition through the ages.

Polo, of which Manipur is the motherland, represents another aspect of Manipuri culture. According to the mythology of the land, the game used to be played by the gods. Its local names are 'Marjing', 'Thangjing', etc. and it has been regularly played in the present polo ground since almost the beginning of the seventeenth century. The game was introduced in India by the military in 1863 from Manipur and taken to England six years later by the 'Tenth Hussars'. Polo is still the national game of Manipur where it is extremely popular.

Economic Features

Industries

Manipur continues to strive forward for rapid industrialisation of the state. The State Government has taken up steps to revitalise a few industrial corporations in the priority areas and to wind up or privatise the remaining ones. The Government of India has also, all along been taking keen interest to invigorate industrial development in the state. Apart from taking up many centrally-sponsored schemes, particularly in handloom and handicrafts, food processing industries, Prime Minister's Rozgar Yojana, etc., the Central Government has granted Rs. two crore for construction of two Trade Centres in Manipur.

The Central Government has granted and released Rs. 1.50 crore for one Industrial Growth Centre at Lamlai-Napet in Manipur. Further, the Central Government has also released another Rs. 1.60 crore for setting up one Food Park in Manipur. The Centre for Electronics Design and Technology has established its branch at Imphal to provide training inputs and basic technical facilities for the prospective entrepreneurs of the state in the field of computer and electronics.

Manipur is industrially backward, primarily due to its locational disadvantages. However, it is now making rapid strides towards industrialisation and has registered 8,043 village industrial units by March 1993. Manipur Drug and Pharmaceutical Project- a joint sector project of Government of Manipur and Government of India has been Commissioned at Nilakuthi, in Imphal district since January 1993.

Large units include a steel re-rolling mill, plywood factory, bamboo chipping unit at Jiribam, spinning mill, cycle corporation, cement plant, Shree Flour Mill and Vanaspati manufacturing plant in the joint sector. A Master plan for industrial development of

Manipur up to 2000 AD has been prepared through National Industrial Development Corporation (NIDC) and profile of 99 feasible industries in the state has also been compiled. An area of 461 acres has been identified at Kanglatongbi in Senapati district for the purpose of setting up one industrial growth centre at a cost of Rs. 17 crores. Preparation of project feasibility report in draft stage is completed.

Manipur Electronics Development Corporation Limited manufactures large number of both colour and black and white TV sets. The Centre for Electronic Development and Technology and Central Institute of Plastic Engineering and Technology has been established by the Government of India at Imphal. A number of successful units have also come up in the private sector.

Agriculture

Agriculture is the single largest source of livelihood of the majority of the rural masses and is also the mainstay of the state's economy. From a modest beginning in 1946, the state has now got sufficient number of trained manpower of its own to implement various schemes and programmes in agriculture.

Agriculture and allied activities is the single largest source of livelihood of majority of rural masses and is also the mainstay of the state economy. From a modest beginning in 1946 the state has now got sufficient number of trained manpower of its own to implement various schemes and programmes in agriculture. Production of rice has gone up to 2,262 kg per hectare for high-yielding varieties.

Consumption of fertilizers up to 31 March, 1993 reached 90 kg per hectare. Total area under forest cover is 15,154 sq km of which 1,463 sq km fall under reserved forest while 4,171 sq km is protected forest reserve and the remaining unclassed forest. Manipur is the abode of Shiroy Lily, the paradise flower which is not found elsewhere in the world. It is also the home of the brow-antlered deer, one of the rarest species in the world.

Irrigation and Power

Within a short period of one and a half decade introduction of major and medium irrigation in the state, remarkable progress has been made bringing 62,000 hectare land under irrigation. The state has so far taken up seven projects under the major and medium irrigation programmes. These projects on completion will provide an annual irrigation benefit of 1,10,770 hectare with water supply and power components of 19 mgd and nine MW respectively:

Power development began in Manipur with the installation of first hydropower house at Leimakhong in 1930 having two sets of 100 KW and 56 MW capacities. Installed capacity was 12,023 KW as on 31 March, 1993.

One thousand six hundred and ninety-seven villages have been electrified as on 31 March, 1993. Power supply position in the state showed a market improvement with the recommissioning of Loktak Hydro- Project in August 1984.

Within a short period of two decades of introduction of major and medium irrigation schemes in the state, remarkable progress has been made bringing 54,100 hectares, under the major and medium irrigation programmes. Currently three major/medium irrigation projects are in progress.

The installed capacity was 47,845 KW and 2,001 villages had been electrified by March 2002. Power supply position in the state showed a marked improvement with the availability of share of power from the Central Sector Generating Stations, i.e. Loktak HE Project, Kopili HE Project, Khandong HE Project and AGBPP, Kothalguri and AGTPP, Ramchandranagar (all NEEPCO). A heavy fuel based power project (6×6 MW) at Leimakhong was completed during April 2002.

Transport

Roads: The State has 7,172 km of roads both metalled and unmetalled. The length of roads consists of national highways 957 km, state highways 675 km, district roads 1,977 km and village roads 3,563 km. National Highways No. 39 and 53 pass through Manipur for a distance of 434 km.

Railways: The state is now included in the railway map of India with the opening of railhead at Jiribam in May 1990. Proposal has been mooted for circular railway line connecting the towns along the foothills of the state.

Aviation: Imphal airport is the only airport which is linked with other stations in the region by Indian Airlines and Jet Airways. The Indian Airlines flights connect Imphal to Silchar, Aizawl, Guwahati, Kolkata and Delhi. The Jet Airways flights connect Imphal to Guwahati, Kolkata directly. From 1 May, 1993 Imphal is linked with Kolkata, Guwahati and Silchar.

Festivals

Thirteen festivals in twelve months, thus goes a popular Manipur saying. Every month is associated with a festival or two and Manipur festivals mean songs and dances and sometimes sports. Important festivals of the state are: Lai Haraoba Rasa Leela, Chieraoba, Ningol Chakkouba, Rath-Jatra, ld-ul-Fitr, Imoinu Iratpa, Gaan Ngai, Lui-Ngai-Ni, Id-ul-Adha, Yaosang (Dolijatra/Holi), Durga Pujah, Mera Houchongba, Diwali, Kut and Christmas, etc.

Tourism

Manipur is the state with glorious history and rich culture. Manipur tourism beckons tourists with its breathtaking beauty, serene lakes, soaring hills, refreshing waterfalls, and exotic orchids and amazing heritage. Tourism in Manipur is growing day by day. The

Manipur Tourism Department is taking major initiatives to develop the state in a prime tourist destination of North-East India. Besides improving tourism infrastructure, and tourist facilities, Manipur tourism is also planning to promote new tourist circuits like Loktak Tourist/Wildlife Circuit and Ethnic/Adventure Circuit.

These travel circuits envisage a major water-sports and recreation facility at the unique Loktak Lake, and offer a mix of ethnic tourism and adventure sports in the hilly districts of Ukhrul, Senapati and Tamenglong inhabited by various Naga tribes. Manipur tourism has tourist information centres in several states that provide information about Manipur travel and offer a wide range of services that include an accommodation booking service, information on places to visit, places to eat and events. Amongst the vast range of information on Manipur tourism the Manipur tourism centres, a wide range of local maps, Manipur tourism guides and books are available for sale.

Tourist Centres

Some important tourist centres in the state are: Shree Govindji Temple Khwairamband Bazar (Ima Market), War Cemetries, Shaheed Minar, Nupi Lal (Women's War) Memorial, Imphal, Khonghampat Orchidarium, INA Memorial (Moirang), Loktak Lake, Keibul Lamjao National Park, Bishnu Temple at Bishnupur, Sendra, Moreh, Siroi Hills, Siroi Village, Dzuko Valley, State Museum, Kaina Tourist Home, Khongjom War Memorial Complex, etc.

Tourist Attractions of Manipur

Shri Shri Govindaji Temple: This temple adjacent to the palace of the former rulers of Manipur, is a sacred centre for Vaishnavites. It is a simple and beautiful structure with twin gold domes, a paved courtyard and a large congregation hall. The presiding deity, Radha Govinda is flanked by idols of Balaram and Krishna on one side and Jaganath, Balabhadra and Subhadra on the other.

Shaheed Minar: The imposing Minar of Bir Tikendrajit park standing tall in the eastern tall in the eastern side of the Imphal Polo Ground of the state's capital commemorates the indomitable spirit of Manipur martyrs who sacrificed their lives while fighting against the British in 1891. The eye-catching Minar also serves as an ideal background for photo shoots.

War Cemetery: The British and the Indian Army Cemeteries commemorating those who died in the Second World War are serene and well maintained with little stone markers and bronze plaques recording brief accounts of their anguish and sacrifice. These graves are maintained by the Commonwealth War Graves commission.

Manipur Zoological Garden: About 6 km from Imphal towards the west, lies the Zoological Garden at Iroishemba, hidden half-a-mile from the Imphal-Kangchup road. Graceful brow-antlered deer (Sangai), one of the rarest species in the world, can be seen there in sylvan surroundings. A trip to this garden at the foot of pine-covered hillocks in the western-most corner of Lamphelpat will be an affair to remember.

Singda: At an altitude of 921 metres, Singda is a beautiful picnic spot 16 km away from Imphal. The scenery is inviting. There is an Inspection Bungalow to convenience visitors. Greeted by a breeze-ruffled artificial lake, every visitor is tempted to revisit with packed lunch and a bunch of bum-chums. Kangchup is a beautiful health resorts on the hills overlooking the Manipur Valley. The site is picturesque and worth seeing. With the construction of Singda Dam at Kangchup, the place has become one of the important picnic spots.

Langthabal: It is 6 km from Imphal on the Indo-Myanmar road. Langthabal is a small hillock rich in the relics of an old historical place, well-planned tempted to revisit with packed lunch and a bunch of bum-chums.

Red Hill (Maibam Lokpa Ching): It is a hillock about 17 km south of Imphal City on Tiddim Road. The place was an action-packed location where a fierce battle took place between the Allied Forces and the Japanese Forces in World War II. Japanese war veterans constructed a monument at the foot of this hill and it was significantly named "India Peace Memorial"

Bishnupur: Bishnupur is 27 km away from Imphal City on Tiddim Road. Here stands the conical temple of lord Vishnu built in 1467 during the region of King Kyamba. It is interesting because of its antiquity and architectural design which was influenced by Chinese style. Bishnupur I is also known for its stoneware production. The bustling district headquarters is popular for hill-grown oranges, yongchak (tree-bean) and vegetables. Shoibum (fermented bamboo-shoot) scents the air around the town market.

Loukoipat: It is a hot-favourite tourist spot in Bishnupur District lying just in the outskirts of the district headquarters. A small but aesthetically satiating lake surrounded on all sides by green foliage-rich hillocks, is the main attraction of the spot. Boating facility is also provided to the tourists. A cool greenery-hedged IB built on an elevated site overlooking the lake awaits to host visitors on the look-out for a night's stay.

Phubala: A Charming resort on the western fringes of the Loktak Lake is situated 40 km south of Imphal. It is joined to the mainland by a low causeway. From there, life in and around the gigantic expanse of the Loktak lake can be viewed vividly.

Moirang: Moirang is located 45 km away from Imphal city on Tiddim Road. The ancient temple of the pre-Hindu deity, Lord Thangjing stands there. Every May, men and women in bright traditional costumes sing and dance in honour of the lord there in an eventful festival called Moirang Lai Haraoba. It was from the village of Moirang that the graceful, Khamba Thoibi dance originated. It was also at Moirang that flag of the Indian National Army was first hoisted on Indian soil on April 14, 1944. There is an INA Museum exhibiting letters, photographs, badges of ranks and other articles associated with INA. A bronze statue of Netaji in uniform stands proud in the lawn.

Loktak Lake: Loktak Lake is like a miniature sea. It is the largest freshwater lake in the North-East. Sendra is a hillock of an island of Loktak Lake, 48 km away from Imphal City on Tidim road. From the Tourist bungalow, set atop Sendra island, visitors can get a birds eye-view of the unique Loktak Lake and the floating mass called "Phumdis".

Keibul Lamjao National Park: The Park is located in the south western part of the Loktak Lake. This is the last natural habitat of the marsh-friendly brow-antlered deer (Sangai) of Manipur. Keibul Lamjao National Park is the only floating park in the world. Shooting for game is prohibited there.

Kaina: It is a beautiful hillock about 29 km from Imphal on Imphal-Yairipok Road. Kaina is a sacred place of the Hindus. According to legend, one night, Shri Govindaji appeared to his devotee Bhagyachandra, Maharaja of Manipur, in a dream and asked him to build a temple enshrined with his image carved out of a Jackfruit tree which was then growing at Kaina. Hill shrubs and natural surroundings give the place a saintly solemnity. Ceremonial dances depicting the divine dream are performed as Ras Lila at the Mandop.

Khongjom: It is situated on the Indo-Myanmar Road, 36 km away from Imphal. It is a place of utmost historical importance. Khongjom was the venue where Major General Paona Brajabashi and other brave Manipuri warriors proved their worth in warfare against the mighty force of the invading British Army in 1891. Khongjom is regarded in awe as a symbol of patriotism and valour. A war memorial laid on the top of this venerable hill adds the historical ambience of the heroic site. Khongjom Day is observed as a State Function every year on April 23.

Andro: Andro lies 27 km east of the state capital Imphal. The small town is an ancient village of the state. A cultural Complex was established there by the Mutua Museum, Imphal. It exhibited potteries of the Northeastern Region of India. There also is a Doll-house wherein dolls of various Tribes of the state are displayed.

Churachandpur: It is the second biggest town of the state spreading out on both sides of the Tiddim Road, 60 km away from Imphal. It exhibited potteries of the Northeastern Region of India. There also is a Doll-House wherein dolls of various Tribes of the state are displayed.

Tengnoupal: Sixty-nine km away from Imphal on the Indo-Myanmar highway, one comes across the highest point in altitude on the way to Moreh, the border town with Myanmar. Over there, one is at advantage point to have a full view of the valley portion of the state. To stay at or pass through the elevated peak of a village, one needs warm clothing in any part of the year.

Moreh: The international border town is located on the Indo-Myanmar Road 110 km southeast of Imphal. Being a commercial town, it attracts a large number of people far away from Tamu, its Myanmarese counterpart which was of late given face lift. The recent opening of the Border Trade turned Moreh into an important commercial hub in the

North-East. Right on the other side of the border, at Namphalong, there's a big Myanmarese shopping complex selling all kinds of Thailand and Chinese consumer goods. The shopping complex serves as a poor man's alternative to Bangkok's National Stadium Shopping Arcade. Things come much cheaper there. Conducted Tours are organised from Moreh to Myanmarese towns like Kalimiew and Mandalay. Such a tour is of the rare opportunities.

Ukhrul: The district headquarters of Ukhrul District is situated 83 km away from Imphal in the east. Undoubtedly, one of the highest hill stations of the state, Ukhrul is famous for a peculiar type of terrestrial Lily, the Siroy Lily (Lilium macklinae sealy) which is grown on the Siroy Hill. Khangkhui Lime Caves are interesting places for excursion. Ukhrul wears gay and festive appearance during Christmas. Known for the natural hospitality of its people, it is the place where pioneer missionary, William Pettigrew was first offered a foothold.

Tamenglong: It's the district headquarters of Tamenglong District situated 156 km from Imphal. The region is known for its deep gorges, mysterious caves, refreshing waterfalls, exotic orchids and oranges. The Tharon Caves, Booming Meadow, Zeilad Lake and Barak waterfalls are interesting tourist spots in Tamenglong District. There's nothing to beat the Tamenglong brand of oranges and cane-mats.

Mao: Mao is one of the oldest hill stations of Manipur bordering Nagaland located midway between Dimapur and Imphal on the National Highway-39 at an altitude of 5,762.02 feet above sea level. The Mao IB, built by the Royal Military engineers in 1897 is more than hundred years old. The cultural mosaic of Manipur is not complete without the colourful Mao-Naga dance. Other places worth visiting is Makhel, the historical place of Naga dispersal and the legendary places worth visiting is Makhel, the historical place of Naga dispersal and the legendary place of common origin of the Meiteis and the Nagas, which has the oldest pear tree memorial of the dispersal. Dzuko Valley with its pristine beauty blooms with a rare lily between May and July known as Dzuko Lily.

Koubru Leikha: Koubru is one of the pious mountains of Manipur and is located on NH-39. A three hundred years old temple of Lord Koubru Mahadeva is situated in the foot hills of "Awang asuppa yoimyai khunda ahanba Mountain". The devotees offer rituals in the name of Koubra Baba or the Lord Shiva.

3

History

Manipur is a gateway to South East Asia. This geographic situation influenced the course of its history and cultural development. Manipur literally means city or the land of gems. According to a Manipur historical work, Sanamahi Laikan, the name Manipur was first officially introduced in the early eighteenth century during the reign of Hinduised Garibanisaz (1709-48). 'Mekhala' was another name of the Kingdom as indicated by a coin of the same King describing him as Kekhaleswar Lord of Mekhala or Mekhale.

This name did not occur in the Pre-Hindu literatures, especially the chronicles of the Kingdom. However, this land and its people were known by different names to its neighbours; the Shan or Pongs of Upper Burma, with whom Manipur had political and cultural contacts called it 'cassay' the Burmese, another eastern neighbour and rival, power called it 'Kathe' perhaps derived from Cassy (Manipuris settled in Burma were also known as 'Ponna' the Assamese name for Manipur. In the first recorded treaty between East India Company and Jai Singh in 1762 the Kingdom was recorded as Meckley' But the coins, issued by Jai Singh and his successors adopted as 'Manipureshwar' Lord of Manipur, while 'Meckley' was discarded. Thus as a direct consequence of Sanskritisation, these three names — Mekhala, Meckley, and 'Manipur' were used as the names of the country in the 18th century.

Later on, a Sanskrit work, Dharma Samhita which was written during the reign of Gambhir Singh (1825-34) popularised the legends of derivation of Manipur and Mekhala. It records the legend of Shiva Parvati-Anant, according to which Shiva and Parvati performed the Ras Dance in Manipur after draining away the water in the valley through a tunnel which was made by Shiva's Trishula. Ananta, the serpent god was overjoyed and sprinkled the sparkling gems; hence Manipur (*Mani* = gem: *pur* = city or land). Vijoy

Panchali, a 19th century history of Manipur says that the land was called Arya Nagar, Mahendernagar, then Mekhala and finally Manipur.

Old Sources

Manipur in Mahabharata

Reference has been made to a Kingdom named Manipur in the great Indian epic, Mahabharata, while describing the adventures of the Pandava Hero, Arjuna, who married to Chitrangada a Princess of Manipur, who gave birth to Babhuruvahana, who became the King of Manipur.

The royal family of Manipur after their conversion into Hinduism claimed descent from the son of Arjuna and preceding him, many hoary Puranic figures as indicated by the royal shelly, prepared after Hinduisation. But there was no mention of Babhruvahana or Arjuna in the Pre-Garibaniwaz chronicles and geneologies of the royal family, which was founded by Nongda Lairen Pakhangba. Manipur's alleged Aryan connection should be viewed as an aspect of Sanskritisation and an attempt to gain respectability in the Hindu world, especially among the royal families of India which was the normal practice of all converted ruling families, either Hindus or Buddhists of North-East India and South East Asia. As S. K. Chatterjee has rightly, observed, "The legend of Arjuna and Chitrangada which is very well known in India, became one mightly say, the pivot for linking up Manipur with Brahmanical Purana Tradition."

Apart from the concocted royal genealogy, serious attempt was made to imbibe this tradition in the popular mind of the people. It may be mentioned that the Aswamedha Parva of the Mahabharata, rendered in Bengali by Gangadas Sen was translated into Manipuri and entitled "Cangoi Shagol Thaba" and sung in a ballad form. The Aryan origin of Manipuri's royal family and their Hindu subjects is now an exploded myth.

Manipur in Ptolemy's Geography

Ptolemy, a Greek geographer and astronomer of Alexandria in his Geography of Further India has referred to a number of places cities and tribes in North-East India and Burma. His references are vague and the identification of these toponymies and ethnonyms is by no means easy. G. R. Gerini made an elaborate attempt at such as identification. For instance, Kirrhadia of Ptolemy is identified with the land of the Kiratas the Indo-Mongoloid tribes covering Meghalaya, the Barak and Surma Valley and Tripura where the best Malabathrum (Tezpat) was available. One may naturally include the western hills of Manipur which are inhabited by the said group of tribes where Tez pat is available in plenty.

Ptolemy mentions three principalities namely, Tugma, Triglypton and Mreura. Tugma has been correctly identified with Tammu, a former Shan principality, now a small township in the Kabaw valley of upper Burma, which became a part of Manipur in the fifteenth century. But Gerini's further surmise that it might be a city of Manipur or Kachar is redundant and unnecessary. Triglypton is located by Gerini in Kale, another principality in the Chindwin basin south of Tammu or in Upper Kuladhan in Chin Hills while Yule located it in Tripura. With regard to Mreura, supposed to have flourished in the Kabaw valley is referred to in the Burmese chronicles. But P. C. Chaudhry identifies Mreura with Manipur, only because of its proximity with Tammu and Kale.

Meiteis, the Old Settlers

Manipur has three major ethnic groups: the Meiteis of the Valley, the Nagas and the Kukis of the surrounding hill tribes. They are predominantly Mongoloid, with strains of other non-Mongoloid elements, who from the pre-historic times till today speak Tibeto-Burma languages. Historical reasons greatly influenced the independent growth of these social groups with varying degrees of cultural development and civilization, of which the Meiteis among these autochthons are the most dominant and advanced community.

The origin of Meitei is shrouded in mystery and the study on the subject is greatly influenced by the religious faiths and political ideologies of the Meiteis themselves, thus, making the problem highly speculative and controversial. The ethnic name Meitei, B. H. Hodson thought in mid nineteenth century, as a combined appellated of Siamese "Tai" and Kochin Chinese "Moy" (Moy + Tai = Moytai = Moitai = Meitei) and that the "Meiteis" belonged to the Moi section of the great Tai race. Chongtham Budhi Singh proposes that this ethnonym is a blending of two tribes of ancient China: Mei and Ti = Mei + Ti = Meiti = Meitei.

However, it is well known that historically, the word Meitei was used during the period of the establishment of the Ningthouja Dynasty by 'Pakhangba', to mean this clan or dynasty and those ethnic and social groups who were politically and socially integrated within the suzerainty of the Ningthouja. Greatly influenced by the linguistic and cultural affinities between the Meiteis and the hill tribes of Manipur and their folklore, W. McCulloch advanced a theory that the major tribes of clans of Meiteis appeared to have been the descendents of the Naga and Kuki tribes. He observes, "From the most credible tradition, the valley appears to have been occupied by several tribes, the principal of which named Koomal (Khu man), Looang (Luwang), Moirang and Meiteis (Ningthouja), all of whom come from different directions. The Meiteis being the most powerful subdued the others and the name Meiteis has become applicable to all the people of Manipur plain.

The Kuki tribes of Manipur are a group of the great Kukichin family of people, while the Nagas also belong to the Indo-Mongoloid tribes of eastern India.

Ancient Period

The source for this era comes from the Chaitharol-Kumbaba, the royal chronicle of Manipur or Kangleipak.

Nongda Lairen Pakhangba (33-54 AD): Nongda Lairen Pakhangba was an extraordinary gifted ruler. Pakhangba was truly the maker of Manipur (or Meeteileipak or Kangleipak). He was the first coroneted historical ruler. According to "Cheitharol Kumbaba" Pakhangba's date has been fixed from 33 AD. *Cultural Development – Sagol Kangjei (POLO)* — The Meetei culture took its roots during the reign of Pakhangba. Sagol Kangjei (Polo) was started during his reign with maiden match between the chiefs of different regions. This game was played in the imitation of the old game played in the traditional age known as Hayachak. Laisna took a great role in organising the game.

Khuiyoi Tompok: Pakhangba was succeeded by his son Khuiyoi Tompok in 154 AD. His reign was peaceful. He was known as the inventor of the Drum (Pung). Technical innovation in metallurgy was also recorded in the chronicle. During the reign of Naophangba (428-518 AD) the treatise on the construction of Kangla, Kangla Houba is believed to be written by Ashangba Laiba.

Loiyamba (1074-1122 AD), the Great Law Giver: Loiyamba's reign was an important period in the History of Kangleibak. Along with the military consolidation of the Kingdom Loiyamba introduced administrative reforms which provide the steel frame of the administration of the kingdom for about seven centuries. He systematised the administrative divisions of the country by creating six lups (Division). He introduced the Pana System. Loiyamba Shinyen has projected a well organised society and economy of Meeteileipak.

Medieval Period

Meidingu Ningthou Khomba (1432-1467), the Conqueror of Tamu: His earlier name according to Ningthourol Lambuba, was Charairongba. On of the most romantic events of Charairongba's reign was the raid of the Tangkul tribe from Tuisem village in his absence and the courage and skill demonstrated by his Queen Linthoingambi in the hoodwinking the raiding tribesmen into defeat and captivity. The Meitei state was completely formed during his reign.

Meidingu Kiyamba (1467-1508 AD), the Conqueror of Kabaw Valley: Thangwai Ningthouba was the earlier name of Kyamba. The credit for the military and territorial expansion of the kingdom was rightly given to King Ningthoukhomba and his illustrious son Kiyamba who was a worthy son of worthy father and equally colourful mother, Linthoingambi, the warrior Queen of Manipur's history. The Medival Period in the history of Manipur brings forth the name of Medingu Senbi Kiyamba, who became King in 1476 AD, at the age of 24. He was a friend of the King of Pong (Shan Kingdom), who presented him with a stone, known as PHEIYA (Almighty). It was after this that worship of God, in the form of a sacred stone, was started.

Meidingu Khagemba (1597-1652), the conqueror of Chinese: He was really a great conqueror who consolidated his father's kingdom and expanded the Kingdom of Meitrabak and defended her successfully from the several foreign invaders like the Muslim, Kachari and the Shans of the Kabaw Valley. Khagi Ngamba means (khagi = Chinese, Ngamba = conqueror) that means "Chinese conqueror". According to chronicle, the Meetei King attacked the principal Chinese village (or town) along with the many brave Meetei warrior and defeated their chief Chouopha Hongdei. Khagemba introduced bell metal currency in the kingdom. Some coins of his reign have been discovered. His reign was considered to be the golden age of Manipuri Literature. He was a great patron of Traditional Lainingthou Cult. A contemporary text, Khagemba Langjei is the expression of the supremacy of Sanamahi as the Universal God of the Meeteis. The Learned scholar who were well known authorities and religious and theology and who attended his court were Apoimacha, Konok Thengra, Salam Sana, Yumnam Tomba and Langon Lukhoi – sort of six jewels of Khagemba's court. He was succeeded by his son Khunjaoba in 1652 AD. Khunjaoba was engaged in the fortification of Kangla and excavated the moat in the front of the brick gateway constructed by Khagemba. Paikhomba ascended the throne in 1666. Paikhomba consolidated his power in the valley. His kingdom extended as far as Samjok in the east and Takhel Tripura in the west.

Meidingu Charairongba (1697-1709): With the dawn of eighteenth century, Meitrabak achieved the full development of her culture, economy and state system. In this revolutionary change in the Meitrabak's life, three Kings, father, son, and a great grandson: Charairongba, Pamheiba and Chingthangkhomba played very significant roles, the stamp of which was imprinted on the history of Meitrbak. After the death of Paikhomba, his nephew Charairongba, the son of his younger brother Tonsenngamba ascended the throne in 1697 AD. His reign was the beginning for the transition period from traditional Meetei social situation to a Hinduised Meetei Society. There was constant trade contact and social relationship between Manipur and Burma. In 1702, the of Toongoo dynasty of Awa (Burma) sent emissaries asking for the hand of Meetei Princess. Charirongba gave his daughter Chakpa Makhao Ngambi in marriage to the Burmese King. He constructed several temples for Meitei deities like Panthoibi, Sanamahi and Hindu deities. The relation with Burma deteriorated and more strengthened with India after conversion into Vaishnavism.

British Period

Anglo-Manipuri Relations

The Anglo-Manipuri relations between 1762 and 1947 may be studied in two phases:

- a period of independent status and,
- a period of subordinate status.

From 1762 to 1891, Manipur State enjoyed an independent and sovereign status, expecting for an interregnum of seven years (1819-26) during which Manipur was occupied by the Burmese forces. As regards the other phase, from April 1891 to August, 1947, Manipur was a subordinate state under British paramountcy, as the Manipuris were defected in the Anglo-Manipuri War of 1891.

The British paramountcy over Manipur lapsed on 15th August, 1947 with the passing of the Indian Independence Act 1947, by British Parliament. It would be interesting to note the chain of the national and international events that developed the Anglo-Manipuri friendship, and side by side, those others which led to the Anglo-Manipuri War, 1891. It would be of equal interest to study the British control over the administration of Manipuri state as a native state under the British supremacy after 1891.

Anglo-Manipuri Treaty

The first Anglo-Manipuri Treaty was signed in 1762. The narrative relating to how it came to pass runs as under: Ajit Sai, having succeeded to hatch a plot for murdering his own father, Garibniwaz, the reigning King of Manipur, and brother, Sham Sai, the heir apparent, became King of Manipur in 1751. But, after some time, the secret came to light that Ajit Sai was implicated in the murder of his father and brother. The people therefore, became averse to the rule of Ajit Sai. Taking advantage of the political situation, Bhorot Sai, the younger brother of Ajit Sai, gathered his men and forced Ajit Sai to abdicate the throne. Ajit Sai fled the country and took asylum at Tippera (Tripura); and Bhorot Sai ascended the throne.

Bhorot Sai also conspired against the lives of Gourasham and Jai Singh, the two sons of his late brother, Sham Sai. As the conspiracy got exposed before it could be launched, Ananta Sai the brother of Bhorot Sai collected his followers and planned to revolt against the ruling King. Bhorot Sai could smell the danger and left the country without any attempt to fight the imminent revolt. Thus in 1753, with the consent of the people, Ananta Sai made Gourasham, the elder son of Sham Sai, King and Jai Singh, the younger son Yuvraj. It may be mentioned that Ananta Sai made an arrangement for alternate kingship between the two brothers for a period of five years each. Thus in 1759, Jai Singh became King and Gourasham Yuvraj.

In 1762, Jai Singh was the King of Manipur. In that very year Ajit Sai, the deposed King who was taking refuge at Tippera, had sought British assistance for regaining the throne of Manipur. Jai Singh having learnt the situation, sent his Vakil Haridas Gossam, to Mr. Verelhst, the British Chief at Chittagong whom Ajit Sai also requested for help. The Vakil tried to convince the British officer of the guilts of Ajit Sai for which he has been deposed. Besides the Vakil also asked for military assistance on behalf of Jai Singh to get redress of the grievances, the Manipuris suffered in the hands of Burmese. He further held out that there could be an extensive British trade from India to China through Manipur and Burma when the two were on amicable terms. To meet both ends, the Vakil had proposed a trade and defensive alliance between Manipur Government and the British East India Company Government.

The British authority at Chittagong made a practical review of the situation so as to protect British interests in Eastern India and Burma. During those days the Burmese, helped the France, had persistently harassed the British in the parts of Negrais and Pegu in Burma. So with a view to making best use of the opportune movement, Mr. Verelhst recommended acceptance of the proposal for a trade and defensive alliance with Manipur (without taking cognisance of the request from Ajit Sai for British help) to Mr. Vansittart, the Governor General of Bengal and the President of the Board of Directors of British East India Company.

After minute discussions the Board expressed itself in favour of availing themselves of the opportunity for a vengeance upon the Burmese by having alliance with Manipur. It was resolved that a force consisting of six companies of sepoys commanded by three officers should be sent to take a post at Manipur. Apparently, such a decision was taken in the hope that the British and the Manipuri forces might jointly fight off their common foe, the Burmese and also in consideration of the extensive trade prospects as hinted by the Government of Manipur.

The expedition under Mr. Verelhst left for Manipur in the month of January, 1763, and reached Kashipur in Cachar in April. The troops however, suffered much hardship because of disease, incessant rains, pestilential swamps, etc. Being unable to proceed to Manipur, the remnants fell back and returned to Bengal. The British made no further attempt to send troops to Manipur to fulfil the terms of the treaty.

In 1763, Goursham confirmed the same treaty after he became King. But it was of no avail. The old friendship could only be revived in 1824-25, when the Burmese authorities threatened the British frontier in the North-East India.

Manipur Levy

The Manipur levy was the result of the compelling circumstances under which the British and the Manipuris had their common enemy — the Burmese. In 1819, the Burmese had invaded and swayed over Manipur and Assam. Chourjit, Marjit and Gambhir Singh, the Manipuri princes, and Purandhar Singh and Chandrakanta the Princess of Assam, fled their countries and took shelter at Cachar and Sylhet (now in Bangladesh). After sometime, the three Manipuri princes, the fugitives in Cachar, succeeded in deposing Raja Govindchandra of Cachar and usurped power in Cachar. Meanwhile they also tried to free their state from the threshold of the Burmese.

Raja Govindachandra sought for British help to regain his throne from the Manipuri princes. The British Government could not give a quick and ready response to the request of Govindachandra because they had their own immediate problems. The Burmese Government, who was in occupation of both Manipur and Assam by that time, had asked the British to surrender the Manipuri and the Assamese princes who were taking shelter in the British territory. They further wanted that if the British failed to do so, the Burmese forces would capture them without any hesitation to fight the British if they resisted the Burmese action. But in spite of the Burmese threat, the British did not surrender the princes saying that it was contrary to the British custom to deliver up any person who had sought their protection.

Raja Govindachandra, being desperate at the British attitude, turned towards the Burmese for seeking help. In their response the Burmese sent an army to restore Raja Govindchandra to the throne of Cachar. In the meantime the British made an arrangement by which Raja Govindachandra was reinstated and the Manipuri princes were given compensation. As the Burmese reached the Cachar frontier, the British expressed their unanimity in restoring Govindachandra to the throne of Cachar. But they resisted the entry of the Burmese forces in Cachar as the Burmese intervention in the affairs of eastern India was considered undesirable. Thus there ensued a fight between the Burmese and the British forces in the Cachar-Manipur border.

In 1823, the situation became more tense as the Anglo-Burmese relations suffered a strain, and a fatal war was unavoidable. In 1824 January, the Burmese even hoisted their flag at Shahpuree and made a formal demand for withdrawal of the company's sepoys from that island.

With a view to saving such a momentous situation, the then British authorities felt that it would be indispensable to raise a corps of Manipuris or other border people for service in the Sylhet frontier and Cachar. David Scott, the Agent to the Governor General in Assam and North-East India, decided to employ Gambhir Singh the most courageous and skilful among the Manipuri princes, for such service to the British. David Scott recommended raising of native force under the personal command of Gambhir Singh with British and an assistance. In return Gambhir Singh was assumed of regaining the state if he succeeded to fight out the Burmese. The British East India Company Government approved of the scheme as recommended by David Scott. With the British help Gambhir Singh raised his troops consisting of 500 strong of purely Manipuris and Cacharis. The force was named Manipuri Levy.

The British objective of raising the Manipuri Levy was that the establishment of an independent government in Manipur as an ally of the British would prove the most effectual check on the Burmese. It may also be mentioned that David Scott had a great reliance on the soldierly qualities of the Manipuris, and admiring their courage and skill, he reported to the government that "excepting the Manipuris none of the natives or tribes on the eastern frontier could be relied upon the defend their state. Truly indeed, the Manipuri Levy played the key role in driving out the Burmese from Manipur and the subsequent regaining of their independent status after the signing of the Treaty of Yandaboo at the close of the Anglo-Burmese War in 1826.

Treaty of Yandabod

The first Anglo-Burmese war of 1825 ended in February, 1826. A peace treaty was signed between the British and the Burmese on 24th February, 1826 known as the Treaty of Yandabo. Manipur was not a party to the said treaty. However, an article referring to the political status of Manipur had been inserted in the Treaty. Article 2 of the Treaty of Yandaboo provided, among others, that "with regard to Manipur it is stipulated that should Gambhir Singh desire to return to that country he shall be recognised by the King of Ava as the Raja thereof."

The erstwhile British policy towards Manipur and the above stated provision of treaty, if read together, necessarily lead to the inference that after the signing of Treaty of 1826 referred above, Manipur became an independent State. The British had to accept such a status of Manipur as a necessary evil for the fact that Manipur could be used by the Burmese as a screen for molestation of the British territories in the Northeastern India. Maintenance of a buffer State like Manipur, whose people and Kings were hard-core enemies of the Burmese by then, was a dire necessity to protect the British interest against the Burmese hostility.

In fact, the British embassy at Burma had also committed that Gambhir Singh "is declared by the Treaty of Yandabod to be the sovereign thereof. Manipur is, therefore, an independent country and will descend as such to Gambhir Singh and his heirs according to the laws and usage of the Cassay people (the Manipuris). The British Agent in Burma has further assured that they would not give assistance in money, men or advice to Gambhir Singh which would be prejudicial to the Burmese." Thus, the Treaty of Yandabod is a landmark in the political history of Manipur State. The Treaty, however, could not prove to be a foolproof device for Anglo-Burmese friendship. Two successive wars broke out and the Burmese belligerency could be tamed only after the British annexation of Burma in 1886.

Jiri Treaty

It had been already mentioned in the preceding paras that the British managed to restore Govindachandra to the throne of Cachar by giving pensions to the Manipuri princes. However, Raja Gambhir Singh continued the possession of the Chandrapura Ilaqa of Cachar. He had established the Thana (police station there and a large number of Manipuris housed in Chandrapur. But the right of occupation of the area by the Raja of Manipur and his people was a controversial issue. Govindchandra, the Raja of Cachar alleged that the area had been forcibly occupied by the Manipuri Raja.

He even asked for British help in compelling Gambhir Singh to vacate the area. Gambhir Singh, on the other hand, claim that the area was his paternal property as his father received the land as a gift from Raja Krishnachandra, the brother of Govindachandra and former ruler of Cachar. David Scott, the agent of the Governor General in Assam and the North-East India, dismissed the claim of Raja Gambhir Singh for want of documentary evidence. The agent, however, made a plan to allow Gambhir Singh to use the land. He persuaded Raja Govindachandra to lease 50 hals (about 240 acres) east of Baskandi to Raja Gambhir Singh for a period of 15 years for the purpose of establishing a magazine and stationing of men for carrying the military stores to Manipur. A document was also executed to that effect in 1830 between the two governments.

Lieutenant Pembertom, who surveyed the eastern frontier of India along with captain Jenkins, recommended cessation of the tract of land east of Jiri river in Cacher to Raja Gambhir Singh for effective control of the tribes inhabiting the area.

There were also opinions opposing such transfer of the land. Lieutenant Fisher the Magistrate and collector at Cachar, and Mr. T. C. Robertson, the successor of David Scott, strongly objected to the said transfer. It may be noted that since the British annexation of Cachar in 1830-31 the question had become purely a British concern by that time. In view of the two contrary opinions from the servants of the Company itself, the British authority kept in abeyance their final decision on the issue. Meanwhile Lieutenant Pemberton was sent to Manipur to feel the sentiment of Raja Gambhir Singh in this matter.

In his report Pemberton reiterated his earlier proposal for transfer of the area as stated above. He further reported that asking the Raja to vacate the land and go beyond the Barak river, as suggested by Robertson, would be an insult to the Raja. Under the circumstances, the East India Company Government had finally accepted the transfer. But in lieu of it, the Raja was to relinquish the Chandrapur Ilaqa. A trade and defensive treaty was signed between Gambhir Singh and the East India Company Government on 18th April, 1833. The Treaty provided for *inter alia*:

- Transfer of Jiribam (Jiri) to Manipur;

- Withdrawal of Raja Gambhir Singh's Thana at Chadrapur in Cachar;

- Supply of porters by the Raja for the British troops going through Manipur either for protection of Manipur or war with Burma;

- No obstruction to the British trade by the Raja, no imposition of heavy duties and monopoly of goods by the Raja;

- Repairing of the Cachar-Manipur bridle path by the Raja;

- Assistance by the Raja with his own troops in case of any disturbance in the eastern frontier of British India; and

- The Raja should be responsible for the arms and ammunitions received from the Government of the East India Company.

The Jiri Treaty of 1833, thus represented an instrument for exchange of territory, and side by side, a trade and defensive alliance between Manipur and the Company

Government. It had made easier to demarcate the boundary between Cachar and Manipur. The Jiri river and the western bend of Barak river have been regarded as the inter-state boundary.

Kabo Valley Treaty

The seeming generosity the British authorities had shown to Manipur in handing over Jiriban in 1833 turned out to be a calculated purposive move when the British opened the Kabo Valley question in 1834. Kabo Valley, a small valley between Manipur and Burma had been a bone of contention between the two states even before the Treaty of Yandaboo. It became a part of Manipuri territory by virtue of the right of conquest as Raja Gambhir Singh succeeded in driving away the Burmese from Manipur and beyond the Ningthee river (Chindwin) in Burma in 1826. But the Burmese Government nursed for long their eagerness for repossessing Kabo Valley and did not stop the pursuit.

The British East India Company kept themselves engaged in finding out formulas to make their ports at Pegu and Shahpuree safe from Burmese hostility. With a view of appeasing the Burmese, the Governor General-in-Council, under the influence of Colonel Burney, the British Commissioner at Ava, decided on handing over Kabo Valley to Burma as a mark of 'expediency and gratification'.

Captain Grant and Lieutenant Pemberton were instructed to proceed towards Kabo Valley with a deputy from Gambhir Singh representing Manipur state. Lieutenant Pemberton had been especially instructed to make all endeavour to reconcile the sentiments of Raja Gambhir Singh to the relinquishment of Kabo Valley by reminding him of the liberal considerations of the government in making over to the tract of Jiriban Territory.

The Governor General also informed the British Resident at Ava to announce to the King of Ava the stand of the Supreme Government that it will adhered to the former position that Ningthee river formed the proper boundary between Ava and Manipur. However, in consideration of the Burmese feelings and wishes and in a spirit of amity and goodwill, the government consented to restore Kabo Valley to Ava.

The agreement signed between the Government of Burma and the British Commissioners at Ava was initially called 'Agreement Regarding Compensation for the Kabo Valley, later on it came to be known as 'Kabo Valley Treaty'. The agreement provided that Kabo Valley should be transferred to Burma with effect from 9th January 1834 Manipur Government, in return, should get a compensation of 500 Sicca Rupees per month from the date of transfer. In the event of retrocession of Kabo Valley to Manipur, the payment of compensation should also be stopped from the date of such retrocession. It is noteworthy that the compensation was paid by the British Government and not by the beneficiary, the Government of Burma.

In signing the treaty a deviation from the standard rule was that though Manipur was to part with a portion of her 'territory' no tripartite meeting was arranged for discussion on the matter. Without such time being given to the Raja of Manipur for consideration the document was brought to Manipur for the signature of the Raja. The document bear the signature of Major F. J. Grant and Captain R. B. Pemberton as the Commissioner at Manipur. The Raja probably could not sign it due to his death shortly after the document was brought to Manipur. It may be noted that Manipur State continued to get the Kabo Valley compensation even after the defeat of the Manipuris in the War of 1891 and till the lapse of British paramountcy in 1947.

After the signing of the Treaty of Yandaboo in 1826 followed by the British appeasement policy towards the Burmese by handing over Kabo Valley, the British authorities remained complacent, unmindful of the future impasse of the unmitigated Burmese hostility culminating in the second and the third Anglo-Burmese wars. Lord William Bentinck, the Governor General, elected by the idea that the Burmese would not wage a war against the British had decided withdrawal of all supports to Manipur in 1835. It was felt that such a spending as in the form of support to Manipur to check the Burmese was unwise.

The Governor General established a political agency in the state in 1835 itself for the purpose of maintaining the earlier link in safeguarding British interests. In addition to his duties of being agent, the political agent was to act as a communicating link between the Government of Burma and the Government of Manipur so as to prevent all border feuds between the two states. Major Gordon was appointed political agent in 1835 for the first time.

Initially the political agency at Manipur was placed under the Government of Bengal Presidency for correspondences relating to the matters of the state and for receiving instructions from the Government of India. Later on in 1836, it was transferred under the immediate control of the Government of India as the matters were of British relations with foreign and independent States. Since 1879, on the recommendation of the Government of Assam the political agency in Manipur was placed under the Government of Assam in view of the interrelated issues that existed in Manipur and the surrounding hill tracts of Assam. Such a practice of maintaining political relations between the Government of Manipur and the Government of India through the Government of Assam continued even after the merger administration in the central administration of India in 1949.

British Protectorate

A number of untoward incidents occurred in Manipur between 1844 and 1851, on the issue of succession to the throne. Maharani Kumudini, the widow of Raja Gambhir Singh failed in her plot to murder Nara Singh, 'the Yuvraj and Regent. She fled to Cachar alongwith the reigning minor Raja. Chandrakirti Singh. Nara Singh became Raja in 1844. After a reign of only six years Nara Singh died in 1850. His brother Debendra Singh was made Raja Just after three months of his rule, Chandrakirti Singh, who had attained majority by that time appeared in Manipur and claimed the throne. Chandrakirti Singh defeated Debendra Singh in a fight and succeeded to the throne of Manipur in 1850-51.

Colonel McCulloch, the political agent in Manipur, informed the government that British interest could be effectively exercised if troops were posted at Manipur. However, he initially recommended only formal announcement of recognising the ruling Raja. He pointed that only a declaration that the British would protect the Raja against any attack would deter others from attempting a revolt against the Raja.

The Government, in reply informed the political agent that it had decided to refrain from interfering in the succession issue in Manipur. However, for that occasion the political agent was authorised to announce the British policy of upholding the Raja. Colonel McCulloch announced such decision of the government as to protect the Raja in a public avowal. Since then Manipur had been treated as a protectorate of the British Government as to protect the Raja in a public avowal. Colonel McCulloch announced such decision of the government as to protect the Raja in a public avowal. Since then Manipur had been treated as a protectorate of the British Government; and she had been referred to as an "Asiatic Power in alliance with the Queen."

It may be noted that the British Government did not declare Manipur as a British protectorate on the request of the Raja of the State. To be true, the British Government was afraid lest the Burmese should exert greater influence on Manipur and jeopardise British interests in the North-East India. Insofar as the internal revolts were concerned, Chandrakirti was confident that no Prince could dethrone him as he was the rightful heir to the throne and as he became King with the support of the people. Reference may be made to the case of Khaifa (Keifa) Singh's arrest by the then British Government as Keif a tried to revolt against Chandrakirti. But when the British authorities demanded the amount of expenditure incurred in connection with the arrest of Keifa and the cost of detention in the jail, Chandrakirti Singh refused to pay the amount as the arrest was not affected on his request.

Maharaja Chandrakirti died in 1886. He was succeeded by his eldest son Surchandra Singh. It was during Surchandra's reign that the dark days of Anglo-Manipuri relations set-in.

In September 1890, a fight took place between the two groups of the Manipuri princes (four on each side among the eight sons of Maharaja Chandrakirti Singh) the fight resulted in a palace revolution. Mr. Grimwood, 'the political agent in Manipur, tried his best to bring about a compromise; but without success. Suchandra Singh, the ruling King, abdicated the throne in favour of his next brother, Kullachandra Singh, the eldest of the opposite group. Maharaja Surchandra Singh along with his brothers in his group, decided to leave for Brindavan. Kullachandra Singh became the King and Tikendrajit, the former Senapati and leader of the revolt, was made Yuvraj. As Surchandra left for Brindavan, the political agent reported the fact to the Government of India. But after reaching Calcutta, Suchandra submitted a representation to the Government of India that he had been forcibly dethroned by his rebel brothers. He also requested for British help to regain the throne in the true spirit of the British being the protector.

On receipt of detailed report from the political agent, the government was convinced that Surchandra was not worthy to be rethroned. They resolved to recognise the ruling King, Kullachandra Singh and Tikendrajit, the leader of the revolt should be deported. The British Government instructed Mr. Quinton, the Chief Commissioner of Assam, to proceed to Manipur with a force and settle the matter. Mr. Quinton reached Imphal in March 1891.

He conveyed the decision of the government recognising the Raja and asked the Raja to surrender Tikendrajit Singh for banishment. On the refusal by the Raja to surrender Tikenderjit Singh the British tried to capture him by force of arms. The British forces launched a surprise attack at night at the Manipuri palace.

The Government of Manipur took the British attack as an unwarranted interference in the internal affairs of the state; and therefore, the Manipuri forces resisted the invading British forces. The British could not succeed in their attempt to capture Tikendrajit Singh and tried for a negotiated settlement. The attempt also failed. Five British officers were murdered by the Manipuris. Enraged by such action, the British sent three columns from Kohima, Silchar and Tamu. The British forces defeated the Manipuris and took over the state administration on 27th April, 1891. Manipur became a subordinate State since then.

Provisional Government and Annexation

After the occupation of Manipur the British adopted the normal practice. Since 27th April 1891, Manipur administration was placed under General Collett, the Commander of British army in Manipur. Major Maxwell was made the Chief Political Officer under General Collett. However, such a form of military rule was short lived. On 13th September 1891, the administration was transferred to a civil authority headed by Major Maxwell. Thus Major Maxwell, the Chief Political Officer, was authorised to discharge both civil and political duties in the state independent of the military command.

On the issue of annexation of Manipur by the British all the divergent views were debated in the British Parliament at London. Mr. Ward, the Chief Commissioner of Assam, strongly recommended annexation. There were also the views of Lord Ripon and Lord Northbrook the Ex Viceroys of India, objecting the policy of annexation. Lord Derby also expressed his views that the policy of annexation would create mistrust of the natives of India towards British rule. Moreover, public opinion in the British press and the Indian press were unanimous against annexation. Ultimately, Lord Landsdowne, the Viceroy, while appreciating the British right of annexation the state, remarked that Manipur had not been annexed as a mark of clemency.

The state was regranted to the native Raja Churachand Singh, a minor from a collateral branch of Manipuri Kings. The exact loyalty and with a view to imposing British suzerainty, a Sanad was issued to the Raja. However, the handing over of the state administration to the natives was only nominal. All powers of administration were centralised in the hands of British officers.

British Power during Raja's Rule

The investiture of the minor Raja, Churachand, took place on 29th April, 1892. The major departure from the earlier norms was that Manipuri was allowed to be the regent to the minor Raja. The British Government nominated the political agent in Manipuri as regent. Major Maxwell the political agent assumed a dual role of political agent and Superintendent of state. Thus, the British officer was administering the state virtually in his own right.

Raja Churachand Singh attained majority in 1907. In the same year, the administration of the state was transferred to the Raja assisted by a durbar called *Manipuri State Durbar*. The Raja was to act as ex-officio President of the durbar. The Government of India framed and implemented a set of rules for administration of both the valley and the hills of Manipur. Under the Manipur administration rule, 1907 the durbar was bestowed with greater amount of power than the Raja. The Vice-President of the durbar was necessarily to be a British officer who really played the key role in the administration of the state. The Maharaja was only a nominal head. The political head was delinked from direct administration of the state.

In 1916, the administration rule was amended. The vice-president of the durbar was made president and the Maharaja was to be kept aloof from the durbar. The Raja was given the power to override the decision of the durbar only with the approval of the political agent.

As regards the financial matters, the Government of India had full control. The State Budget, both for the hills and the valley, was prepared by the durbar. It was to be operative only with the final sanction of the Government of India. The Government of India was free to make any alteration if found necessary. The more remarkable feature of the administrative control was that the British had brought in a dichotomy in the state administration. The Maharaja and the durbar were not given any power in the administration of the hills. They were to administer only the plain areas. The Hills and the Hill tribes were to be administered by the political agent and the assistant political agent (Vice-President of the durbar). This form of a dual government virtually separated the people of the hills from those of the plains.

However, after the amendment of 1916 rule, the Maharaja was given a consolation by inserting in the revised rules that the President of the durbar would administer the hills on behalf of the Raja. But, the durbar still remained devoid of power about hill affairs. The final authority in the state was still the political agent.

The durbar did not have any jurisdiction in hill affairs. They were simply to prepare the hill budget for the satisfaction of the government. Not only durbar, no Manipuri official was associated in any high ranking office in the hill administration. Even after the opening of four subdivisions in Manipur, only British officers from the Assam Provincial Service Cadre were appointed as subdivisional officers. It was only after the Naga unrest of 1931 that one Manipuri official was appointed as Assistant to the President of the durbar who was in charge of hill affairs. As regards the role played by the Maharaja in the hill matters, such gap remained between the letters in the rules and the practice in the field. The control continued till 1947.

Maharaja Bodhachandra (1941-55), became the ruler of Manipur ceremonially on the 15th Sajibu (March-April, 1941), on the approval of the Viceroy of India. In view of the strategic importance of his state during the Second World War Manipur became the first line of communication and later a war zone. Flushed with victory against the British in East Asia, the Japanese occupied Burma, Andaman Island and reached the vicinity of Manipur as the ally of the Indian National Army (INA) raised by the Netaji Subhash Chandra Bose. The Japanese planes made a series of air raids on Imphal between 1942 and 1944. The civil administration was paralysed; inhabitants of Imphal fled to villages for fear of life. Imphal looked like a deserted place.

The INA and Japanese troops had occupied about two-third of Manipur and Nagaland from the clutches of British Imperialism. A large number of young Manipuris, hill-chiefs of the Nagas and Kukis, because of their security reasons, went to the Japanese. They distributed INA leaflets and also secret meetings were held. In their estimate, a happy life was promised with the quickest capture of Imphal by the Japanese. They knew the differences of complexion and character between them and the white men. The people believed and repeated what they were taught by the old Purana saying "Non gpok Thong Hangle" (the eastern gate has been opened) by which they meant the western rule and culture would be replaced by the eastern rule through Japanese invasion. They started propaganda about the immortality and invincibility of the Japanese.

Gen. Shah Nawaz Khan was the first man to hoist the INA flag in Mourang (56 km to the southwest of Imphal).

The Allied powers strengthened the defence of Imphal by means of intelligence, anti-aircrafts and forces of SEAC. Some of INA officers defected to the British side and gave all secrets resulting in the setback to the Japanese. There were sharp fightings in Bishenpur, Nambol Maibam Lokpaching, Palel, Kohima and Dimapur Road after which the Japanese showed signs of losing ground. They thought that once they got across the Manipur border the Congress people in Imphal valley would help them in capturing Imphal. But things were not happening as they had expected. They were driven out of Imphal after a series of reverses. It is estimated that about 26,000 brave INA soldiers laid down their lives on the soil of Manipur and Nagaland. The Japanese left Imphal leaving thousands of their comrades dead in the battle fields.

The Maharaja cooperated loyally with the Allies in all phases of the war effort. The Indian refugees who passed through Manipur from Burma were housed in Korengei camp, entertained by the Maharaja and Maharani Iswari Devi, and many thousands of troops received the fullest help even at great trouble to the state in 1942. The morale of the people was high enough in the dark period. It was during this period that the Maharaja received Lord Mountbatten. Air Marshall John Baldwin, General W. Slim, British war officers and Indian rulers of British India.

The bombardment on Imphal killed many civilians and destroyed their properties. Victory celebration of the British was held in Imphal on the Vijaya dasmi day in 1944. They were immensely helped by the Assam Rifle Association. Compensation for war damages was paid to the affected people by the British Government. The war brought in great changes for the people of this land as they learnt how to adjust themselves in such a situation. Roads and bridges to enable the allies to move the army were constructed in different parts.

Remission of Tribute

In recognition of the steadfast loyalty displayed by Manipur state and people, the annual tribute of Rs. 50,000 payable to the British Government was remitted in perpetuity in 1945 by his Majesty, the King Emperor. It removed the misunderstanding between the British and the ruler of Manipur. The scene was occupied with bright and joyous hearts of Vishnu Ia grat a (invocation to Lord Vishnu). His Majesty declared the 8th October of every year as a state holiday under the name of Bodha-Leisemba "Renovation Manipur during Maharaja Bodhachandra" in commemoration of this gift from His Majesty. The people of Manipur decorated the ruler with the Title of Meidingu Leisemba (Maker of Manipur).

By 1947 Manipur became a part of the Indian Union. Manipur State Durbar was redesignated as Manipur Council and its members were named as Ministers from July 1, 1947. The inner-line permit system issued by the Political Agent for the outsiders visiting the state was transferred to the Home Minister of State Council.

The Maharaja ushered in a new era in the state by his administrative reforms for associating the people with the governing of the state and announced the formation of a committee to make the Constitution with 17 members, 6 members from the hill areas and five official members. It formed two subcommittees to draft the Constitution. The reports of them were duly passed. They obtained the approval of the Maharaja and Interim Government of India. It became an Act called the Manipur Constitution Act 1947. Manipur was the first native state in India to introduce assembly elections on adult franchise.

Elections were held in March 1948. The elected Legislative Assembly met thereafter. This act would have been democratic had the person having the largest majority was appointed the Chief Minister. But the Chief Minister was appointed by the His Highness in consultation with the elected ministers of the council although they were elected by the Assembly. It is clear that 90 per cent of full-fledged democracy was introduced on a somewhat imperial model.

With the lapse of British paramountcy on August 15, 1947, the treaty lapsed after 56 years. Captain F. F. Pearson, the former President of Manipur Durbar and sometime Chief Minister handed over the formal charge to Captain M. K. Priyobrata Singh, the second son of His Majesty Churachand Singh. The portfolios were distributed among the ministers with the approval of Governor of Assam.

The post of Political Agent (later Dewan) was created as a temporary arrangement. With the transfer of power there was a corresponding increase of responsibility for the Maharaja and his new ministry. The Maharaja became the master of hill areas which were so long administered by the president of the durbar on his behalf. The silent departure of the British had been predicated as the unsound firing of the gunshot in the Puranas of the Meiteis. It was implied that the British would leave the country without any gunshot. The Maharaja celebrated Indian Independence Day by hoisting Pakhangba flag in front of the Council Hall and with ceremony of Puja in the old Kangla capital.

From his announcement of orders on August 28, 1947, it is known that when the question of enforcement of martial law and cow slaughter during the war time came before the government the objectionable issues were, after a determined opposition from His Highness cancelled it in the interest of the Manipur Hindu Vaishnavas. He heralded a modern era in the political and educational changes by recognising Manipuri as the language of the state and dividing Imphal valley into five subdivisions under the SDOs and establishing a college called Dhanmanjari College and Changing State Military Police into Manipur Rifles and opening a Chief Court.

His reign extended up to 1949 and the state for a brief period functioned as an independent kingdom with him as the ruler and his council of ministers, later only to merge either with Burma or Indian Union. Many voluntary political parties were formed. Strikes, Satyagrahas, Hartal, etc. were adopted from the Indian way of life for the first time. The movements for merger against its independent status gained momentum among such political parties as the Congress, Communist and Socialists, etc.

The Congress workers of West Bengal and Assam moved the merger of Manipur with West Bengal and Assam, the Socialists for its merger with Assam. Congress Party of Manipur was in favour of merging Manipur with India or Purvanchal (Eastern State Comprising Manipur, Cachar, and Lushai Hills). In the last week of November; 1947, the leftist group of Manipur state Congress launched an agitation for a responsible government of Manipur on non-violent lines as the council fell short of their demand. In August 1948, the Mao Nagas demanded the merger of Mao area with the Naga Hills. In the same year

Manipur Kishan Sabha under H. Irabot Singh started agitation for cession of northeastern part of Manipur from Manipur and establishment of an independent Government with Headquarters in Nongda. In addition to their agitation in the valley areas, the communist leaders went to Rangoon to meet the Burmese leaders for inclusion of Manipur in Burma, only ruling local party, namely, Praja Santi Sabh, was opposed to the integration of Manipur with India. The Maharaja went to Shillong in September 1949, for clarification of pending election cases. Shri Shri Prakasa, the then Governor of Assam forced him to merge Manipur with India as the fulfilment of Indian Government desire.

Maharaja Bodhachandra signed Merger Agreement of Manipur with India in Shillong the undue pressure of the then Home Minister Sardar Patel. He was given an annual pension of three lakhs of Rupees from noon of October 15, 1949.

The Constitution Act, 1947, became inoperative, Legislative Assembly was dissolved, Council of Ministers dismissed, the chief court abolished by the order of the Government of India.

It raises certain legal questions as to why the then assembly accepted the order of dissolution although the Maharaja signed the merger agreement without getting the opportunity of consulting his Council of Ministers and the Assembly. The Maharaja was fully assured of the betterment of the people by the free India's Government and the people hoped then that they would get a political set up not inferior to the one they had already enjoyed up to the date of merger. But the unceremonious abolition of the hard earned full-fledged Assembly had produced some adverse effects on the people. The present history of Manipur is the history of struggle of the people, both of hills and plains, for restoration of Assembly and statehood as their legitimate claim.

Maharaja Bodhachandra died on December 9, 1955. The Rulership was given to his second son, Okendrajit by his second Rani, Kamalabati Devi, on the recommendation of the Chief Commissioner. A case of dispute for the successorship was instituted by the sons and near relatives of the deceased Maharaja. A high Judicial enquiry was appointed with Judicial Commissioner of Manipur by the Home Ministry of India. The judicial officer expressed his desire to receive all applications from all the interested people having a right to the Gaddi of ruler. There were as many as nine candidates including the sons, brothers of the Maharaja Bodhachandra, some Rajkumars and Ningthuja clan on the ground that they were the descendents of the ancient line of princes.

The judicial court started examining them along with witness which were presented to it regarding the customs, traditions and manner of the Manipuris. It took sometime for the order of the Government of India to come after receiving the judicial report. The recognition of Okendrajit was upheld. After the abolition of the Privy Purses of the rulers, he became a citizen of Manipur and the Chairman of Shri Govindaji Temple Board.

Religious and Customary Affairs

Like his father the Maharaja Bodhachandra and his durbar ruled the Kingdom with only the least interference from the British authority, that is, the Political Agent and the Government of Assam. The Manipuri ruler is the head of the two major religious creeds-Pre-Vaisnavism and Vaisnavism of Bengal (as it appeared in the state). The ancient cities have been honoured as the Hindu deities since the 18th century. The Manipuri King insisted that every god in Meitei calendar should be celebrated with a public ceremony. There was not much distinction between the religious and secular functions. The people had spiritual and temporal allegiance to the King in an unavoidable way. The Governor of Assam had been conscious enough to dissuade the ruler from the purely religious course of action as it would mean nearly one day in three as holiday. The durbar made allotments of funds for the state in connection with the celebration of the following festivals:

- Chandra Jatra,
- Nar Singh Janma,
- Jalakeli,
- Ratha Yatra,
- Radhashtami,
- Bamon Janma,
- Durga Puja,
- Magha Shri Panchami,
- Shivratri,
- Rama Navami,
- Charak Puja (Meitei Cheiraoba),
- Varuni,
- Dolyatra,
- Pakhangba Chenghongba,
- Sanamahi Chenghongba,
- Nityananda Chenghongba,
- Kali Puja,
- Pakhangba Leikatpa,
- Lai Haraoba, and
- Krishna Janma.

It is to be noted that Hindu festivals are observed in a modified way and a day later as determined by their calendar. Some of them were exclusively conducted by the court Maibas and Maibis of the court. The Maharaja's approval was necessary for all cases covering disputes, social and religions irregularities and admitting outsiders into Meitei community except the Muslims and the Yaithibis (scavengers). The court Pandits and Physicians conducted the annual worship of great gods on behalf of the Maharaja and the kingdom as customary functions. There were various taboos connected' with the person of the' ruler. He was not permitted to go north on Tuesday which was considered inauspicious for travel. Some of the hill tops and sacred groves were not visited by him as the presiding deities were inimical to the royal family.

The effigy of snake god, Pakhangba was worshipped by the King in the Royal Temple the image 'was never allowed to be moved in a western direction, because to do so would have implied retreating from Burma, the traditional enemy. The King thought that it was his duty to safeguard the trust which the people entrusted 2,000 years ago up to Pakhanba who happened to be the founder of Ningthouja (Royal) dynasty. The King safeguarded the sacred trust with honour and full consciousness.

Maharaja Bodhachandra (when he was the Yuvraj) was exiled to Benaras for about three years and one month (1934-37) for his action against his father by Churachand with the consent of the British Government of India. In his exiled period, he drew inspiration from a Hindu monk and led a pious life as ordained by Vedas. He became a devotee of Lord Vishwanath as is evident from his poems written there. One will be struck by the way of life he lived as King of Manipur in later years. His long, black hair and Jata (coil of hair on the head) and use of Banarasi cotton cloth of soft and thin texture reminded certain features of Sadhus in the Holy City. He was a fine composer of poems.

He himself too was a Pung player (drummer) of considerable merit. True to pious generation of Vaishnava rulers he acted as the main singer of Kirtans, Manoharsahi type of songs in connection with the state functions and sacred days of his favourite people.

During the period of Second Word War he is credited with having brought the idol of Royal Deity-Shri Govindaji to the safer places (Khongman and Uchekon), and keeping the daily devotional service of the Lord of the Universe intact.

Under orthodox Hindu influence important state functions were usually marked with Pujas, Sankirtans and chanting of the Slokas of Srimad Bhagavat. Pure Manipuri games of great interest such as polo foot hockey, boat race, wrestling (Mukna) and dances and cycle polo were played various other activities were also carved out.' The ministers were obliged to take Oath in the name of the Bhagavat before Shri Govindaji. The ruler continued to be the authority in giving national awards like Khamen Chapta (Printed silk Dhoti), Sana Khuji (gold bangle), Tal (Jan beads and sequences) to the deserving persons, appointing persons in his court and conferring titles on them. He also undertook a pilgrimage to the hill villages of different tribes who were neither Manipuri nor Hindus.

They enjoyed his protection and were required to obtain his recognition in their affairs. Some of them had begun to embrace Christianity offered to them by the Missionaries with the consent of the British. The Muslims of the Manipuri Valley did not look as active in religion as in the politics. The Meitei Marups had started a number of propaganda activities by the time of merger agreement.

The Maharaja was regarded as the incarnation of God Vishnu or Pakhangba in Manipuri belief. Most of the office holders were the princes nearer to the throne near relations of the ruler were also regarded as divine. The customary and religious rights of the ruler were enshrined in the Manipur State Constitutional Act, 1947, Article 8 says, "The Maharaja's prerogative (a) All family matters which are the Maharaja's sole concern as head of the ruling family, all matters which are his sole concern as the defender of faith and all matters concerned with Titles, Honours and ceremonial shall be deemed to fall within the Maharaja's personal prerogative and in such matters the Maharaja shall exercise full discretion subject to the provisions of the Constitution and the laws of the state. The Maharaja's prerogative shall not, however, be taken to compromise any matter wherein the legitimate interests of the state administration or civil right sustainable in a court of law is involved.

It will be within the prerogative of the Maharaja to remit punishment and pardon to offenders subject to the provisions of the Manipur State Court Act provided that this prerogative shall not 'prejudice the right of any individual to confirmation; (b) It shall be prerogative of the Maharaja and Maharaja's first wife that neither may be made answerable to law nor subject to any legal proceeding in the State Court. Their persons and property shall be inviolable.

The relation between the Maharaja the Rajkumar of ruling house and the people was governed by thou gallon (court manners and language). This use was a courtesy which contributed to the social solidarity and a charm all its own to the Raja's regime. It is one of the aspects of Bhakti Yoga. Formalities like touching the foot, prostration, covering the women's head with a piece of cloth, etc. came into vogue by this time. The use of separate vocabulary lent colour and dignity to the ruling King and princes.

Manipur has the unique distinction of having given right to such Constitution and court manners. The dignity of the Maharaja was also guaranteed by the popular council vide Resolution No. 2 (b) of June 22, 1949. The merger agreement gives the ruler to enjoy the authority as follows: "(a) His Highness the Maharaja shall continue to enjoy personnel rights, privileges, dignities, titles, authority over religious observances, customs, rights, ceremonies and institutions of the same in the state which he would have enjoyed had this agreement not been made. (b) The Dominion Government guarantees the succession according to law and customs to the Gaddi of the state and to His Highness the Maharaja's rights... in charge of the same in the state."

But the merger agreement and the World War II gave the Ex-Maharaja and the people a chance of change, change in social outlook, way of life, change for a new idea-ideal of equality and justice hailed by the modern mind. The people who were orthodox before the war were radically changed. Inter dining going to hotels, new dresses, cinema, theatre, etc., have increased. Band party has become an essential part of sociocultural life such as marriage, ball dance and Laiharaoba. But as far the prestige and influence of the ruler, it rested wholly on the political power and once it was taken away, his eclipse was inevitable.

Under Congress influence, attempts were made by some interested groups to disown his religious rights and authorities over the Ningthou Lai (gods of the King whose Seva is done by him for all Manipuris) and rites. The rulers in the administration by this time violated the agreement of 1949 in their actions and decisions. They held that the old time rights lapsed with the accession of the state to the Indian Union. The Deputy Commissioner instead of referring the matter to the ex-Maharajas undertook to fix the date of Moirang Laiharaoba. The Police Superintendent spoke to the gathering of Moirang to forgo all rights and titles with a view to carve out a society of equals.

The D.C. and the officer of Police attending the festival ignored Maharaja's ceremonious visit and did not show the simplest courtesy of greeting that he could expect of them. The congress agitators began to spread the news that the ink of the agreement was dry. The Maharaja made complaints to the Governor of Assam over the head of local authorities in Manipur for not according him the courtesies that were due and proper. But the new rulers ignored even to reply to his petitions. It takes time to change the traditional state. The old institutions and customary court titles were never abolished as they offered opportunities to satisfy the religious needs of the people or to provide the posts nearer to custom and religion. They retain some status till today. Under his able assistance and encouragement, the His Highness' Pandit Loisang continued to be the authority to shed light on the history of the clans, hierarchy of the clans, concept of common seat and common pipe smoking.

Important events of his reign were entered in the royal chronicle and Cheitharol Kumbaba under his order and every page of its authenticated' by his seal. His Loisang (office) prepared the sacred compilation which has now ceased to be so. Maharaja Bodhachandra began to live the typical life of a pious and orthodox Vaishnava, the life of a Yogi who renounced the mundane pursuits and devoted himself solely to spiritual quests. He sought solace through pious works and prayer though he was not consulted by the new rulers in later life. He retired to the sacred hill of Nongmaiching (Vindhyagiri as its Hindu name) which is traditionally associated with the cult of Nongpok, Ningthou and Panthoibi (Siva and Durga). On 10th Wednesday, January-February (Phairen), 1944, the Jivanyas ceremony of Goloknath and Raseswari took place in the palace on a grand scale. The idols were carved out of the Champaka and Jackfruit tree (grown on Kaina

Hill) by his order. On 22 Wakching (December-January), 1948 he beautified the sanctuary of Nongmaiching and with his worship of Siva evolved the sanctity of this hill.

He dedicated a brick temple to Mahadeva on the top of the Nongmaiching hill on 28th Wednesday, Lamda (Feb.-March), 1947, a stone temple in Gouranagar, on 15 Phairel 1954, (foothill of the same hill) and another at Khalong on 7th Sunday, Ingel (June-July), 1955. Roads, tanks, Kundas, etc. were renovated in Nongmaiching; Kabru Hills which were sacred to the Meiteis. With due Sankalapa he arranged the hearing of sacred Vaishnava text in the hall of Shri Govindaji. In the function which lasted for one (from 1st Sajibu, 1953 to 12th Sajibu - March-April) 1954, texts like Mahabbarata, Ramayana, Vijay Panchali, Vayu Puran, Lakshman Digvijoy, Govinda Lilamrita, GovindItihash, etc. were discoursed in the traditional manner. One person recited the musical metre of the texts according to Raga and Ragini while another translated the passages and the ideas contained in Manipuri. There were no writings in Manipuri in these themes by this time. He patronised this form of art.

The Maharaja as the sole authority, presented the participants with coveted rewards and conferred on them suitable titles. It was on 18th of Friday Hiyangei, just eight days before his death that the Maharaja performed the memorable Mahakirtan of Khallong and on 21st Monday he performed royal feeding of the people with eight types of Palas. He died a sudden death on 26th of the same month.

He was in constant touch with the Manipuris living in Hojai, Cachar, Vrindavan, etc. On his way to Shillong in October 1951, the Meiteis living in 42 villages of Hojai (Assam) requested him to establish religious and customary courts like Cheirap (Civil Court), Garod (Military Courts), Brahmasabha in that area on the model of his ancient courts. He appointed the head of the Brahmasabha and deputed the officials of his court to introduce the system of introducing for Panas (divisions) and set up customary departments so that they might look after their customary affairs.

The Meiteis in one respect or another turned their feet towards him even after the integration of the state to get their custom and belief stamped with his approval as a prerequisite towards their practice. So far as the common old people were concerned they did not know much of the administrative and religious changes. In conformity with the pious ideal, a well-to-do man used to instal a temple, a congregation hall, etc. to organise Sankirtan and visit holy places in his life time.

They made several promises to various deities in the form of dress, ornaments, furniture for temples, in the event of their wishes being fulfilled. It is customary for a high status family to promise Shri Govinda that in the event of fulfilment of its wish, it would organise a Rasa dance as a mark of gratitude to him and also that his or her son would play the role of Radha Krishna in the profound Rasa dance. Sometimes a pious man had a small temple built in a corner of his house. He offered the food which he prepared in a separate kitchen to the favourite deity inside the temple and he alone took the Prasad (rice and vegetable products alone forming a variety free from fish) at the altar. Sometimes a Brahman is requisitioned for the Seva of the deity on payment of paddy salary. Such was the emotional pattern of the time. With the confirmed Vaishnava they are still popular.

Thus the above discussion about the time of the Maharaja Bodhachandra enables us to have a glimpse of the generation gap to compare the situation of the one prevailed on the eve of the war and the merger agreement with the new developments in all fields.

They are involved in making a synthesis between the old and the new culture and making some phenomenal developments.

Post-independence Era

Administrative Changes Since 1947

Manipur became a State under a Chief Commissioner. The annual allowance of Rs. 6270 payable to Manipur for Kabaw valley (a part of Manipur ceded to Burma) was continued by the British Government and the Government of free India up to 1958. The former Maharajas (His Highness Churachand and His Highness Bodhachandra) urged upon the chamber of princes, Government of India and the British authorities for suitable measures for the restoration of the valley to Manipur. A delegation met the Defence Minister and Sardar Patel who refused flatly to open the issue afresh. Under the Chief Commissioner all Central Acts had been extended in Manipur.

In 1950-51, an advisory form of Government was introduced. Socialist Party in alliance with some local parties organised an agitation for installation of Assembly against his advisory Government in 1954. In 1957 following the recommendation of SRC Report, a territorial Council of 30 elected members and two nominated members replaced the advisory rule. The whole state was agitated from time to time for the restoration of an Assembly. The Naga hostiles activity under A. Z. Phizo was also fairly widespread in the Naga inhabited areas of Manipur. The belief in the formation of a separate state had been nicely given expression to by Pan Manipur Youth League, Meitei State Committee, United Natural Liberation Front, Revolutionary Government of Manipur, Kanglei League and Political Organisations of the Hill People.

Territorial Council to Territorial Assembly

With the passing of the Government of Union Territories Act, 1963 the existing Territorial Council constituted under the Territorial Council Act, 1956 had been converted into the Territorial Legislative Assembly in June, 1963. The Act provided a Legislative Assembly of 30 elected members and a council of three ministers for Manipur. Manipur continued to be administered by the President of India through the administration.

The Chief Minister would be appointed by the President and other ministers by the President on the advice of the Chief Minister. They were collectively responsible to the Legislative Assembly. The leader of the Manipur State Congress, Shri Koireng Singh who commanded the largest number of Congress MLAs formed the government.

The Congress with Shri M. Koireng Singh as Chief Minister ruled Manipur till the next election, held on 19th February, 1967 in the Valley and 29th February, 1967 in the hills of Manipur. During the first Koireng ministry, the historic events that took place was the spontaneous non-violent student march on August 27, 1965 to the Chief Commissioner and his ministry demanding distribution of foodgrains to the masses, opening fair price ration shops and curbing the unregulated price rise, the failure of the government to give written assurance to the hungry masses and the subsequent police firing to the thousands that thronged in the Chief Commissioner's compound.

The firing on the crowed led to the death of three students, one AIR driver, injury to hundreds and arrest of the student leaders. The event which was condemned by a large section including members of the Ruling Party was investigated by an administrative enquiry led by Shri Ashok Mitra, which criticised the government action. The combined students' and women movement on the massive scale left deep scars in the mind of the younger generation, reminiscent of state tyranny, the event is yet to be studied in more details.

Second Koireng Ministry

The fourth general election was held in Manipur on 19th February, 1967 in the valley and on 20th February, 1967 in the hills. The net result was out of 30 candidates returned, Congress won 16 seats, SSP 4 seats, CPI 1 seat and Independents nine seats. Of the nine Independents, seven went over to the Congress. Smt. A. Bimola Devi and Smt. R. T. Shining were nominated as MLAs by the Central Government under section 3(3) of the Government of Union Territories Act, 1963. The Congress had a comfortable majority of 25 members in a house of 32 members. Shri M. Koireng Singh, leader of the Congress Legislative Party, was sworn in as Chief Minister on 20 March, 1967. The other four ministers were: (i) Shri Sibo Larho, Finance Minister, (ii) Shri N. Tombi Singh, Education Minister, (iii) Shri Goukhenpau, Medical Minister, (iv) Md. Alimuddin, Development Minister. Shri Salam Tombi Singh and Shri Khwairakpam Chaoba Singh were elected the speaker respectively and deputy speaker of the Manipur Legislative Assembly.

Soon a severe struggle for power ensued within the State Congress Legislative Party. Eight Congress MLAs defected to United Opposition Front on 19th September, 1967 reducing the ruling party to a minority in the 32 member house. The defection raised the strength of the opposition to 17 including the Speaker Shri Salam Tombi Singh and the Deputy Speaker Shri Khwairakpam Chaoba Singh who had joined the opposition front earlier following their expulsion from the Congress Legislative Party for alleged anti-party activity.

As a result of the defection the Congress Party's strength had been reduced to 15 from 25 in the house. But Manipur Tussle took a dramatic turn when both sides claimed majority. Though the Congress ministry in Manipur had been given a fresh lease of life by the postponement of the Assembly Session till October 5, the defection of 8 Congress MLAs to the Opposition United Front continued to cause anxiety.

The political atmosphere in Manipur Continued to be tense reaching the climax gradually. The Assembly was summoned on 5th October, 1967 and the Opposition United Front had given notice of a no-confidence motion against 'Shri M. Koireng Singh's ministry. On 4th October, the Congress had bowed out of power in Manipur with the submission of the Koireng Singh Ministry to the Chief Commissioner. Shri Longjam Thanbou Singh of the United Front was later elected Chief Minister designate of Manipur at a meeting of the United Legislature Front in the wake of the fall of the seven month old Congress Ministry headed by Shri Koireng Singh. At the invitation of the Chief Commissioner, Shri Salam Tombi Singh, leader of the United Legislature Front had a discussion with Shri Baleswar Prasad, who had formally asked the ULF to form a new ministry. Shri Long jam Thambou Singh Chief Minister designate, met the Chief Commissioner and held a brief talk of the formation of the new Ministry. His four Cabinet colleagues were Shri Seram Angouba Singh, Shri K. Envey, Shri Ashraf Ali and Shri Ayekpan Biramangol Singh.

Thambou Ministry

The five men Manipur United Front Ministry of Manipur headed by 64 years old Shri Longjam Thanbou Singh who had 21 years old association with the Congress Party, was sworn in at Imphal on 13th October, 1967, ending ten years of Congress rule in the territory. Of the other four ministers two were defecting Congress and two were Independents. This was the first non-Congress ministry in Manipur.

Shri Koireng Singh, leader of the Congress Legislature Party, however, claimed that his party was well poised for definite victory in the forthcoming trial of strength in the Assembly meeting. He brought a motion seeking leave to move a no-confidence motion against the Council of Ministers on 16th October when the Manipuri Assembly met after two postponement over the ministerial crisis. On October 4 when the Assembly met to debate the motion of no-confidence brought by the Congress against the ULF Government Shri Salam Tombi Singh, speaker, adjourned the Manipuri Assembly till the next day as there was no one to preside in his absence as he had to leave the chair for some urgent reason. In this connection it may be noted that the entire panel of chairman had earlier resigned. On the next day, when the Assembly met the speaker himself resigned. What happened in the Union Territory of Manipur was perhaps without any parallel in the history of the parliamentary government. In the 32 member assembly the ruling United Front and the Congress Party were equally matched which had created a statement that could scarcely be solved through the ordinary democratic process. The Ruling Party and the Opposition Party were so nicely balanced that no one was willing to act as speaker.

Then the speaker resigned, the Chief Commissioner asked the Congress and the United Front which had 16 members each in the Houses, to nominate candidates for fresh election. But both sides refused to do so. Since the Legislature could not function, the Chief Commissioner had no other choice but to prorogue its session. The Centre had then taken over the administration of Manipur following the political developments and a parliamentary crises in the Union Territory. A proclamation to this effect was signed by the President in New Delhi on October 25. The Presidential order suspended the functioning of the Manipur Ministry and the Assembly for a period of six months. Thus the 12 day old Thanbou Ministry was dissolved.

Shri Koireng Singh of Congress tried his level best to consolidate his position. Shri Ch. Rajmohan Singh resigned from the ULF and joined the Congress Party. Some other MLAs who had defected to the ULF except Sarvashri Salam Tombi Singh and K. Chaoba Singh, who were expelled from the Congress, were taken into the Congress Legislature Party. Thus having consolidated his position, Shri Koireng Singh announced on 30th Nov. 1967 that the Congress had regained the majority and could form the Ministry. Shri M. Koireng Singh who had a support of 22 members in the 32 member House, was sworn in as Chief Minister on the 19th February, 1968.

Some of the Congress MLAs soon revolted against the Koireng Ministry as they were not accommodated in the Ministry. The induction of Sarvashri Sinam Bijoi Singh and Waikhon Mani Singh as Deputy Ministers on 4th July 1969 had enraged those Congress MLAs who had inspired for ministership. These MLAs sided with the Opposition Party to overthrow Koireng Ministry. On 23rd Sept. 1969 Shri Y. Yaima Singh of the Opposition Party moved a no confidence motion against Koireng Ministry. As the motion had obtained the leave of the House, the speaker announced that the motion would be taken for discussion on 24th Sept. 1969.

The Prime Minister Smt. Indira Gandhi paid a short visit to Imphal on September 23. This was the first time that she visited Manipur as the Prime Minister of the country. The Prime Minister was to address a public meeting at the Polo Ground which was organised by the State Congress. Along her way to the Polo Ground the students shouted anti-Congress slogans. The police lathi charged the students, both boys and girls to clear the road for the Prime Minister. The crowed retaliated by throwing stones. The violence was touched off by demonstrations in support of the demand of full-fledged statehood for Manipur.

In a series of clashes between the police and the leftist demonstrators three people, including a central reserve police man were killed that evening. Many people were injured. Curfew was clamped on Imphal and the army was called, out to assist the civilian authorities. The situation of the capital continued to be tense on the subsequent day. The visit of the Prime Minister to Manipur had brought to the fore the demand for raising the status of the Union Territory to that of the state. Those champions of this demand at Imphal resorted to the most serious form of violence, described by the Prime Minister as "Premediated."

The eight month old Koireng Ministry of Manipur fell on September 24, when nine dissident members of the Congress voted with opposition of a no confidence motion tabled by the United Opposition. The Congress Government fell on October 16, the President Shri V. V. Giri dissolved the Manipur Territorial Assembly and imposed President's rule in the Union Territory.

Hartal was observed in Imphal the next day to a call given by the United Legislature Front to protest against the imposition of President's rule and dissolution of the Manipuri Territorial Assembly.

Agitation for Full Statehood

The agitation for full statehood continued in full vigour. Many members demanded in the Rajya Sabha on March 30, 1970 that Manipur should be given statehood. The representatives of the five political parties United Action Committee for statehood constituted of SSP, Manipur Peoples Party, PSP and CPI sent a delegation to New Delhi in the second week of April, 1970 to call on leaders of the different Opposition groups in Parliament in order to apprise them of the latest political situation in Manipur and also to get their active support to the demand of statehood for Manipur. The delegation also met the Prime Minister and the President of India.

Twenty Congress Municipal Commissioners of Imphal Municipal Board including its Chairman resigned on August 1st in protest against the decision of the Union Government to grant statehood to Himachal Pradesh ignoring the demand of Manipuris for the similar status.

Immediately after the announcement of granting statehood to Himachal Pradesh the All Parties Statehood Demand Coordinating Body gave a call for Manipur Bundh to express their resentment and anger against the attitude of the Government of India towards Manipur. In Imphal and other adjoining areas, normal activities were completely suspended.

People of Manipur boycotted the Independence Day celebration on 15th August at the call of the All Party Statehood Demand Committee as a mark of protest against the centre's refusal to grant statehood to Manipur.

The Prime Minister Smt. Indira Gandhi announced in the Lok Sabha on 3rd September that the Central Government had accepted 'in principle' the demand of the people of Manipur for statehood. She however, said that the details had to be worked out "keeping in view the importance of a coordinated approach to the problems of development and security of the Northeastern Region." The announcement in both the houses was welcomed by all parties.

Formation of New State

With the passing of the reorganisation of North-East India Action both the Houses of the Parliament in 1972, necessary arrangements were made for inauguration of statehood for Manipur on January 21, 1972.

January 21, 1972 is an epoch-making event in the political history of Manipur. On this day, Manipur emerged the political map of India as a full-fledged state.

The Prime Minister Indira Gandhi inaugurated the 21st state in India on 21 January at the Palace Ground Imphal. Hundreds of thousands of people from all over Manipur attended the colourful ceremony and warm reception to the Prime Minister.

The New Governor Shri B. K. Nehru was sworn in at the Raj Bhawan by the Chief Justice of Assam, Shri Goshwami as the first Governor of the new State just before the inauguration of Manipur State by the Prime Minister Shri D. R. Kohli who had served Manipur for about two years and who was saying good-bye to the people of Manipur was asked by the Prime Minister to continue to aid and advise the Governor of the new state in consideration of the situation, particularly to bridge the gap till the elections to the State Assembly which would facilitate the formation of a Council of Ministers.

4

Geography

- -

Manipur is one of the smallest states of India. It is located at the extreme eastern corner of the country. It lies in between 23°47' N and 25°41'N latitudes and 93°6' E and 94°48' E longitudes with an average elevation of 750 metres above the sea level. In the north it is bounded by Nagaland, on the east lie the Sorma tract and the upper Chindwin districts of Burma; the south is surrounded by the Chin Hills of Burma and the state of Mizoram; while its western boundary is formed by the Cachar District of Assam. It has a total area of 22,327 sq km and a population of 22,93,896 (2001).

Manipur is essentially a mountainous state. Physiographically, it can be divided into three well-defined regions: (i) the Manipur Valley, (ii) the Manipur Hills, and (iii) the Barak Plain.

The Valley

The Manipur Valley, also known as Imphal Valley is one of the Himalayan, Midlands, like the Valley of Kashmir, the Dun-Valley, and the Kathmandu Valley. The Valley of Manipur has an area of about 1,800 sq km.

It has a flat land topography, formed by the alluvial deposits after the Tertiary Period. For its height of 700 to 900 metres above the sea level, the valley has been described as a little plateau surrounded by the hills on all sides. It is drained by the Manipur River and its tributaries. Imphal, Iril, Thoubal, Nambul and Naibol are the main tributaries of the Manipur River which drain their valley southward.

The Mountains

Belonging to the Himalayan Mountain System, the mountain of the state are the parallel ranges of sharp relief running across the state, roughly in a northeast to southwest direction. The Mount Japvo 3,016.5 metres (9,890 feet) a peak of the Barail Range of Nagaland, not far from the Manipur. Nagaland border acts as a knot from where mountain ranges branch out in different directions. In Manipur, there are long continuous parallel ranges often culminating in peaks. Many spurs and ridges project in different directions and sometimes connect the ranges.

There is a labyrinth of ridges and valleys. Scores of peaks are more than 1,500 metres in height. These ranges are quite young in age and highly folded and faulted in character. The numerous ridges produce a criss-cross pattern of ridges and defiles. A narrow river valley flanked by two ridges provides the general pattern. The hill-crests and valley-bottom provide the extent of local relief. The land is full of sharp slopes and there is hardly any flat surface.

There is reason to believe that the mountains which had higher elevation in the past have since been lowered in elevation and are being worn down. The ranges, ridges, and spurs have no definite name. But in certain sections they are called by some names which may either be the name of the village or the dominant tribe inhabiting in it.

The heavy rains during summer monsoons on the soft sandstones and shales acting through the agency of hundreds of streams has sculptured and lowered the surface beyond recognition. But there is no big stream capable of obliterating the upstanding masses of mountains, which so far have only been worn down at the edges. This is evident from the absence of flood plains. In general, the river valleys are narrow defiles. In some cases there are broad valleys which can be ascribed to structures. In such cases the ridges stand for apart. The ridges and valleys in general, follow the strike and the mountain slope is influenced by the dip of the formations. Between the plain of Cachar and the Kabaw Valley of Upper Burma there are a number of parallel ranges separated by the river valleys. A brief description of the main ranges of Manipur is given below:

Along the western part of Manipur the first range is called *Nunjaibung Range*, which extends from the tri junction of Assam, Nagaland and Manipur southward up to Tipaimukh. This range is almost parallel, to the western boundary of Manipur and a few kilometres east of it. This range is flanked on the west by the line of Jiri and Barak, and on the east by Mukru, and Barak rivers. It continues uninterruptedly up to the confluence of Tuivai and Barak rivers. At the tri junction in the north its elevation is above 2,135 metres. In this region near Thingobol the triangulation station has an elevation of 2,081.3 metres.

There are several peaks with elevations exceeding 1,500 metres. Southward its elevation decreases steadily. At the place where Cachar road crosses it, the elevation of the crest is merely 330 metres, but further south the elevation goes on increasing up to 989 metres near Phulpui. The average elevation of this range is 869 metres.

The second range is called the Kala Naga Range. It can be traced from the Manipur-Nagaland border in the north where it attains an elevation of 2,125 metres. It is almost parallel to Nunjabung Range and east of it. The average crow fly distance between the crests of both the ranges is about 8 km. This range rapidly loses height southward. The Cachar road crosses it near Oinamlong. A few kilometres south of Cachar road the Barak river cuts across this range. In this section its general trend is southeasterly.

The Barak bed at the point of crossing is 77 metres above the sea level. This range bends southwestward and attains elevation exceeding 1,220 metres. The Irang (Irung) river cuts across its 8 km south of Gallon. From there it extends southward and runs parallel to Barak river. The Churachandpur Tipaimukh road crosses it at Parbung. South of Parbung it extends parallel to Tuivai river up to the state's border. In this section Senvon Peak attains an elevation of 1,342 metres. South of Tolbung this range bifurcates into two ridges, both rising gradually southward. The western branch runs parallel to the line of Barak and Tuivai but the eastern branch passes through Khongjang, Tinsong, Pherjol, Jhangkum, Thlanship and Vongkot up to the Manipur-Mizoram border.

The intervening land between the eastern and western branch which are progressively further apart towards south forms the Tuibung Valley. The western branch may be treated as the real continuation of Kala Naga Range. Thus the Kala Naga Range runs parallel to Mukru (Makru) river up to its confluence with Barak and further south it runs parallel to the line of Barak and Tuivai up to the state's border. The average elevation of this range is 1055 metres.

In the northwestern part of Manipur there extends a mountain range between Barak on the west and Irang on the east. This is the third important range of Manipur. It passes through Makuilong, Kuilong, Kadi, and culminates in the peak of Vallelbung (2,158 metres). It has a northern spur named Sintonbung which extends northward having two unnamed peaks of 2,440 metres and 2,435 metres above the sea level. It has another peak called *Laikot peak* 2834 metres above the sea level. Further north this range is called *Yangpuilong* culminating in an unnamed peak 2,456 metres west of Rajamei. The intervening land between these two ridges is occupied by the valleys of Inhuki and Ngehaki rivers which are the tributaries of Barak, called *Tuilong River* in this section.

The Vallelbung range extends southwestward through Langmei, Taloulong and Sonparain. In this section it is to the west of Irang, very close and remarkably parallel to it. Thereafter, it bends westward and is close to Tamenglong from where it extends southward and has Pangkibot peak 1,659 metres above the sea level. The New Cachar Road crosses this range at Nungba. Nungba, situated on a saddle is nearly midway between Barak and Irang rivers. South of Nungba this range is closer to Irang than Barak. The Irang cuts across it west of Nathelbok where the bed of Irang is at an elevation of about 76 metres. Southward there is a peak called *Thangnangbung* with an elevation of 1,113 metres above the sea level. From here up to Tolbol (26 km) this range loses height appreciably.

The Churachandpur Tipaimukh road crosses this range at Tolbol. South of Tolbol this range bifurcates into two branches, one western branch which has a peak attaining an elevation of 1,525 metres hardly about 3 km to the south of Tolbol village. The two branches enclose the Tuijam valley. The average elevation of this range is 1,553 metres. This is a long continuous range from north to south across the state connecting Rajamei-Laikot Sintongbung-Vallelbung-Tamenglong Nungba-Thangnangbung-TolBol Sumtuk. Between this range on the west and Indo-Burma water parting on the east there are innumerable ridges and spurs enclosing big and small river valleys which are tributaries of Irang river. In fact, this area presents a maze of ridges and valleys.

The fourth mountain range of Manipur extends from Manipur-Nagaland border in the north where Tenipu Peak within 8 km west of Mao, attains a height of 2996 metres. This is the highest peak in Manipur. Further south in this range there are two unnamed peaks with elevations of 2,694 m and 2,499 m. Southward it runs parallel to the line of Nukhi and Barak near Thongjong its elevation is 2,334 metres. This is the source of Tiki, Nukhi and numerous other rivers with a spur and a saddle a few miles north of Kangpokpi, this range joins the Indo-Burma divide east of Imphal-Kohima Road (NH 39).

There is a central branch of this range along which the Imphal-Kohima road (NH 39) passes. This is rather the central ridge and is flanked on the east and west by the two bends of Barak. The hair pin bend occurs at Karong. Therefore, near Karong all the three branches come closer to each other. Craval deposits occur just south of this crossing. The central ridge attains elevation of nearly 2,135 m west of Mao and steadily decreases in elevation southward to about 1,373 metres near Karong. The average elevation of this ridge is 1,678 metres above the sea level.

The fifth range is the Indo-Burma divide which may be traced from the northern border about 8 km west of Zhamai in Nagaland where the peak on the border attains an elevation of 2,492 metres. From there it extends southeastward. There is another peak 2,504 metres above sea level from where the range extends towards southwest for a distance of 19 km where it has another peak 2,229 metres in elevation east of Kangpokpi. From there this range takes a northwesternly bend through a saddle up to another peak east of Thongiang 2,334 metres in elevation.

From there it bends southward and passes through Koubru peak 2,563 metres and the range is called Koubru. It extends through Loiching 2,015 metres. This range is on the west of the central plain of Manipur. This is a continuous range across the state. The average elevation of this range is 1,937 metres. The drainage to the west of this divide passes through Ganga-Brahmaputra system, whereas, the drainage to the east passes through Chindwin-Irrawaddi system.

In the eastern half of the state there is one continuous range which may be treated as the main range of Manipur. It extends from the bend of Tuzu (Tizu) river in the extreme northeast of the state in a southwesternly direction up to Ukhrul. It passes through Jessami. South of Jessami it has a peak 1,711 metres high above sea level. It extends through Kharasom. Chingin peak in this region is above 2,135 metres high and extends up to the bank of Marou or Marang Lok, which cuts across this range. In this region it is flanked on the west by Lanier and on the east by Chingai of Ringna rivers. It is about 50 km long between Tizu and Marang Lok. Southward it passes through Paoy (Paowi) Peak 1,687 metres Phungcham and Furing and extends through Ukhrul, Sirohi Kashong 2,570 metres towards Khyangbung. North of this range there are a number of ridges.

The intervening tract between these ridges are occupied by the valleys of rivers like Wondi, Meshakui, Marou, Chingai, Chamu, etc. all flowing from southwest to northeast. A very large number of ridges and spurs branch out from the main range, which, however, extends southward through Sangjing, Sangshak, Sokpao and Kasom.

Further south this range is known as Maphitel (Nupitel) Range and culminates in a peak 2,055 metres in elevation. It extends southward through Manwungyan, Tonghlang, Gomi, Samukom, Sitachingjao to Tengnoupal. The Imphal Morch road crosses this range at Tengnoupal.

One special feature of this range is that it throws numerous ridges and spurs on either side of it. There is a labyrinth of ridges and valleys in Ukrul region. The average elevations of the Maphitel range is 1,678 metres. West of this range a ridge can be followed west of Chakpikarong passing through Heika elevation 1,451 metres, Shelkui Khunao southward culminating in Nangle Vum 2,375 metres above sea level. This is the highest peak in this region. This ridge is bounded on the west and east by rivers like Kana Lok and Tuiyang respectively. There is another ridge east of Manipur river and very close to it, extending through Nungshira in the north to Yangdung in the south.

The eastern most and last important mountain range of Manipur extends along the Indo-Burma border. This can be followed from Mol He, a peak in Surma tract 3.2 km east of the international boundary extending southward. In this section there is a peak 2,400 metres in elevation. Further southeast one comes across another peak called *Khayangbung* 2,838 metres in elevation. This is the second highest peak of Manipur. From Kachao Bung to Nampanga crossing it is called *Kassom Range*. It is a precipitous rocky range bounding on the east the Chattik or Phou Khong valley.

But for this intersection its natural prolongation is the Angouching Range. Further south the Nam Panga river cuts across it. Inside the state between Nam Panga and Nam Aya which are small streams, the hills are known as Mulain Range. The average elevation of the Indo-Burma bordering range is 2,031 metres.

The Central Plain of Manipur would have been a monotonous featureless plain but for a number of hills and mounds rising above the flat surface. In a way they reduce the area of flat surface, nevertheless profoundly add to its scenic beauty. Among the hills of Manipur may be included: Chingmeirong, Langthaban, Waithou, Langathel, etc. Among the small mounds and hillocks may be included:

Pishum, Chinga, Nongmeibung, Lalambung, etc. The hills projecting about the surface of Loktak Lake are Karang, Thanga, Ithing, Sendra, etc.

The following are the main characteristics of the plain of Manipur.

- It is absolutely a flat plain resembling a flood plain.
- The bordering ranges surrounding this plain lack talus deposits except where the rivers debouch and deposits coarse sediments.
- The hills and mounds projecting above the plain are also without talus and the plain or swamp reaches right up to the foot of the hill or mound.
- There exist a number of lakes and swamps in the process of being silted up and obliterated.
- Large tracts of the plain, especially in the southern half are subject to recurrent floods.
- For averting floods high embankments have been constructed and are being maintained.

The Khoupum Valley provides another high level small plain surrounded by steep precipitous hills in Tamenglong District. It is an isolated plain with only one outlet to the south. The stream draining it has cut an outlet across a ridge in the south side and passes through a gorge with rapids and falls and joins the Irang river. It is a miniature of the Central Plain.

The Hills

The Manipur Hills which encircle the Central Valley, comprising about 91 per cent of the state area and one-third of the population, are strategically and ecologically the most important region of the state. Formed of tertiary deposits and having general ridge and valley character, these hills have a gradual slope towards south.

The altitude in the hills varies from 3,000 metres in the north to 900 metres towards the valley and to the southwest, and 1,200 metres to the southeast. The rivers of the eastern and southern section of the hills drain into Chindwin, a tributary of Irrawaddy, but the rivers of the northern and western part flow into river Barak, which emits into the Bay of Bengal. Clothed with dense humid forests, and inhabited by numerous tribes, these hills always posed a problem for the state for lack of transport and communication.

Drainage and Rivers

The State of Manipur is drained by a large number of streams. Nearly half of the state lies west of the Indo-Burma Divide. The main stream of the western half of Manipur is the Barak River. It has many tributaries, important among them being the Jiri, the Makru (Mukru) and the Irang. The Barak has its source near the Manipur Nagaland boundary about 19.3 km east of Mao. It receives many tributaries and flows in a southwesternly direction up to Karong. In this section, it is called by the name of Sangu Lok.

At Karong it makes sharp intersection across the ridge and takes a hair pin bend and flows in a northernly direction, enclosing the ridge, through which the Imphal-Kohima Road (NH 39) passes. The Barak bends westward south of Maramei and cuts across the western ridge overlooking the valley after which it receives a tributed named Kozeri Lok. The Kozeri Lok originates from the southern slopes of the mountain range which encloses the Tenipu peak. The Barak river then joins the water of Majatki Lok.

Another tributary from south called *Majakoi-Nadi* joins it and the elevation of the confluence is 767 metres. From there the Barak flows north-westward and receives another tributary named Karuioi Ki where the elevation of confluence drops down to 463 metres. From there the Barak flows westward up to the boundary of Manipur and takes a southwesternly bend. In this section it acts as the boundary between Manipur and Nagaland up to the point where it receives Sulen or Maguiki river coming from north. In this section it is called Barak or Tuilong river. The Barak flows in a southwesternly direction with numerous bends usual for the mountain streams. It cuts across the Kala Naga Range and establishes its antecedence beyond doubt.

Thereafter it flows westward, and about 19 km downstream it receives Makru river. The elevation of Barak-Makru confluence drops down to 59 metres. The Barak flows between Kala Nag and Nunjaibong range in a southwesterly direction and receives its biggest tributary, the Irang, the confluence being at an elevation of 48 metres. It then flows up to Tipaimukh where it receives another tributary from the south, named Tuivai. This point is of political significance as it marks the tri junction between Mizoram, Manipur and Assam states. At this confluence the Barak river takes a sharp bend northwards and flows along the western foot of Nunjaibong range up to its confluence with Jiri river from the north.

From here the Barak bends north-westward, crosses the low hills of Bhubon range and enters into the Plain of Cachar at Lakhipur. In the Cachar plain (Surma Valley) it meanders and makes numerous bends which are the characteristics of a river in flood plain. At a place called *Bhanga* it bifurcates into two branches, i.e. Surma and Kushiara. Finally it enters Bangladesh and empties its waters in Brahmaputra river near Bhairab Bazar.

Erang River

The main branch of Erang or Tuilang rises from the western slope of the divide west of Kangpokpi. It receives numerous small tributaries big and small, many of which are unnamed. Among the more important streams a few may be mentioned from the source downstream. One of the small streams is Asikade Nadi. Leimatak from south is comparable to a big stream. The confluence of Erang Leimatak is at an elevation of 180 metres.

The other tributary is Tuipi the elevation of confluence being 90 metres. All the big tributaries of Erang carry the drainage from south and join it. Erang is the largest tributary of Barak. It drains a large tract of the hilly region of the districts of Tamenglong and Churachandpur. Erang flows through very steep sided valley and gorges.

Makru River

Makru or Mukru river is an important tributary of the Barak. It drains the land between Nunjaibong and Kala Nag ranges. It has its source near the watershed between Nagaland and Manipur. It flows from north to south and receives many small streams on its way and discharges its water in the Barak about 10 km south of the point at which the Cachar Road crosses it.

Jiri River

The Jiri river rises near the tri junction of Assam, Nagaland and Manipur. It flows southward and acts as part of the western boundary of Manipur. It takes numerous bends in its course and reaches Jirighat, from where it moves southward with many small bends. It empties its water in the Barak river near Jirimukh. The drainage of the eastern half of Manipur passes to Chindwin-lrrawaddy System. The Mapithel (Nupithel) range acts as water-parting. Many streams flow west of this water-parting and pass through the central plain of Manipur. The combined water flows south of the plain through the hills. This is called *Turel Achouba* or Manipur river. It crosses the southern border and joins the Chindwin river in Burma. The main tributaries of Manipur river are the Iril, the Imphal, the Thoubal, the Khuga, the Sekmai, etc.

Iril River

The Iril river is the largest stream coming down to the central plain. It originates in the high range near the northern border of the state at a height of 2,600 metres above the sea level and from the source up to the confluence with Imphal river has a long course of about 120 km. It has a drainage area of about 1,300 sq km before Imphal-Iril confluence at Lilong. It has steep gradient in the hills and discharges huge quantities of water silts and sediments.

Imphal River

The Imphal river has its source in a ridge east of Tongiang at an elevation of about 2,335 metres. It flows through Kangpokpi, Kanglatongbi, Imphal to Lilong where it meets Iril. In its upper course it is called *Tiki River*. It has a course of about 75 km above the confluence and a drainage basin of about 500 km.

From the confluence downstream the river is still called Imphal. In the central plain it is almost devoid of gradient and has a negligible silt carrying capacity. It flows along well maintained embankments, which sometimes fail to contain the swollen stream.

Thoubal River

Thoubal river is another important tributary of the Imphal river. It originates in the high ranges near Fumi and follows a southwesternly course between the two ridges, the eastern ridge being the Maphitel itself. This stream enters the central plain east of Yairipok and passes through Thoubal town. It follows a zigzag course and joins Imphal river at Irong about 4 kilometres to the east of Mayang Imphal.

From the source to confluence it has a course of about 105 kilometres. Its catchment area is about 1,050 sq km. It has a steep gradient in the hilly section. It carries heavy load of sediments to Imphal river. It often results into devastating floods and deluges.

Khuga River

The Khuga is a grand tributary, of the Imphal river. It meets Imphal (Manipur) river near Ithai. The Khuga rises in the high hills near the southern border of Manipur and flows between the two ridges. It flows from south to north. After reaching the central plain south of Moirang it takes, an easternly bend, flows south of Loktak and discharges its water in the Manipur river. The Khuga has a course of about 80 km and a drainage basin of about 620 sq km. It is a mountain stream of steep gradient. During rainy season it is heavily loaded with sand land coarse sediments and interferes with the normal flow of the Manipur river when in spate.

Chakpi River

The Chakpi is another important tributary of the Manipur river. Its source lies in the hills far to the south, follows a northernly course between two ridges and carves out a steep sided valley. It has a course of about 60 km and a drainage area of about 800 sq km. Being a mountain stream it is fully charged with debris which is discharged into Manipur river.

Lanier River

The Lanier river originates in the north of the mini-divide. It has several tributaries flowing parallel to its course. The main tributaries are Wondi (Akung Lok), Meshakui (Meshaku Lok), and the main branch of Lanier which has its source near Ukhrul. The Lanier is called *Marou* or *Marang Lok* in this section. The valleys of these streams are confined between the parallel ridges. The Lanier turns near Nambi and cuts across the ridge. The confluence of Wandi Lok and Lanier is at an elevation of 860 metres. From this point the Lanier flows in a north easternly direction and finally joins the Tizo river near the extreme northeast corner of Manipur. The Lanier is the main stream of northeast

Manipur. After merging into the Tizo river it enters into Burma and after a long sinuous course merges into the Chindwin river.

Chingai River

A tributary of Tizu the Chingai is an important river of Manipur State. It drains the extreme northeastern parts of the state. The Chingai flows east of the Jessami-Kharasom-Chingjaroi ridge. It originates from a ridge east of Nambi. In its upper reaches there are a few salt springs.

A ridge separates its valley from that of Chammu Turel. It receives many small tributaries. One of important tributaries is Viratai which flows for a long distance along the India-Burma boundary. After flowing for about 16 kilometres along the boundary the Chingai merges into the Tizu river.

The mini-divide already referred which extends a few kilometres west of Ukhrul and joins the Maphitel (Nupitel) Range. The land to the south of this line and the Maphitel (Nupitel) range is drained by a number of small streams. All these streams are the right hand tributaries of the Chindwin river. There are a number of spurs branching out of the divide and a river valley occupies the intervening land between two spurs or ridges. Among such streams the names of Nam Panga, Yu Lokchou and Tiwan Lam are worth mentioning.

Phou Khong River

The Phou Khong is an important stream draining the tract of land between the eastern bordering range and the east-west extending ridge — the two meet at Khayangbung. The Phou Khong and a smaller stream flowing west of it and called *Chai Khong* drain this area. The confluence of Phou Khong and Chai Khong is at an elevation of 438 metres above the sea level. Down stream the river follows a southernly course and is known as Sana Lok. At the international boundary another big tributary called Khunou Khong joins it and the combined water flows east ward across the Angouching Range of Burma to Chindwin river under the name Nam Panga.

Yu River

A ridge branch out from Nupitel Range and passes through Sangshak, Hundung Goda, and Phaisat. Between this ridge and Nupitel is an enclosed valley of Tuyungbi. It Joins another stream known as Maklang and the combined stream is called the *Yu River*. Taret river is a small tributary. It Joins the Yu river near Hlezeik in Kabaw valley. The Lokchao follows a southernly course and crosses the international boundary at Moreh and joins the Yu river.

The southeastern hilly tract of Manipur is drained by the Lalim Lok, Chichapao Lam and Tiwan Lam. All these streams follow a southeasternly course and discharge their waters in the Yu river. The most unique geomorphic feature of the state of Manipur is the existence of a levelled plain in its centre. This plain covers an area of about 1,800 sq km which is nearly 8 per cent of the total geographical area of the state. Being most fertile it supports over 66 per cent of the total population of the state. On all sides it is bounded by steep walls of the ranges of the young folded mountains. The southern part of the plain is occupied by the Loktak Lake which during the rainy season acquires a size of 150 sq km. The drainage of the plain passes southward through the Manipur river which passes through a gorge in the southern ranges of the state.

The origin of this plain has been a point of contention among the geologists. According to E. W. Dun the flat elevated valley was formed due to a stream being blocked by some culvulsion of nature. The commonly held view is that the plain was formed as a result of a lake being filled by a river borne sediments. The present Loktak Lake, in fact, a shallow lake occupying the southern part of the plain is said to be the remnant of the original lake, that once occupied the site of the central plain.

According to another opinion the formation of the Central Plain of Manipur is closely connected with uplift and down cutting in south Manipur hills and the behaviour of the Imphal river and its tributaries which drain the Central Plain. Whatsoever, the reason of the origin of the plain may be it is a highly productive plain and the economy, culture and society of the state are dependent on the prevailing milieu of the central plain.

Barak Plain

The Barak Plain, on the western border of the state, is the smallest physiographic region of Manipur State. It covers an area of 227 sq km, i.e. about only one per cent of the total area of the state. It is dotted with low sandstone hillocks. This plain has been created by the headward erosion and subsequent deposition of river Barak and its tributaries. The diluvial fringe of the plain is filled with loose talus which are borne by the rivers during the period of heavy rains of the summer monsoon. This region is covered by bamboo forests and alluvial soils which provide immense potential for future development.

Natural Resources

Minerals

The State of Manipur is not very well endowed in basic minerals. The known minerals of the state are limestone, lignite, copper, chromite, nickel, cobalt, asbestos, clay and salt. Unfortunately, these minerals have not been exploited on a commercial scale. The future development of these minerals lies on the estimates of their reserves and quality aspect along with their exploitability.

The State of Manipur has rich lignite seams in the southern hills. The exploitation of lignite deposits can help appreciably in the regional development as it provide fuel to the secondary and tertiary sectors.

The mineral resources of the state are not fully explored and much less exploited. According to the results obtained from the surveys conducted by the Geological Survey of India which has so far covered about 10 per cent of the total area of the state. Manipur has deposits of limestone, lignite, nickel, cobalt, chromite, asbestos, clay and salt. Limestone occurs at Ukhrul, Hundung, Lambui, Sokpao, Kasom, Toupokpi, Chakpikarong regions. The total mineable reserve at Ukhrul is estimated at about 48 lakh tonnes. The rest of the deposits account for an additional reserve of 15 lakh tonnes. Lignite mixed with clay is found at Kangvi; while chromite is found in the Shiroi hill of Ukhrul. Small quantities of nickel and cobalt associated with copper ores are found at Nangu and Kongal Thana areas. Nickel also occurs in Nampesh and Kwatha areas of Tengnoupal District. Salt springs are found at Waikhong, Shikhong, Chandrakhong, Keithal Manbi, etc. The springs are being tapped for the manufacture of mineral salt in small quantities.

However, the potential for a number of minerals like chromite, nickel, etc. are yet to be assessed. The entire Indo-Burma border area in the state has remained 'Terra-incognita' for obvious reasons. There are indications that petroleum will be found in Manipur. The Oil and Natural Gas Commission is doing exploratory survey and drillings in the various parts of the Valley of Manipur.

Forestry

Forests cover an area of nearly 15,155 sq km or 66.7 per cent of the total geographical area of the state. Nearly 50 per cent of the total forest area is under tree forest, 23 per cent is under bamboo forests, and the remaining is under open forests.

The forests of Manipur can be classified into five major types:

(1) Tropical-moist semi-evergreen,

(2) Tropical moist deciduous,

(3) Subtropical pine,

(4) Dry temperate, and

(5) Teak garjan forests.

Forests in Manipur and their Areal Sprawls

Type of forest	Area in sq km	Percentage
1. Wet temperate	1,451.01	12.36.
2. Pine forests	2,442.77	20.81
3. Wet hill forests	6,590.59	56.1
4. Semi-evergreen forests	644.79 5.49	
5. Teak Garan forests	610.59 5.20	
Total	**11, 739.75**	**100.00**

Source: Forest Dept., Manipur.

Nearly seventy commercially valuable species including teak, garjan, uningthou, etc., are found in the Manipur forests. The forests provide timber, round wood and fuel alongwith bamboos and canes, turpentine and resin, Daichini, gum fibres, oils, honey, wax, and medicinal herbs.

The tropical moist semi-evergreen forests in the Barak basin, on the western flank, yield rich bamboo, which are planned to be used in the paper and pulp mill to be set up in the region. In the tropical moist deciduous forests, near the Burma border, grow good varieties of teak, while pine forests thrive in the northeastern hill tracts. The central deforested valley has dry temperate vegetation scattered in patches.

The total value of the annual out line of major and minor forest products is about Rs. 30 lakhs. Forest revenue is however, very low, being only Rs. 200 per sq km as compared with Rs. 868 per sq km in Nagaland and Rs. 644 per sq km in Tripura.

The wet hill forests cover 56.14 per cent of the total tree forests of the state. Pine forests have the second largest areal strength being about 21 per cent. The wet temperate occupy 12.36 per cent, while teak and semi-evergreen forests have over 5 per cent of the total tree area of the state.

The Environment

The State of Manipur has a unique climate. In general it has a pleasant subtropical climate but there are micro-level variations in the temperature and rainfall regimes. In fact, the climate of Manipur is closely controlled by orography, the local mountain and valley winds and the reversal of monsoon winds. The mountain being a better absorber and emitter of heat, it is heated or cooled more speedily and efficiently than the surrounding air and this exerts a thermal influence. Consequently, the mean daily temperature range in the hilly places is higher than in the plain areas. Imphal in the heart of the valley, registers an annual rainfall of 1,410 mm but in the hills in the north and west it swings between 1,600 and 2,000 mm annually.

In Manipur the rainy season generally lasts from May to September. In the period of retreating monsoon, i.e. October and November the rains occur occasionally. December to February is the cold weather season. January is the coldest month, the mean maximum and mean minimum temperatures at Imphal in this month being 20°C and 4°C. At the occurrence of cold waves the minimum temperature goes below freezing point. Occurrence of fog and mist during winter season is a regular feature.

The temperature starts rising in the month of March. It is the hottest month of the year in which the mean temperature reads up to 22°C. The mean maximum temperature ascends further and reads up to 34°C in April. The night temperature in April, however, remains around 18°C thus the nights generally remain cool. The subsequent months of May and June do not show any upward trend. The day temperature in June at Imphal reads around 32°C and the night temperature about 23°C. Thus, nights become comparatively warmer in June.

From July to September the cloudy weather and intermittent rains reduce the mean maximum and the mean minimum temperatures. Nearly 75 per cent of the average annual rainfall is recorded from July to September at all the rainfall recording stations of Manipur.

From October the temperature drops steadily. In October the mean maximum and the mean minimum temperature reads around 25°C and 15°C respectively. The sky generally remains overcast in October also and in this month Imphal receives about 20 cm of rainfall. In the winter months (December-February) about 32 cm of rainfall is recorded at Imphal. Occasionally the winter rains are accompanied with hailstorms, thundering and lightning. Of all the seasons winters are most invigorating and enjoyable in the valley of Manipur.

The average annual rainfall at Imphal is 210 cm and the variability of rainfall is low, being around 10 per cent. The cropping patterns and the production per unit area largely depends on the timely arrival of rainfall. Excessive rainfall in a single downpour may leads to deluge and floods while long rainless interval may result into drought like conditions. At the failure of rains for about ten to fifteen days forces the farmers to irrigate their paddy and other high moisture requiring crops.

5

Society

Manipur with an area of 22,327 sq km and a population of 22,93,896 (2001) has an average density of about 111 persons per sq km. An important feature of the population of the state is its rapid rate of growth, more rapid than the corresponding all-India rates. Thus the growth rate of Manipur's population was 3.4 per cent per year in 1981 as against 3.7 per cent in 1971, 3.5 per cent in 1961 and 1.4 per cent in 1951. The corresponding all-India rates were 2.5 per cent (1981), 2.5 per cent (1971), 2.2 per cent (1961) and 1.3 per cent in 1951. The spatial distribution of population is highly uneven. The valley of Manipur has a very high concentration of population while in the remaining ports, especially in the hilly and mountainous areas it is most sparest and thinly populated. The unevenness of the distribution may be appreciated from the fact that 67.5 per cent of the total population lives in the central valley. Comprising nearly 10 per cent of the total geographical area of the state.

At present there is a considerable unemployment and underemployment in the state because of the inadequate utilisation of natural resources. In June 1985, there were about 1.90 lakh job seekers on the live registers of the employment exchange in Manipur. Although unemployment in an all India problem, its intensity is much greater in Manipur than that of in other parts of the country. The proportions of the total population works out to 7.9 per cent in this state as against 1.8 per cent of all India. If the natural resources are fully and judiciously utilised, the present socio-economic backwardness of the state could be removed easily.

Significant Society

The historical evidence demonstrate that Manipur has always provided a broad-socio-political framework for integration and frequent assimilation of tribes into the Meitei social formation. To this extent the change of identity or the shift of alliance with other groups is not novel development. In Manipur, there are examples, of groups giving up old identities and accepting the new ones. But there is a significant qualitative difference between the part and the present kind of changing orientation observable among the tribesmen; whereas in the olden times (i.e. in the days of Kings) the movement was essentially Meiteicentric, in the post-independence times, the tribes realising their identity in what may be said as 'tribe-centric' manner.

Thus there is no longer the question of a tribe seeking admission into the Meitei fold nor the Meiteis have any political machinery like the former royal pressures to integrate tribes within its fold. Moreover, after the Scheduled Tribes Act-1956 the change in tribal names have become rather difficult. Each tribe has become more or less a distinct unit of official and formal reference.

The broad tribal labels like the Naga, Kuki, Mizo, have appeared as the loci of alignment and grouping. In reality, the identity projected by the people concerned carries more meaning. In the light of it, one observes the claims of the Hmar, Paite, Vaiphei or the Gangte in aligning themselves with the Kukis or Mizos; one finds it to be justified for they have much affinities in common.

Even within the Naga groups of people common history and ancestry are nothing but the myths. The thirty two Naga tribes occupy geographically contiguous and extensive areas within the territories of Manipur, Nagaland, Assam, Arunachal Pradesh and Burma. Though most of the Nagas claim their origin from Meikhel or Makhel (a small village about 16 km south - east of Kohima), the Kabuis and Maring claim their origin otherwise. The Kabuis and Maring claim their origin from caves at Haobi Peak in upper Burma. This is an indicative of the fact that all the tribes under the ethnonym 'Naga' need not share the same origin or possess similar cultural symbols. However, they stand as loosely integrated groups. Thus among the Nagas the integrative factors are other than the common history.

The tribes of the Kuki-group which migrated from the Chin Hill region of Burma in the south at a relatively earlier period are referred to as the old Kuki tribe, while the Thadous came from Chin Hills of Burma in the middle of the 19th century. The Kukis both old and new speak language which are understandable to many tribes including those which have already identified with the Nagas. In this context, the Kukis must have got better grounds for organising themselves into large ethnic groups. With regard to mythical origin, majority of these tribes claim their origin from cave.

In the post-independence period, various tribal communities in Manipur are engaging themselves in various social movements. This becomes more plausible because of the fact that almost every tribe had a stage of religious transition from animism to Christianity. This is leading to a new era of association among the various tribal groups. In fact, the regular contacts of the people through religious activities laid the foundation for a perpetual bond between the co-religious groups.

Thus the Nagas are distinct linguistic-cultural group vis-a-vis the Meiteis, Manipuri speaking Muslims and the Kuki-Mizo groups. Their identity consolidation has territorial meaning since all Naga villages are contiguous to one another. On the other hand, the Kukis are the groups of people possessing common language and common culture but which show little organisational compatibility into a compact ethnic group. It is a picture which emerges when they are seen in isolation. When viewed in the context of large socio-political milieu, the Kukis vis-a-vis the plains Meiteis or Nagas, they constitute a discrete ethnic group.

The Mizos have separate ethnos of great significance. They have many things in common with the Kukis and their concentration in Manipur lies many in the southern parts. In recent years, they have shown a tendency for becoming a willing member in the 'Mizo ethnic club.'

The differences of stature, dress, and weapon make it easy to distinguish between the members of these tribes. In colour they are all yellow brown. The nose also varies, for there are cases where it is almost straight, while in the majority of individuals it is flattened at the nostril.

Complexion of People

Majority of the women have fair complexion of a yellowish colour. They belong to the Mongoloid race and very much resemble to the women of Burma, China, Thailand, Malaysia and Japan. They have jolly brown eyes, and flat nose. A few exceptions, are however, there.

The dress of the Meitei women is quite different from those of women in other parts of India as well as the western women. The female dress consists of a cotton or silk cloth passed round the body and a jacket or a blouse and a sheet of cloth or Chadder — the traditional two pieces. The cotton or silk cloth passed round the body is called the Fanek (Plianek). The Phanek is of three types. The first one is of striped nature of different colours, i.e. red with green strips, green and black, blue with black and white stripe, yellow and brown, dark blue with green and white stripes, etc. At the top and bottom of the garment is a broad margin on which geometrical figures of various kinds indicating the feasts in arts and crafts and sewn by hand with floss silk in various colours.

This type of phanek is usually worn at occasional functions like marriages feasts, festivals, and other important social functions. The second type is of a simple variety made of cotton in different colours. Women usually wear this type for day to day work. The third type is also made of cotton, but it is one colour without any border. It is generally used at the time of mourning, religious functions, etc. Widowed and old women also use this type of phanek.

The Phanek is open except at the bottom where it is stitched together by the edges for a few inches. This is folded round the body, under the armpit and over the breast, and tucked in by the hand at the left side of the body. In length it reaches the ground, but as it would be inconvenient in walking, it is hitched up half way to the knee. Young girls at earlier times folded the Phanek round the body at the waist and not over the breast. Nowadays, however, the urban educated women folded the Phanek at a days, however, the urban educated women folded the Phanek at the waist. The Manipuri dress is colourful, picturesque and pleasing. Manipuri tribal women also wear clothes like Phanek. The colour and stripe differ from tribe to tribe. Most of the tribal women do not wear the sheet round the body. Modern educated women prefer western dresses like pant-shirt. The dress of Manipuri women needs modification in the modern scientific manner.

Women's Role in Economy: The role and contribution of the Manipuri women in the economy and society is overwhelming. It is a common sight in the rural areas to see women working in the paddy fields. Rice transplantation depends heavily on women's labour. Women also work as hired labour. Most of them earn money by working extra-hours in the paddy fields of others.

In Manipur every household in the village has a vegetable-garden in the surrounding campus. In their leisure hours women of the family look after the garden. In the evening, the elderly women go to the Keithal (Bazaar) to sell the products of their gardens. Every afternoon, streams of women walk about two to three miles with basket loads of vegetables to the market to earn money. Thus the Manipuri women contribute substantially in the economy of the society and are not mere luxurious parasites.

Wearing, trade and commerce are the other economic activities in which the Manipuri women remain engaged. They are famous for their five weaving. Both the old and the modern methods of wearing are used by women. In the part loom used to be an essential part of dowry of every women.

Embroidery, rice pounding, fishing and helping in house-building are the other economic activities of women. On the whole the Manipuri women has a good status in the society. Their position in the society is undoubtedly much superior to that of the Hindu and Muslim women.

The Manipuri women are quite conscious politically. From the ancient times, Manipuri women always led non-violent and peaceful movements. They even corrected the injustice done by the King or by any officials of the state by reporting the matter to the King. They were able to get the scheduled programme of the King if the royal programme affects the interest of the state.

Nowadays, educated working women have greater political awareness. But this is not always reflected in participation. Majority of the women feel that politics has not solved the problems which affect their daily lives such as poverty, rising prices, unemployment, breakdown of law and order, etc.

Levels of political awareness are also greatly conditioned by the political culture of the area, approach of political parties to women and the quality of the local political leadership. Women organisations and women groups have also a very important role in importing the rear political education to women. Among the factors which deter women from active participation in politics are the increasing expenses of election, threats of violence and pitiable recourse to baser tactics like character assassination.

Ethnic Groups

The ethnic groups of Manipur dominate the state's populace. One of the elite members of the egalitarian society has a cosmopolitan culture.

Amongst the various tribes who reside in the state the Meiteis and the Tangkhuls deserve special mention. The Meiteis inhabit the Manipur valley and are an industrious lot. The Meitei men have a sinewy and portly physique. The natural beauty of the Meitei woman is accentuated by their fashionable clothes and gold jewellery.

The Tangkhul tribe is another tribe that originates from Nagaland and inhabits extensive portions of Manipur. Locally known as Hao, the tribal people converse in a variety of dialects. The literacy rate marked in the tribal community is exemplary and the children are conversant in a variety of languages.

Meiteis: The picturesque state is inhabited by a wondrous montage of several tribes that include the Meiteis, the Tangkhuls, the Kukis, the Anals and the Monsangs.

The Meiteis, one of the most eminent ethnic groups hail from the Manipur Valley and are an industrious lot. The men are robust and have a strong, sinewy physique. The tough build and slightly corpulent frame enable these tribal men to endure tremendous strain, physical hardships and fight against unfavourable climatic conditions. The Mongol features and the jet black hair are distinctive characteristics of the Meitei men. The men have coarse hair but refrain from growing beards or moustaches.

The Meitei women, however, are extraordinarily beautiful. Their faces are rather striking with sharp and angular bones and slightly Mongoloid features. The flat and stub noses and the full lips are distinct features that characterise the Metei woman. Their complexion is usually slightly tanned and whitish. Some women also have an ebony coloured skin and long luxuriant black hair that cascades down their backs and presents a fine spectacle. Some of the young maidens also sport a short stylish bob with a cut fringe across their forehead. The matronly women, however, prefer to keep their hair hanging down their back with a prominent centre parting.

The Meiteis also have their archetypal costume that reflects their cultural heritage. The clothes are rather ceremony specific and depict the aesthetic taste of the people. The women love to embellish their garments and look their best and are adorned in chunky and elaborate jewellery.

Tangkhul: The Tangkhul tribals originate from Nagaland and inhabit a large portion of the state of Manipur and the Ukhrul District. Locally known as Hao, these tribesmen are very industrious and have a penchant for enhancing their education and knowledge.

The Tangkhul tribesmen are mostly polyglots who converse in a variety of dialects. However, the most popular language happens to be the Tangkhul dialect. In fact, the linguistic diversity of the Tangkhuls is reflected by the fact that the residents of each and every Tangkhul tribal village and bucolic hamlet speak a different dialect. Although these mediums of speech and communication do have some semblance, some of their distinct traits make it difficult and almost unintelligible for a person hailing from the northern provinces of the Tangkhul tribal belt to decipher the speech of his southern counterpart.

The Tangkhul dialect is very similar to the dialect in vogue with the villagers hailing from the Langdang and Shirui villages. The Tangkhul community records an exemplary literacy rate. The children are proficient in English as well as the Roman script.

The people mainly depend on agriculture for their economic subsistence. Besides agriculture, they also run poultry farms and rear livestock to earn their livelihood.

The Tangkhul tribes, one of the principal ethnic groups of Manipur, provide a wonderful insight into the quintessential tribal legacy of North-East India.

People

The characteristics of the Manipuri people vary according to geographical divisions. The population comprises different social groups. They are Meiteis, Nagas, Kukis and miscellaneous groups. The entire population is distributed into two regions: the hill population and the valley population. The valley people are supposed to be the descendants of four old tribes called *Khuman, Luang, Moirang* and *Maithai*. The hill people are broadly divided into Naga and Kuki tribes. The Meiteis inhabit the plains, and the Kukis and Nagas live in the hills. Early Manipuris were followers of Hinduism, and believed in the hierarchy of the Gods. Many of the hill-dwellers have converted to Christianity, while the majority of those residing in the plains continue to be Hindus. Older forms of worship, however, continue to exist in the veneration of forest deities known as Umang Lais.

They are represented as metal masks, similar to the deities of other Himalayan people such as the Himachalis of Kulu. Like the Nair women of Kerala, the women of Manipur are trained in the fierce local Martial art known as Thang-ta. Dressed in black, they look like lithe, vicious felines. When their swords clash, sparks fly. The concept of unity in diversity was a remarkable characteristic of this state. In the history of Manipur, there has not been even a single instance of communal or ethnic dispute. But in recent times, it has been the scene of bitter ethnic conflict. The ethnic animosity between the Kukis and the Nagas stems from xenophobic insecurity. Over 1,000 have been killed, more injured, houses burnt down and thousands rendered homeless, in the conflicts in the past six years. The people of Manipur are simple and largely untouched by the pollution of modern living. Their wants are few, they love outdoor life, find communion with nature and depend on the gifts of nature like rice for food, fish to supplement their dish.

The general facial characteristic of the Manipuris are of the Mongolian type. There is a great diversity of the features among them. The people are very good looking and fair. It is not uncommon to meet girls with brownish black hair, brown eyes, fair complexions, straight noses and rosy cheeks. The Manipuris are decidedly a muscular race. Fat people are rare. They have good chests and well formed limbs. These are the people whose folklore, myths and legends, dances, indigenous games and martial arts, exotic handlooms and handicrafts are infested with the mystique of nature.

Population

Manipur has a population of 2,293,896 (2001 Census). Of the total population, 58.9 per cent live in the valley and the remaining 41.1 per cent are in the hill areas. The hills are inhabited mainly by the tribals and the valley by the Meiteis (including Meitei Muslims known as Meitei Pangal or Pangal).

Social System

The Meiteis settled in the Manipur valley are essentially farmers and their mode of life is different to that of the tribes' living in the hilly tracts of the state. The villages in the valley are large and semi compact. The houses generally extend on either side of the road at varying distances from it. The houses are separated from one another and there is no congestion or crowding. The houses in general face either to the east or to the south. This is to ensure more sunshine which keeps the house more cosy, warm and lighted. The houses-big or small have a rectangular plan with gable or slanting roof. In the hilly areas they need relatively level land for the construction of house. In case suitable site is not available, the slopping land is levelled with spade and terracer.

Some houses have open verandah. Many households maintain one or two separate small out-house for keeping cattle, pig or poultry. Such houses, for their small size are animals' use are generally constructed of very inferior material. In fact, there are mere shades to accommodate the cattle and pigs.

The house of Nagas and Kukis who live in the hills have almost identical layout of the house. A noticeable feature of Nagas and Kukis house is the way which variations in structure indicate precisely the status of the owner. The details vary much from village to village, but a man with knowledge of the local custom can tell by a glance at a house exactly wheat status the owner of the house has in the community. The variations, however, are confined to the front of the house and the decoration of the roof; the plan of the main structure is always the same. It consists of a small front room on the ground level, a large main room on piles, and at the back a sitting out platform, also on piles.

The villages are being built in such a way that the houses face towards the top of the ridge, the bamboos supporting the platform are often very long and a pedestrian passing along the back of a row of houses sees nothing but a forest of poles crowned with platforms far above his head. Wealth is on the whole so well distributed among the Nagas and Kukis of the Manipuri that apart from the wretched hovels of old windows the house vary little in size. The sites, too in the crowded villages are so restricted that, even if he would, a man cannot spread himself much. An average house of a tribal measures 8 metres long by 5 metres broad with a platform at the back measuring two metres long by five metres broad. The back and front are square and the roof of thatching grass or palm leaves. The ridge of the roof runs out along the projecting roof-tree and forms a little flying gable in front.

Planks are not used at all, the walls and floor of the house being made of strong bamboo matting, save the floor of outer room, which is of pulverised earth. In this outer room are kept the rice pounding table, cut from one piece of wood and exactly resembling that of the Angamis, Aos and Lothas of the Nagaland Bamboo containers for water, spear stuck up by the centre post, and an odd assortment of baskets and other cumbrous years. The flour of the sleeping room is of interlaced split bamboos supported on poles. In the middle is a hearth, furnished with three stones for supporting cooking pots. The ceiling is of bamboo matting, and in a well to do man's house has stuck into it many skewers of dried meat, half-cured pig's fat, dried skin, dried fish and other dainties, put there to be out of the way of rats. From the main ceiling beam immediately above the hearth are suspended one above the other three bamboo trays.

Meat to be smoke-dried is hung under the lowest tier, and they are crowded with pots, spoons, parcels of salt, baskets of chillies and numerous other things which the household wife wants ready at hand at the time of cooking. One corner of the main room is after partitioned off and used as a little store room. The beds are hewn out of one peace of wood. A ridge of wood serves as a pillow and the head-end is often on slightly longer legs than the foot.

The husband's bed is by the fire, and there is often another bed for children by the wall. From the main living room a door leads directly on to the back platform, which is used as a general sitting-out place by the family. The daily supply of rice is spread out on mats on it to dry, ready for pounding, and here the wife sits and weaves while the children play. There is nothing in the way of railing, but it is very, very rarely that a child falls over. A simple house which a young man builds at the time of his marriage have to follow the tradition structural design. The only rules are that house may not be built exactly opposite a house across the street, or evil influence will be wafted straight out of the door of one house into that one facing it. Moreover, the house should be so built that the sun cannot strike directly through the back door on the hearth, obviously because it would seem to put the fire out, though no such specific reason is given for the custom.

The relatively well-off tribals and Meiteis have started the use of galvanised sheets, Iron-nails, cement bricks and stones in their house. The building material like wood, reed, thatching grass, paddy straw, etc. are locally available while galvanised sheets are purchased from the market. A variety of tall grass (imperata cylindrica) grows in the forest. During winter this grass attains full size and is harvested. Villagers cut it with sickle, bind it into bundles and store the bundles for use when needed. It is also sold in the market.

The Characters

The Meiteis are sturdy, honest, hard working and people of commitment and integrity. They are brave like Rajputs and adventurous. Most of them are depend on agriculture and have the generous attitudes of mutual cooperation.

The Nagas have a well built stature and dedicated people. They however, believe in ambush and guerrilla tactics and 'therefore' they cannot be said as brave people as the Meiteis and Rajputs are. The Nagas very often attack by surprise and lose no time to withdraw if they find the enemy well prepared. They are not the people who can fight and finish to the last under adverse circumstances. "All Nagas are brave enough when things go well, but subject to panic when plans go away." Throughout the Naga History one finds that "....normal methods of carrying on was undoubtedly characterised by stealth and ambuscade rather than the open fighting...."

As regards to their sex morals, it has been observed that Nagas have an uninhibited attitude in the matter. Nagas are exagamous and do not have intra-clan marriages. Even intra-clan extra marital relations except where custom permits are look down upon. Though most of the Naga and kuki communities are permissive in matters of sex but only so far these are carried on stealthily. In the case of women turning disloyal to her husband, she has to part with her ornaments and her paramour is also to pay a fine to the husband. All this does not mean that the Naga moral is loose. In fact, whatever, latitude is given or deviations allowed are all within the framework of accepted social rules and conventions.

The Manipur's are fairly orthodox and follow their religious with Catholicity. They adhere to religions practices and even the dances and cultural gatherings are marked by religious rituals. In fact, the religious traditions and rituals have great importance in their social life. It has an added importance but rituals cut across the religious, tribal and linguistic differences. The moral character of Manipuris and the gamut of their life are would around the orthodox traditions.

Place of Women

Manipuri women are considered as most industrious. 'In facts, most of the work of the country except the heaviest is performed by them. It would be difficult to find a more industrious woman in India than the Manipuri.

In the primitive period women held a very high social status in Manipur. There was equality between men and women-the latter even enjoying even higher status than men. Women were the head of the families. The society was matriarchal. The position of women in a subordinate status has been legitimised with the coming of Hinduism in Manipur.

Cleanliness is another virtue of Manipuri women. Majority of them are early rivers. In every house, one always find the floors of the house very clean. After cleaning the utensils they usually have bath. They wash their hair with rice water and sometimes boiled rice with herbs. Younger women up to the age of 35 are always engaged in domestic work irrespective of their class and status. School and college going girls have to do a lot of domestic work before going to classes. Even the educated working ladies have to bear the responsibilities. The burden is, however, more in rural areas.

Uneducated elderly women above the age of 50 years usually go out from home to do buying and selling of the products of the land. Very often, one may finds even old women our 70 years of age selling commodities in the market. After independence, the literacy rate of females has gone up. Educated women take up government service and teaching. But most of them are still engaged in small internal trade and commerce, weaving, agriculture and other domestic works. In the part as Manipuri manual force was engaged in constant warfare with neighbouring powers, her women become involved in almost every aspect of life.

In the present-day society of Manipur, the number of women who belonged to the above category are also increasing in large numbers and women as a collective group, e.g. Meira Paibi, Nisha-Baudh, etc., are also contributing a lot for the eradication of social evils. Most of these women are maintaining their families and educating their children.

Castes in State

The peopling of Manipur has a long history. Ethnic groups and people coming in the form of waves from Burma, Assam and Nagaland have intermingled to form the complex mosaic of population of the state. According to the cultural anthropologists and demographers, four categories of people have mingled together in the formation of Manipuri-speaking people and they are:

- People living in the valley before AD 33;
- People colonising the central part of modern Imphal and west in AD 33;
- Immigrants from other parts of India;
- Immigrants from upper Burma.

When Pakhangaba arrived in Imphal in AD 33 with fire and sword, the valley was sparsely populated. In consolidating his principality, he thoroughly exterminated his enemies. Those who did not like to face liquidation, either fled to the cold hills of the northeast or the north or surrendered to him and accepted his authority. Those who fled to the cold hills mostly perished in the cold climate while some merged with the hill population. Those who surrendered to him inter-married with the colonisers and thus became Manipuri speaking people. Pakhangada seems to be an Indian Prince seeking his fortune on the Indo-Burma border. In the first and the second centuries of the Christian era, there were many such princes.

Pakhangaba's successor annexed, in the course of centuries, the other principalities in the valley and all the hills round it and extended their territory in the Kabaw valley and beyond the upper course of the Chindwin called Ningthee by them. All those settlers who came by about the close of the 19th century were absorbed in the local population, and went into the formation of Manipuri speaking people. The Shans who came to Manipur during the 15-17th century probably merged among the Manipuris. The immigration from the rest of India continued up to the end of the 19th century and is still continuing. This amalgamation of various ethnic groups explains the great diversity of facial features and the differences in the stature of the various people of Manipur.

About one third of the total population of the state belongs to the category of scheduled tribes. The scheduled caste population is small, being about 2 per cent of the total population of the state.

On the basis of caste and religion the population of Manipur may be classified into (i) Meiteis (including Hindus and Muslims), and (ii) the non-Meiteis. It is worthwhile to discuss the salient features and sprawl of the Meiteis and non-Meities people of the state.

Meiteis: The ethnogenesis of the Meiteis has long been muddled. The dominantly Mongoloid features of Meiteis, their Tibeto-Burman linguistic affinity and the oriental base structure of their cultural system-all, however, may be considered together pointing to an association with early Chinese history at least for a certain early phase of the history of the origin of the people.

In 1908, Hodson stated that 'Meiteis' has been derived from Mi = Man and Theie = separate. "In the Moietay of Manipur we have the combined appellation of the Siamerse 'Tai' and the Cochin-Chinese 'Moy'. In other words, the Manipuri tribe, called 'Cossiah' by the Bengalis belongs to the Moi section of the great tribe called the Tai by themselves, and Shanvel Syan by the Burmese, the sectional names being also foreign and equivalent to the native."

Chatterjee (1946) in his famous work "Kirata-Jana-Kirti" stated "the Meiteis or Manipuris are the most advanced section of the Kuki-Chin people." They have their kinsmen in Burma and appear to have settled in ancient time in Manipur and the Lushai Hills, as well as in the Chittagong Hill tracts. There Indo-Mongoloids are known to the Assamese as Chins and the Kuki-Chin has been adopted as a composite and inconclusive name for them. Singh (1975) describes the Meiteis as:

"The people of Manipur in the valley, speaking as their, the Manipuri language, is known in the local language as the Meiteis. Whenever, references have been made about them in any book, the word Manipuri has been used to denote the Meiteis."

As stated at the outset the Meiteis are broadly divided into Hindus, Muslims, and scheduled castes. The Meitei Muslims or Manipuri Muslims have many things in common with their Hindu counterparts, in respect of language, dress and construction of huts. The caste rules in Manipur do not appear to be very rigid and differ very much from those in the rest of the country. The present Manipuri race is composite one formed our of several tribes. The fertile Valley of Manipur witnessed the invasions of different tribes from time immemorial. At different periods the Nagas, the Kukis, the Shans, and the Chinese came and settled in this land and merged themselves into the Manipuri community.

Kshatriyas: The majority of the Manipuris call themselves 'Kshatriya' and wear the sacred thread. Among the Kshatriyas, there is a community known as Bishnupriya Manipuris. They are said to be the descendents of 120 Hindu families of different castes, who were brought into the Valley of Gharib Nawaz in the later half of the 18th century to teach the indigenous inhabitants of the valley the customs of the Hindus. They intermarried with the people of the country but after a time the Meitei or the original Manipuris came to the conclusion that the new comers were of inferior stock". According to another version the Bishnupriyas are supposed to have been the first ruling race, and the Meiteis are supposed to have been the next immigrants.

Their language is distinctly different, the Khalachai (Bishnupuriya) language is more akin to the Bodo-Chinese group. It is quite a reasonable surmise that the Austric Kha-Chais (Kharis) who had submitted to the influence of Bodo and the Asura culture and stayed in the plain of Kamrupa. When that country was overrun by those races, they gradually turned into a mixed race with a mixed culture and language. At a later time due to fresh political turmoil in Kamrup, instead of migrating to the Khasis and the Jaintia Hills where they were socially banned by the orthodox group of their race, they migrated further eastwards and settled in the valley of the wide Loktak Lake or Khala and even know as Khalachais. The headquarters of there people were at Vishnupur, so named after the tutelary deity Vishnu.

The Bishnupriyas claim the status of bona fide Manipuris of their formation of section of the Manipuri population. This has to be examined with emphatic references to their position in Manipur and the affinity of the language and other ethnic factors. They have a dialect absolutely strange to the Manipuri language in structure and in original character. The emergence of this community in the context of the recent history of Manipur must have been subsequent upon the contacts between the Kings of Manipur and the other Indian communities, especially of the eastern region (Assam and Bengal). Their dialect looks more deformed Bengali than Manipuri.

Among the Kshatriyas there is a class known as Rajkumari. They are the descendents of the various Rajas of Manipur. A Rajkumar is not allowed to marry a Rajkumari. The title of Maharaj Kumar is borne only by the sons of the ruling chief.

The Brahmins enjoy a very high position in Manipur. The ancestors of the Brahmin family came and settled at different times in Manipur mostly from Bengal. At present they are endogamous, although formerly they used to intermarry with the Kshatriyas. There is a class of people who do not wear sacred thread and still retain the Bengali titles. They are known as Lairikyengbunl. They still retain titles like Basu and Das. But in other respects they have been absorbed into the general mass of the Manipuri population.

The Loi caste is not recognised as a pure Manipuri. They appear to be the descendents of the former inhabitants of Moirang, one of the original tribes which formerly occupied the southern parts of the valley. They are mostly engaged in salt making, fishing and silk manufacturing.

The ancestors of Muslims of Manipur came at different times from Sylhet and Cachar. They took Manipuris as their wives and settled in Manipur. They took Manipuri as their mother-tongue but in dress and customs quite often they maintain the Islamic standards. The population which left Manipur in the exodus towards the west, also included Manipuri Hindus (the Bishnupriyas) and the Manipuri Muslim. Thus one can see big pockets of Manipuri Muslims living in close neighbourhood with Manipuri Hindus as members of the same family in Kachar, Tripura and Sylhet.

Tribes in State

There are numerous tribes in Manipur. Most of the tribes have their abodes in the hilly and mountainous tracts of the state. The present-day tribal populations have now been better known by their official names. The 'Tangkhul' for example, represents one of the scheduled tribes of Manipur.

In the 1981 census, Manipur has a list of 29 scheduled tribes ranging in size from more than 57 thousand Tangkhul to 70 individuals of Angamis. The 29 tribes of the state are: Aimol, Anal, Angami, Chiru, Chothe, Gangte, Hmar, Kabui, Kacha Naga, Koirao, Koireng, Kom, Lamgang, AnyMizo, Maram, Marnig, Mao, Monsang, Moyon, Paite, Purum, Ralte, Sema, Simte, Sahte, Tangkhul, Thadou, Vaiphei and Zou.

These tribes align themselves with one or the other of the three ethnic tribal categories, viz., the Naga, the Kuki and the Mizo. Among the Naga group of tribes the more populous groups are the Tangkhul, Kabui, Mao, Kacha Naga, Maring, and the Maram. Within the Kuki category, we may place the Thadou, Vaiphei and the Gangte. Among the Kuki groups are such as the Hmar, Paite, Zou and Simte. The Mizos, constitute the third category in the state's ethnopolitical tribal setting.

Housing Pattern

The Meiteis as well as the non-Meiteis after selecting a site, religious ceremony is performed. The frame of the house is erected by using wooden or bamboo poles. Bamboo is invariably used for the frame of the roof. The slanting side of the roof is made of bamboo poles. Thereafter, split bamboo and reed is spread on the slanting bamboo pole and on it thatching grass and paddy straw is spread in thick layers to ensure that the roof becomes room proof. Split bamboo and reed is also used for the construction of walls.

This is fitted tightly to the frame. Thatching grass is also available in the village forest and the neighbouring hills. Once the roof is completed, the major work is over. The rest of the work can be done at ease. This includes erecting the frame of wall with bamboo and reed. Thereafter, straw is mixed with semi-liquid clay and plastered on the bamboo reed frame. When this plaster dries up, a thin layer of fine clay is spread on the walls to make it smooth and more attractive to look.

Such walls are prepared on all the four sides and also inside the house. The ground floor is made level. Wherever, necessary, door and window frames are fixed on the floor and wall and later on fitted with planks and locking arrangements. One has to see that water does not remain stagnant near the house and proper drainage is provided.

In the villages of the valley of Manipur, houses may be divided into two types, i.e. Katcha and Pucca, depending on the material used. The Kutcha house is made of locally available building material. In the case of Pucca house, sand and cement is used for flowing and plastering of wall and galvanised/corrugated sheet for making the roof. In such houses, timber is used in place of bamboo. But no house is completely Pucca in the sense that walls have the same bamboo and reed frame to hold the plaster. In place of mud, cement concreting is generally not done.

The thatched roof keeps the house cool during summer, when the day temperature is high. The difficulty with the thatched roof is that a new layer of thatching grass or straw is to be added almost after every third year, otherwise the roof will start leaking. Thatched roof easily catch fire during the hot dry parts of the year. Contrary to this the galvanised sheet roofs are strong and durable. Once used, it lasts for decades. Its only repair cost is in annual painting to enhance its durability. Its main disadvantage is that the roof becomes too hot in summer during the day time. The cost of construction of the Pucca house is prohibitive and beyond the reach of most of the rural people. But compared to Kutcha houses, it is far superior and durable. People are now slowly replacing thatched roof by galvanised sheets.

Style of Life

Dress

The people of Manipur have distinct dress from that of the people of Assam and the Aryans of the North India. The clothing of Manipuris is closely influenced by their eastern neighbours in Burma and the Naga tribes of the north. Though the general pattern of the dress is uniform, variations in clothes may be observed during the winter and the summer season.

Children below four years of age are not very particular about wearing clothes, especially in the rural areas, but during winters they put on woollens to protect their bodies against cold and inclement weather. They use homemade cloth or tailored clothes, especially shirts and bush shirts. Grown up men use home made cloth for lower part of the body and wrap themselves with 'shawl' which is home made. Now the use of pants and shirt among the youths has increased and even the elderly/men put on modern dresses. This is necessary to keep themselves at par with urban people. The older generation of people prefer to wear homemade 'Dhoti'. This is a loin cloth called 'Kutei' in Meetei dialect.

The Kutei is about two and a half metres long and less than a metre wide. Females wear tailored blouse as garment for upper part of the body. For lower part they wear homemade 'Phanek' which in Chiru dialect is called as Panbe'. Two pieces of narrow loin cloth are stitched together lengthwise and the resulting one piece is about two metres long and about one metre wide. 'Panbe' is worn by unmarried girls around the waist and over the breast of married women. Both men and women wear a white cloth of 'shawl' type on occasional functions. This is called *Panchi* in chiru dialect.

Panchi is a home made cloth. In the preparation of Panchi two pieces of cloth are stitched lengthwise to give it the size of two metres by nearly one metre. Its striped border makes it distinct. Men and women use 'Hawai Chappal', shoes and sandals. The younger generation, however, makes greater use of Hawai chappal and fashionable shoes. The students both in the urban and rural areas wear shoes.

A women's skirt is a sheet of cloth by rolling it along the waist which loops down to cover the legs, a bodice covers the breast. An apron is worn by fastening either on both the sides of the collarbone or one end is fastened along one side and the other is suspended below an armpit. This dress often keeps the hands bare but they girdle a shawl by suspending it from one of the shoulders.

In the hilly areas as well as in the Valley of Manipur, weaving and colour combination art differs from tribe to tribe, but the dress pattern is intrinsically the same. Many of the cloths are striped on the corners or their width and entire length; the strips run parallel, but sometimes introverted with geometrical designs and embroideries within the stripes or outside. Stripes are generally of different colour from the main background of the cloth. The ceremonial costumes have more complex colour formations on deeper lining.

Dress without ornaments is incomplete. Ornaments are profusely used, those worn by men are derived from metals, cowries, shells, cane, leather, orchids and wood. Neck ornaments are strings of beads, shells, cornelian stones, etc. An opaque red stone serving as a necklace suspended by a thread or cane string is highly prized and worn by the rich Nagas and Kukis. A conch-shell worn with a chain of beads implies social status.

Among the tribes, women's ornaments are earring, wristlets and bracelets of brass or copper, but sometimes of lead or silver. They use copper earings. Naga ladies have their necklaces, bracelets and opaque red stone as a set of their ornamental dress while beads, introverted with pieces of buffalo's horns are also the highly valued neck ornaments. Aesthetic as they are, both male and female use further personal decorations of wild flowers.

Dancing dress is yet more colourful. Ceremonial male body garments differ from place to place. The hand woven sashes or baldrics of mixed hues are worn as scarves which, wide enough, crossing on the chest, cover the body but make the arms bare. The waist is rolled by a belt. White cotton robes are looped down the kilt by the Nagas. On the elbow, ivory armlets or red and yellow and checkered cane gauntlets adorned with cowries and shells or sleeve-guards coloured in red with horizontal stripes are used by the tribals. In fact, dress implies status. Therefore, there are variations in the way of dress from one person to another as from one group to another. But in principle, dress patterns of all the tribes resemble to each other.

In the urban areas, although scarves and blouses of modern designs are used as supplementary dress items of mill-made fabrics, ladies still keep intact their original skirt woven locally. In Manipur's villages and towns men have used modern dress patterns although they still love to suspend from the shoulder their age-old mantle which shelters them from cold said to be as warm as an overcoats. Schools have adopted a shawl as school uniform. In fact, primitive, indigenous and modern dresses go side by side which provide a spectrum of the vast changes.

Mention may be made of rain shields. There is a rain hat made of fibres suspending by a string. Another rain shade is of straw sewn lengthwise the bamboo frame, with cane strings and buttons for tightening it to the body. Both men and women use this sort of rain shade at cultivation in the field.

The tribals both men and women have a traditional style of hair dress. Among the women, while the virgins are hair-cropped, the married on the contrary keep their hair long but regularly combed. Men have a traditional fashion of haircut, it is a round cut style. Now modern fashions have become rampant for which, the service of saloons and expert barbers has become necessary.

Food and Drinks

Rice is the staple food of the people of Manipur. Manipur has a mixed population of vegetarians and non-vegetarians. The Vashnavite Hindus largely take rice, pulses, potatoes and vegetables, while the Kuki and Naga tribals relish the rice with animal proteins. The tribals domesticate animals both for food and sacrifices. Pork is more relished as pigs are more in number than the other kinds of breed. Slices of meat with entrils of animals slain are dried by suspending on kitchen racks, meant for longer preservation. Fish both fresh and dried in taken. Pork, beef, chicken, fish and mutton are prepared into various curries both in the indigenous and modern systems.

Meaty soups boiled with vegetables or herbs are the favourite traditional dishes taken with rice. Bamboo shoots prepared into vegetable curry is a favourite dish. Kachu and other vegetable herbs are common. Condiments prepared with wild vegetables salads and tuber roots are used. Dais (pulses) are also the major ingredients of the people of Manipur valley. Generally, they prefer the hot tastes with chillies. Chutneys of beans, chillies, are considered as refreshing. Vegetables adopted recently have supplemented the indigenous ones.

Out of the beverages, tea is more relished. Milk and milk products are largely consumed by the Meitei farmers. Areca-nut, and Pan (betel nut) is taken by almost all people. Indigenous rice beer is a favourite drink of the Manipuris. In the preparation of drinks rice is soaked first in the water for one day when next it is thrashed until it becomes completely powdered; the preparation is next laid inside an enclosure generally an elaborately compressed basket which holds the water and does not let it pour out.

Powdered yeast is mixed and the basket is kept in that way for two to three days. Generally the undissolved grains are left but the addicts say that the beer taken together with them is quite refreshing.

Familial Matters

Marriage

The Hindus and the Muslims follow their traditional ways of marriages. Among the Muslims it is a social contract while the Hindus take it as a religious ceremony in which the two souls have to meet each other birth after birth. The marriage ceremonies of the Hindus and Muslims are celebrated with festivity and decorations, depending on the socio-economic status of the parties. Dowry system among the Hindus is getting increasing popularity. Some of the Muslims have also started imitating the Hindus in the dowry matters. Different tribes follow different systems and traditions of marriage. The Nagas, especially the Kabui found in the hills between the Cachar District of Assam and Manipur and in the Valley of Manipur have a distinct marriage system. The Kabui Nagas have come under the direct impact of Meiteis.

The Kabuis have to seek his spouse outside his own clan. Intra-clan marriage is prohibited. Marriage within the clan is called *Tanpui-Tanpu*. If such a marriage takes place, the spouses are fined with a pig initially. A rite is performed (Mai-Khoumei) to regularise the marriage. But even then certain socioreligious restrictions are imposed on them which remain valid throughout their married life. In some cases, stricter measures are employed by the village council, which does not leave for any scope for regularisation.

The villagers perform a rite called *Neimei* which literally means purifying or driving away the evil. The spouse are required to give four pigs and two pitchers of rice beer to the villagers. A cloth worn either by the husband or by the wife should also be given. The headman and the village elders set it on fire at a spot away from the residential houses of the village. The half-burnt cloth in then held by the headman with a stick, who would pronounce the expulsion of the couple from the village. It is possible that same new sub-clans were formed as a result of this type of excommunication by the parental village. The same clan partners cease to be members of their respective clans. They are not allowed to interact with other-members of the clan.

Normally, marriage (Nousonmei) among the Kabui is a contract made between the parents of the two parties. Some elderly persons are engaged by the boy's parents to act as the go-between (Nouthanpou). In such a contract, the consent of the boy and girl is seldom taken into account. When agreed upon the parents of the bridegroom approach the parents of the bride in the latter's residence with a small hoe and two bottles of locally prepared rice beer. The acceptance by the bride's parents or the presents offered by the bridegroom's parents symbolises fixation of the marriage. Traditionally, most of the marriages had to be arranged by the parents. While this still continues to be the practice, in many cases it is no longer a rigidly observed rule. But in any case, approval of both the parties is necessary including an agreement on the payment of bride price (Manthing-Lemmei).

In the former days, the bride price was quite high and consisted of seven buffaloes, two bill hooks or Dacs, two dining stringes of beads of conch shell, two pieces of ornaments, two pieces of black cloth, two dining plates, two hoes. Should either party break the engagement, he or she had to pay compensation to the other, besides returning the bride price. The question of returning the bride price arose only in the case of a girl.

Marriage by negotiation is followed by the payment of bride price is known as Khamsang-Batengmei. In some cases the boy comes over to stay with the girl's family. He is expected to serve the girl's family in the best way he can, after which marriage in performed. In the type of marriage (Noumangmei), bride price is put off or reduced to half. Although girls were more or less isolated in former day, amorous adventures were not uncommon. This is evident from stray cases of marriage by capture, i.e. Nimjaimei. In case of Nimjaimei a tussle between the two parental groups occurs. Today, young people have the opportunity of meeting girls regularly in schools, colleges, and public places. Many of these meetings ultimately result in marriage (Jaipakmei).

Society is not very much against such marriage proceeded the rules of exogamy and incest are not isolated. There is another type of irregular marriage, Chamimei. Here a girl is given in marriage even against her consent to a family with whom the girl's parents are in debt or have some other obligations. The most tabooed form of marriage is called *Tankhi*, which includes marriage of a boy with his father's sister's daughter. Forced separation is the inevitable consequence of such a marriage. Marry Mo Br Da is considered to be the most preferred union. Clearly, the Kabui patrilineal elans are linked with materilateral cross-cousin marriage, It is almost obligatory on the part of a man to serve his mother's brother, and the best way he can do so is by marrying his daughter.

It also reinforce the tie between the brother family and sister's family. Such an alliance is called *Kangi-pi-Kadoimei*. This alliance further epitomises the obligatory relationship between a girl and her Fasi. A girl is under obligation to serve her Fasi. It must be remembered here that in a patrilineal system a girl automatically belongs to the same clan of her father's sister and she represents her unilateral group in the continuation of marital alliance. Among the Kabui, the rule permits a man to take his wife from his mother's lineal group. Some of the Naga groups also supposed to have a wife-giving and a wife taking relationship.

Widow Remarriage

Widow marriage is a normal customary practice among the Nagas. It is difficult to come across a widower in a village. For a widow, who has crossed the marriageable age, it is not always possible to find a partner. For that reason there are more widows than widowers. The bride price of a widow is just half of a girls price, i.e. every item of the price is given in single, not in pairs as in the case with the girls. But when the younger brother takes the widow of his deceased elder brother, no bride price is required. Such a marriage is called Kakhaomei, which means looking after the family of the deceased brother.

Divorce is permitted, but it is not common. Infidelity of the wife, bad temperament and barrenness are the reasons for divorce. If the husband seeks a divorce, he is required to pay a cow and a metal disc to the woman. Should the divorce be sought by the wife, she has to refund the bride price to the man. Sometimes a guaranter money (Changamjang) is to be deposited with the Peikai (council of elders) by the party who initiates divorce.

Remarriage of the divorced wife and husband is a taboo, unless purified by a rite called Chuksumei. After divorce children should remain with the father. The little one remain with the mother. When the father wants to take the child back, he is required to pay a buffalos which may compensate for the cost of bringing up the child (Nagongjang). Although divorce is permitted, the Kabui and Kuki societies lay strong emphasis on the husband-wife relationship. This is evident from a custom called *Mundan*, which is performed by the husband on the death of his wife. He is to pay the price of her bones to the nearest kin of his dead wife.

Marriage according to Meitei law is called *Luhongba*. The expression combines the words Lu and Hongba, means to solemnise or to change. So it may be "head changed or solemnised," or "bone changed or solemnised." Marriage is the mandate of Sanamahi religion, which is a part and parcel of Meitei family law. A male or a female if born is bound to solemnise marriage, and he or she must leave his image before departing from this world. The lives of issueless or impotent couples are bad omens in the eyes of others. When they die, there shall be always a specoa; rote of Chipsaba at the time of cremation. The belief is that an unmarried or impotent dies thrice.

The most important ingredient of Meitei marriage lies in the concept of Kujaba. It consists of four elements, viz., the earth, the foodgrains, the cloth and the accessories. Khujaba is an unavoidable act of marriage giving freely the daughter to another Yek-Salai without changing her own. It is the blessing for stating a new life by changing the head of the family from father to husband.

As to the number of forms of marriage, opinions vary from one scholar to another. We may consider only four forms of marriage. They are Hainaba (engagement), Chen ba (elopement based on love and consent), Chin gba Phaba (capture), and Loukhatpa (recognition of unsolemnised elopement). The purest form is Hainaba, but the most accepted one is Chenba. However, in any form of marriage, virgin marriage is regarded as divine marriage.

Conditions of marriage between any two Meiteis are as follows:

- Neither party has the same clan at the time of marriage.

- Neither party falls within the prohibited degrees of Shairuk; Tin naba; Pendinnaba, Pudinnaba or Fomnaba.

- The parties are not within the degree of prohibited relationship and are permitted to marry each other by their customary law.

- The parties have attained puberty.

- The bride is not a wife of somebody and the groom if previously married has taken permission for the marriage from his mother (if alive), or from his wife (if the mother is not alive) at the time of marriage, and lastly,

- The groom has not more than four wives at the time of marriage (because only five wives are permitted).

A Meitei marriage may be solemnised in accordance with the customary rites and ceremonies of either party thereto. Such rites and ceremonies include the Lei Chaiba or Lei Koiba. It is the flower offering for three times or the taking of seven rounds by the bride alone before the sacred water, Isaiphu. When the third flower offering is made or seventh round is taken, the marriage becomes complete.

Divorce (Khainaba)

In Meitei law divorce is known as Khainaba. The method of divorce of the Meiteis is one of the simplest in form. In ancient Meitei law, there were conditions permitting the husband to commit polygamy and tolerating the wife who establishes secret cohabitation with a person other and lastly, the legal positivism sanctioned some sort of penalty for infringement of such laws.

There are ancient records enumerating the grounds of divorce:

- When the wife does not please her husband,
- When the husband dislikes the character of his wife,
- When any of the spouses becomes insane,
- When either of the spouses becomes insane,
- When the wife is issueless, disobedient, immoral, outcaste or handicapped, and lastly,
- When there is any circumstance compelling either of the spouses to divorce.

The procedure for divorce is very simple. Either spouse, may initiate divorce. If the divorce is initiated by the husband, he shall give bride's price to the wife. If the divorce is initiated by the wife, the wife shall give groom's price to the divorced husband. If the divorce is done by mutual agreement, the children should be taken by the husband. In case if children below 4 years in age, the mother is the custodian of her children. In such cases, her husband shall give her maintenance of nearly twelve bags of paddy, which is equivalent to the consumption of one person for one year. Strictly, there is no fixed amount of maintenance allowance.

It must be sufficient to maintain both the mother and the child. In case of female children, the option of residence is given to the children. For the sons, the father is the rightful claimant. Even for the daughters the father has better rights about the claims of residence of the children. At present there is no such system. For rehabitation or restoration of married life a simple form of mutual agreement between the two spouses is required. When the wife likes to desert her husband, she may quarrel for a cause with her husband and then she may divorce him. This method of desertion may be applied by her husband too.

Wa-Loithoknaba is the 'confirmation of divorce'. Divorce requires a binding force only after this formality. In observance of this formality both the parents, the Sagei Pibas and elderly local men together orally require the spouse. They decide whether divorce is proper. It is a simple form of social recognition of divorce. If any divorce has been confirmed by Wa-Loithoknaba, shall be still treated as only an absentee to their cohabitation. Such absence may run for years, or for only one day. If the wife dies at her parental house before Wa-Loithoknaba, her husband must perform all rites of her death as her lawful husband.

During the Pre-Wa-Loithoknaba stage, she cannot marry another person. If she does so, the latter husband must pay a fine called *Mangkat* (usually half of the expenditure of the earlier marriage ceremony) to the earlier husband. If the earlier husband does not agree with her act of remarriage, then there arises a matrimonial dispute between the divorces, and its final decision shall only be given by the law court. Hanjinnaba is the re-cohabitation of both the divorcees or the coming back of the divorced wife to her husband's house. However, their act of re-cohabitation is free from any binding rule because it is always at the choice of both the divorces. They may establish their married life ignoring all their prestige and marital status. In the meantime, any divorced woman who is staying at her parental house is commonly known as Mon Hallakpi, who is again treated as an unmarried wife.

In re-cohabitation, the woman has more rights than the man, because the divorced wife even after having had a remarried life or, having lived as a concubine of another person, may again become his wife. However, the practice is regarded as social evil. In this regard the following rules may be noted:

- The conjugal rights may be restored within three years from the date of divorce.
- The divorced wife belongs to the surname or family of her husband until a remarriage with another person is resumed.
- There shall be no formal marriage ceremony for any remarriage of married or divorced woman. Her second husband is always abhored by the society.
- The formal marriage is only once in woman's life. However, a woman without a husband has a social stigma and, therefore, remarriage of such woman because permissible.
- There is no hard and fast rule in divorce, became it is complete when the wife has gone or escorted to her parental house, provided her husband was consented to it.
- If the divorce is not confirmed within three years, then such divorce shall be presumed to have been automatically confirmed.
- Any claim of either bride's or groom's price (if arises) shall be made within three years from the date of divorce, and such claim shall be abided, if it is made after the lapse of three year's divorce.
- No claim of any type shall be made or given by the wife of the husband is case the latter is unwilling to the restitution of there conjugal life. If the divorce is caused due to negligence of the husband who dislikes to any restitution, then he is liable to pay claim or compensation to his wife. In such cases also the limitation is three years.

Property Issues

The Meitei concept of property is quite completed. Individuals were treated as the property of the King. The King could give and take certain individuals as his own property, and such individuals acquired the prescribed status as servant, slave, maid, attendant, bride and reward. Sometimes, the sons or daughters were given as security for debt to the money lender.

Slavery may be said to be one of the oldest institutions of property. It is called *Naithang*. It extends even to the next generation as a hereditary one, if the father of a person who was a slave died indebted. The law was that the survivors of a debtor are liable to pay the debt incurred by the father. The survivors of the deceased debtor, who left unpaid principal and interest, became the property of the creditor.

The husband is the master and is entitled to deal with the woman in light of his title inherited in his cattle or slaves. It is because of the fact that in patriarchal society marriage is always marriage of dominion and it always leads to the acquisition of an amount of authority over children, who are looked after by the father rather as an acquired property. The same was the position of the ancient Roman-law. Land belongs to the King. The produce of the land was collected as land revenue. Land was divided into two divisions, viz. homestead and gardening land and paddy fields. Revenue was charged only on paddy fields. Paddy produce was given as land revenue.

The village pasturage was free from land revenue. Every village was to have a fixed boundary of pasturage. The villagers were collectively responsible for any incident or crime that occurred in the pasturage.

Transfer and Succession

There existed no distinction between ancestral and self-acquired property. A father is the absolute owner of all the property in his possession, whether ancestral or self-acquired — movable or immovable. In his lifetime, a father can deal with his property in any way he likes. He may give away some or all of his property to any one he likes even to the exclusion of all or some of his sons.

In case of a fractional share in a joint estate is sold, the purchaser has a right for the partition of that property only and for possession of the share bought by him.

A mother cannot herself demand partition, but if a partition takes place between her sons, she is entitled to a share equal to that of a son after deduction of the value of the woman's wealth if any, which she may have received from her husband or father-in-law. A wife is not entitled to any share in the property of her husband and cannot demand a partition during his lifetime as he is the absolute owner of the property in his possession.

Brothers take equally on portion between themselves. The share of a deceased brother is taken by his heir. If any property or money is earned by any unmarried woman or a widow by her own efforts, she is its full owner. Similarly when a woman receives a gift from her father, mother, brother, husband or some other relatives, she is the full owner of that property. Even if her husband gives her his landed property, she becomes the full owner of it. Gifts given by stranger to a married woman during the husband's lifetime are her property and she becomes the full owner of the property given to her as gift (dowry) by her parents and other guardians at the time of her marriage.

The same becomes her property. The same becomes her by her property. A girl becomes the full owner of the articles given to her by her husband, parents and other relatives on the eve of her marriage. A wife is the full owner of the property given to her by her husband after her marriage with him and she can claim the same at the time of her divorce from the husband. And so also she becomes the full owner of the property given by the relatives of her husband after her marriage with him. Unchastity is not a disqualification against a woman inheriting property nor does it affect the extent of her control.

Among the Meiteis a significant institution is the law of primogeniture, in which the eldest son of the eldest wife stands first as the legal heir, in preference to any other son of the wife or co-wives. But this law was confined to the royal families.

Inheritance is traced through the male line. The headship of the family belongs to the father. Such family consist of father, his wife or wives, his descendants, and adopted son and the aged dependent parents. The expansion of the family is done along the lives of agnatic kinship, as kinship is counted through males only. It there is an adopted son, the male line of the deceased husband of the widow shall be established through the male descendents of the adopted son. The agnates of the deceased are in the second category, as the widow and his children are in the first. Husband cannot inherit or dominate the whole property acquired or earned by his wife.

A brotherless daughter marries a man who will stay at her residence under uxorilocal system as Ningol Mawa without sacrificing his surname.

Distribution of Property

The distribution of movables are done through the principle of Chakthung Phithung. It is the giving and taking of all permissible shares for movable properties which are so essential to a separate family. The immovables are distributed in accordance with the concept of Sharuk Tamba.

The daughters are not entitled to take property during life time of their brothers. However, the brothers will maintain her and provide for residence. It is obligatory under the Meitei law that a daughter is allowed to stay in the house of her brother as a matter of right.

Inheritance Law

The law of inheritance in respect of sonless Parental Intestate property is still a debateable one. The ancient law is that in the absence of daughter, the intestate property goes back to the King. It was primitive or a lately living law. The family relatives had no right to take the property under there was a sanction accorded by the King and his country.

The inheritance of property of the deceased is done according to the law of the land in the sedentary population of the state of Manipur. There are, however, some variations in the law of succession among the tribals. Among the tribals, there is no written or statutory law in force regarding the inheritance of property. The tribal people are guided by the customary laws which have been in vogue from the very early times some inherit the property, movable or immovable, and share as far as possible equally among them.

The daughters are given dowry at the time marriage. But there are other considerations quite important, not to be ignored. If the parents, one or both happen to live and there is more than one son, some one has to take the responsibility of the partners. Usually, the old parents like to live with the youngest son, who takes upon himself the task of supporting his parents, in given the larger share of the property. There is yet another situation when one of the brothers has more children and more mouths to feed is given a larger share on humanitarian and sympathetic ground.

In his life time the father would like to divide the property among his sons. However, if it is not done, the sons accomplish this task with the help of the village elders. The property to be divided among the sons of the deceased includes land, cattle, pigs, buffaloes goat, sheep, birds, utensils, clothes and agricultural and other complements. The house is generally not partitioned in the tribals as in the mountainous and hilly areas land is available in plenty, for construction of new houses. With building materials locally available, a small home may be constructed within a few days.

Among the Kukis and Nagas, if a man with only a daughter and no sons were to give land and money to his daughter during his life time, those gifts would remain valid after his death, But all property remaining undistributed at his death would go to his next male heir, whatever, his known wishes might be. They could give the daughter a share if they liked, but need not do so. A man cannot will his property away contrary to custom. If the daughter in the case mentioned above made her father a payment for the land, it becomes her private property. She can sell it or give it away if she likes, but if she does not transfer it during her life it goes on her death to her father's male heirs.

But if she makes no payment she can only have the use of the land for life and may not dispose of it, and after her death it goes back to her father's heirs. All sons inherit equally. A widow receives a portion of the rice crop and the use of the house, and as much as she becomes so infirm that her sons have to support her. Very often a woman lends out and thereby increases the rice she received at her husband's death. Anything she buys with this rice becomes her absolute property. If the widow has to support a young son or daughter the land assigned for her use is increased accordingly.

Land bought by a woman-perhaps with money given by her brother or other male heir of her father. It cannot go to her husband. Of her rice, on the other hand, the greater part goes to her son or to her father's heirs, but her husband's heirs the rest. Ornaments are valuable property and inherited as follows; those bought by her husband are the wife's only for life and go to him or his heirs; those she has bought herself are her absolute property, and she can give them away to her daughter or anyone else she likes; of ornaments she has bought herself any remaining with her at her death go to her father's heirs-her husband, has no claim on them if the beads and ornaments brought with her at her marriage half go to her husband or his heirs and half to her father's heirs.

Hindus have a law about the adoption, the Muslims can do it without any formal custom, while the tribals do adoption very rarely. As stated above among the tribals, wealth is pretty evenly distributed and it is not often that a man is desperately hard up that he will go to another man and call him father in the hope of becoming supported.

Faith and Religion

Manipur has a composite culture and religion in which ancestor worships, Burmese Buddhism and different Hindu cults have been welded together into a peculiar belief. Ancient Meitei religion is not contained in any one sacred book, nor does it have a single historical founder. The legends declared in dreams and the utterances of the Maibis (priestesses) gave order to all sorts of affairs thus legislating through the mouth of dreamers.

In Manipuri thought there is nothing like culture separated from religion and other social traditions. Whatever is culture is also religion or philosophy. Every aspect of life such as politics, fine arts, and crafts are never maintained separate existence from religion. Worship of deities with the help of music and dances to ensure the community welfare is part of their belief. Even polo, for which Manipur is famous as its motherland and also Raslila and Lia Haraoba (Merrymaking of god) and other games and forms of art such as rowing and fishing are understood on the basis of religious beliefs.

The concept of god and fire as a holy symbol are also unique. The ancient Meiteis worshipped most of the Vedic natural deities such as the sky, sun, moon, stars, rivers, and the fire under non-Sanskritic names. They were classified under three deities, such as Imunglai (household deities), Lainlai (gods of the country side) and Urnanglai (forest deities). Another feature is that fire never becomes the forest deity nor it is the god of the country god. It is worshipped in the centre of a dwelling house with an iron tripod called *Yot Sabi* and husks. To them it stands for the substitute of the sun. The flame that burns upwards reminds man his noble nature. It is involved at the time of formal entry into a house.

At the popular or common level there is a great deal of local or regional variation with respect to the worship to the worship of innumerable Umanalais. In the rites and offerings they are so installed that one is never mixed up with other. The particular deity, who is being worshipped, is praised above all others. Pantheism prevails, but all deities are considered to be the manifestation of the same Almighty who has no direct dealing with man and the world. These ideas enabled them to accept all other cults as true. The identification of non-Sanskrit gods with Sanskrit names in Hindu periods makes possible the acquisition of Hindu ideas by the primitive deities.

Gods and Goddesses

All important gods and goddesses are associated with shrines and sacred groves. The lesser deities have only mounds, bush in the past, but temples nowadays.

Hindu temples said to be built in the 18th century occupied a prominent place in the temple and there are also a few minor deities, family members, associations, represented by smaller images or symbols in different parts of the temple. Thus in a Rama temple, Rama would be the principal deity and Sita, Lakshman and Hanuman the minor deities, where as in the Govindaji temple, Govindaji and his wife Rajeshwari would be the principal ones and all other Hindu deities the minor deities. Image worship in the form of wood and metal mouldings was beyond the way of time as the passage of Sanamahi Thirel throws light on it according to some. But some of the images of different divinities are dated as early as the 15th century.

One peculiar feature is that all sylvan deities (Umanglais) are supposed to come from water. They are alive to the point that the gods are eternal and present everywhere. In their belief gods are in a state of quiescence in ordinary times and must be brought into a state of activity through a particular ceremony called *Lai Themgatpa* (enticining). By this ceremony gods are persuaded to show their power by taking possession of their pronounced worshippers. The community festival of Lai Haraoba is supposed to strengthen the god and make him more capable of helping the worshippers. It is the choicest product of Meiteir intellect.

The Universe of Meiteir tradition is similar to that of any theistic system. God (Asiba) created everything on earth. The Biblical conception of the creation of the world in seven days in not known to their mind. The concept of Angels and Devils (evil spirits) is a significant trait of Meiteir thought. The worship of Sanamahi (sun goddess), the concept of seven progenitors of seven clans along with their wives are in line with the concept of Era van in Persian thought.

Their function is to promote birth, nourish, and welfare of the people. The adoration of Laibangthous (male deities), may be compared to the ministering angels to attend to

His call. The ancestral spirits are the group leaders through which the relationship between the living and the dead can be established. Neglect of the adoration of the ancestral spirits is the source of all evils. They are believed to show bad omens, white ants, deformed banana and fruit to the concerned people. In Manipur as in China and Japan, religion is a family rite rather than a personal creed.

Religion as a Controlling Measure

Religion was used as a control measure by Kings and nobles. The cult of the ruling Ningthouja dynasty became the cult of the people of Manipur. The ruling class descended from god (Pakhangba), the divine ancestor, whose reign is coequal with the country's culture and civilization. It may be mentioned as an emphatic expression of the values of Meiteir people attach to god-man relationship preferences about the responsibility of all sinful acts (such as war, flood) as well as prosperous acts (abundance of food, rains and good of all beings) in society and nature are found in a well known text called *Loina Sillon*. The King's sacred person is protected by many taboos pertaining to his royal office and priestly sanctity in view of his direct association with the great snake god Pakhangba. His presence was supposed to drive away the evil spirits from the spot.

King as God

The King was deified as Lainingthou (king of gods), which means a particle of god Vishnu and an agent of Lord Govindaji (the royal deity). Some of the Kings were deified after death. The Pandits maintain that their spirits were emanations from one of the original gods. From time immemorial the Meitei people have been venerating Kings, princes and the title holders as divine-beings to be adored by the common people the King as the head of the polity continued to provide emotional security through the social upheaval. This theory is continued to be propagated for ages by the writers, poets and scholars. This is a fine example of political, religious, and social structure unified under god. So long as the 'unification was perfect, religion could be equated with society.

The performance of various rituals and rites as a means of spiritualising human life is a trait shared by the Meiteis. Manipur being a Tantric belt of Northeastern India has also Tantric Puja. There are no rituals without the art of poetry, singing and inner metaphysical meaning. The rites along with them represent the origin and progression of the world and man's relation to god and the world. A careful incantation as revealed in numerous treatises lend a considerable support to its association with the magic and origin of religion for the people of southwest of China and of Himalayan region bordering Tibet. Under the guidance of priests and priestesses, the large mass shared the worship and sacraments of the deities so that sickness and trouble might be kept out of the state.

They endeavoured to please god by meritorious deeds, gifts of money, land, the temples or places of pilgrimages. A number of temples and shrines have been well-maintained and some that destroyed by fire have been rebuilt under royal patronage. The shrine of Umangiai is remarkable not only because of its cultural heritage but also because of proper care of the village headman or Hari jaba, who on the order of the King does not allow any Prince to approach it, for should any of them contrive to worship there and after gold and silver, he would certainly aspire for the throne and might cause endless trouble to the ruling King.

The Gurus have very special status in the society. Their role in salvation is of immense significance in 'their belief. The Almighty is addressed as Guru sidava (eternal godhead). The stream of knowledge comes from the eternal godhead through three mortal gurus and ten guru pandits. The Gurus in theology, music, dance, and crafts are god-realised souls who have brought a sea change in the disciples and then in the courts of the Kings. The relationship between the Guru and shishya has always been regarded as sacred. All forms of art such as music, dance, story telling, fortune telling, etc. are strictly within the cult of Guru is taken as visible god. There is a saying that one who has the blessings of his Guru is ever triumphant in life, while one who has the blessing of Krishna — the Lord of Universe, may sometimes fail.

Closely connected with the concept of Guru Kripa is also the grace of Lai chakhetpi (the levelling goddess) for one's quick rise in art, politics and business. The Puja of levelling goddess is a feature deeply ingrained in every Meitei heart.

Religions Morals

The development of moral monotheism in India and Mtltei thought is alike. Animals are notable characters in them. The fairies and giants (Deos) play some part in rewarding the virtue and humanity and protecting the weak and the more amiable against the wily and the violent. Most of the stories and dramas were meant for teaching the people Dharma with the help of tigers and elephants.

A major feature of Meitei thought is the ample evidence of polytheism, dualism, monism and henotheism. In Meitei belief there has been a curious blending of naturalism and supernaturalism at every level of experience. Forces of nature like the sun, the moon, stones rivers, hills, etc. have been worshipped. The supernatural ideas have been largely developed under the tremendous influence of Vaishnavism in the 18th century. When they meet they accost each other saying Hare Krishna and by asking the welfare of the other.

Success on the battlefield depended more on the favour of god than in the skill of any army. These ideas lead to the belief that man is but an instrument of god and the universe is his Lila ground.

A significant characteristic of the Meiteir society has been the harmony of humanism and worldliness of early period with the pessimism and mysticism of the 18th, 19th centuries. It is a common place of early thinking to emphasise human effort, family life, material happiness. Community welfare and affirmative world-view through its institutions. A unique feature in their genesis is that of the heroic duel of fighting among the rivals as divine ordeals for any dispute. Appeal to bouts of fighting with spears and swords, etc., was a means to test the innocence of the warring groups or persons.

According to the code of chivalry and honour the loser feasted and took wine with after which he suffered himself to be killed by the victor. Fighting is one of the inescapable duties of upholding the sacred duty of defending one's integrity. Sin is taken in the sense of ceremonial pollution and violation of the approved customs. There are, however, trends about mysticism and pessimism in Manipuri thought. Besides the mysticism of the Tantric and Yogi type there existed the cults Maibas (priests).

The Vaishnava, however, brought certain ideas such as Karma, Niyati (fate), Maya, Heaven and Hell and certain weaknesses of Puranic Hinduism. They are implied in the literature of Vaishnava period as well as in their practices.

The Meiteis are perhaps the most God-fearing people. There is not a single trend of thought which denies the existence of god but arguments against a particular cult or way of religious life by the Sarois (ancestors of the Kuki Nagar) jare to be found in the early myths. A Meitei believes that he can prove the existence of god not as a theory but as a fact provided he follows the correct path of god realisation. The Meitei words for God are Chingu (one who can see the Universe), Khoyum (one who has his abode in the navel). The Meiteis worship 243 gods and 142 goddesses. The religion of Meiteis has the characteristics of animistic, polythesistic and a curious mixture of nature and ancestor worship. Thus their religion has been considered as a kind of naturalism tempered by metaphysics.

While believing in the existence of gods and goddesses the Meiteis exalt Sidava Mapu (Shri Hari) as the supreme. He is assumed as existing prior to anything. The Negative attitude of Sidava (immortal) is used here as in Upanisadic thought. It implies that there are no human beings analogous to His will and pleasure.

The Meiteis believe that god is personal rather than impersonal. There are references to the Tatastha laksana of God in which he is regarded as a person. All that existed come into being by His will, Urn (puff off his breath). Before the creation, everything was in darkness and void. By His second sound Urn, there was water. God brought forth several other gods from His own body-Ashiba (creator), Leishirel Nornungbi (Shakti), nine Laibanngthous (Divine Youths) and seven Lainuras (nyniphs) to execute his order.

The Meiteis in general address the God as father. Yet it is also refers to him as feminine and even as neuter. Masculine address indicates that god is a person. The description of God as father in the front side and as mother in the backside is evidence enough of this concept. Before him men and women are equal, inequalities between the sexes are done away with. God is impartial as all are in the same relation to Him.

The Meiteis address gods and goddesses as their ancestors or progenitors of clans. The continuity between man and God is symbolised by the expression denoting ancestor-descendant relation or parent-child relation. The belief, the Meitei clan extends in unbroken continuity from the divine ancestors down to the present generation is an emphatic expression of the value they attach to such a relationship. God signifies His personal relationship to the Universe as creator, preserver and destroyer of the pantheon. Some of the gods suffer mishaps and hardships. Love which involves suffering is ascribed to God in the Lilas. Merrymaking (La iharaoba) rite is performed to imitate the play of God. In ordinary time God is in a state of quiescence and by enticing to bring His into a state of activity from water in the rite He is activated and persuaded to show power in helping His worshippers.

Henotheism

The Meitei religious system may be characterised as henotheism as distinct from polytheism. In the Laiharaoba rite the deity is worshipped in His own peculiar place as the chief deity of the universe without interfering at all with the claims of any other god. The same oration, hymns and palms are used on every occasion of sacrifice without regard to which a particular god is being addressed from which we may infer that Umanglais are thought to be different forms of the Almighty. The Laiharaoba is the bedrock on which the entire Meitei civilization rests.

The gods and goddess are as real as the shape of water in the vessel. They have the pure human forms, composite forms (partly animal and partly human). The planetary gods were endowed with animal heads, e.g. Mars had the head of a buffalo, Mercury that of elephant, etc. Some gods (chaiba) are born like human beings. Some are created after the likeness of god. The gods are like human beings worked together for the King. Gods have the quality of goodness and truth.

Local variations could be detected when different villagers worshipped different gods and at times the same god in different names and aspects. They assumed the deities presiding over the throne, individual house, forest, mountainous regions, rivers, lakes, directions and occupations.

Some gods like Sorarel have heavenly abode; most of the deities come down to the hills and villages to which they are attached. The Almighty is fabled to live in the sacred hill in the form of a human being. Another thing to be noticed in that the body is regarded as a means of god-realisation, but never as an end in itself.

The Manipuris also pay their homage to the native land, to all the great shrines within their own direct knowledge bearing association of saints and philosophers. The Meitei mind is pantheistic. In everything of this world they perceive divinity and the deity. They are beyond communal narrowness. Naturalistic world view constitutes another feature of their thought. It is written in the sacred books that the gods and goddesses in their incarnation and deeds teach the Meiteis the mystic dances, duties of family life, housing, cultivation and all items of human life.

They have the myths of the underworld, soul's journey to the abode of death and care for the dead, graves and the funeral offerings. An outsider will feel cautious to see a beautiful Meitei cremation with seven layers of firewood (meaning seven goddess), four green bamboo poles and a canopy. Each householder is virtually the priest of some deities such as Sun-god, earth goddess, etc. The priestesses known as Arnaibisare experts in dance, oracles and trance with the bells. They do not eat fish and use clean fire. The Manipuri Devadasis (Ma ibis) are selected from the selected from the selected few who had a tragic call of fate and unusual signs. They get training from a senior Guru. For spiritual works they use white uniforms given by the King of Manipur. The female Ma ibis continue their family life with their husbands, though certain restrictions are imposed on their everyday life. They have nothing to do with prostitution by furnishing a clear example moral life.

Soul or Atma

About the soul it is the deep rooted conviction of the Meiteis that the soul survives the body and does not perish along with the body in pre-vaishnavism as well as Vaishnavism. The Meitei wisdom proves that the old worn out and the soul assumes a new cloth in birth. Later under the influence of Vaishnavism the ideas of the Gita about spiritual life have entered into their philosophical and religious conceptions.

The creation story of man proves that Guru sidaba put the soul into the creature created by Knodin or Sanamahi by his own order. This creature which has intelligence, perception and notion of right and wrong is man, the should comes after the body. A Meitei artist has a view in image making; one is the image with soul and the other image without soul. The nature and the function of the soul has been thought is different ways. The soul is considered as the driver of the body.

It is a belief of the Meiteis that only one dwells in the physical body of every person as the King with power to control the impulses and senses. All souls are alike. The union of immortal soul with the sky means death. The soul is an immortal air. According one belief many souls dwell in human body. One of the souls goes out of the body in sleep. It works in dream and is followed by other souls.

Companion soul is responsible for guarding the individual against diseases, misfortunes, and evil spirits. Black magic against Loinaba while in one's sleep is sufficient for the victims sudden death, nightmare and accident. If this soul leaves the body, the person becomes senseless and utter incoherent words. They believe that there are five souls in a human being which actual the body and control different functions. Each soul is apt to migrate from one part of body to another according to astrological conception which came into prominence with a good number of works in physiological and astrological literature:

Some of the scholars have a different view point on the nature of the soul. The soul goes into the corpse. One of the souls called *Yaibirel* is supposed to go to the sky at the time of burning the dead body. One soul is said to reside in the grave. Another soul is in the physician. Still another lives in a part of the house. The famous Pandits of King Ihagemba could bring back the universal belief the Meiteis hold that after death the good and wicked stay at separate places, the former going to Heaven and the latter to hell. They, however, do not have any clear idea about the Day of Judgement as we find in Christianity and Islam.

Faith in Heaven

The Manipuris have faith in heaven which is attained after death. The pre Vaishnavite heaven which can be reached through a divine ladder is a place of Indra or polestar and is situated on the sky far remote from the regions of the sun, the moon and the stars. Another prevalent belief, however, says that it is ruled by the deity of death. The good souls are allowed to live with the family members in this region. The soul's personal immortality is implied in this conception. The materials of Puja, ornaments, etc. which are put for a dead person will appear in Khamung for him as the soul is subject to human limitations. Some of the souls are thought to be born again in the womb of the woman of the same tribe for another life.

The general trend of later Meitei thought also suggests a belief in paradise where god resides and is protected by his gatekeepers. There the noises of the Hayum Haya (inhabitants) resounds. Their way of life is different from the way of the mortal since they are always free from pains and live in mirth and pleasure.

The radical followers of Bengal Vaishnavism of Vaikuntha where the Almighty (Vishnu) reposes on the coils of snake Ananta with Lakshami sitting at his feet. The description and illustration of celestial place are found in abundance in the Vaishnava scriptures. Nabadwip and Varandavan attract the Meitei pilgrims as abode of god. The holy places are reckoned as a paradise in their candid opinion.

The Meiteis strongly believe in karma and are of the opinion "as you sow, so must you reap." There are numerous proverbs about the theory of fate and the theory of good action, etc. For example "what is lotted cannot be blotted," 'sin breeds sin', ill gotten money is ill spent.

The Manipuris see karma as Shraddha karma (Shradha Ceremony) and karma Yuga (period of Karma) in astrological calculations. The Manipuri text Amabadhi, teaches the Doctrine of Karma, the essence of which was the denial of the existence of Heaven and Hell. It explicitly describes that the happiness and misery are the result of one's virtues and vicious deeds. Karma bears fruit in the present life and does not wait for the next birth. "There can be no ordain of god. Man is to earn the fruit of his own labour as a pot is the product of the pot-maker. Man's individual will turn god's ordain. Do not be down cast, never be idle, that is to say there is no ordain of God. Man succeeds in life according to his own individual work as the potter makes his pot. For mankind, the individual will become the act of providence. Hence, don't be unattended to duty and never be idle. There is no fate apart from the fruit of labour. If fate is, it can never come without labour." It was an article of faith with some men are not helpless puppets of destiny, but masters and creators of their own fate.

The Manipuris believe that troubles in life, such as defeat in war, etc. are the results of their karma. According to them there is a very close connection between the karma of the King or the state and the individuals who are under him. Not only do individuals have Karma but a society of institution also has its karma. According to the Meiteis the change of mankind's karma always begins with the human revolution of one person in his faith in God. While doing our best to attain our personal revolution, and even the entire world.

The rural folk holds that fate is personified, the deity of luck Indra and, therefore, one should not repent for his poverty, or miserable condition. The Sorarel (creator) writes the luck of a baby on the sixth night after birth. They worship Viddhi Vidhata in order to bestow good luck on the baby and to alter the divine decree if there be ill luck.

Closely connected with the theory of karma is the theory of transmigration of soul and of seven or ten births which have prevailed in their mind in a unique way. Previous deeds in past lives determine the present life as amongst a thousand cows a calf knows its mother so the deed done finds out the doer. A man cannot escape his karma, good and bad alike.

The Meiteis hold that through confession, repentance, expiation, atonement, prayers one can cleanse his karma.

Concept of Mukti (Salvation)

The Meiteis believe that the soul is imprisoned in the body. The soul is described as a bird in a painful nest and longing for its native land, i.e. heaven. It is unable to quit the mortal coil in the body case. The ultimate purpose is to fly to God from where the soul was sent. In Meitei belief the body is the temple which the soul manifests itself and, therefore, has to be kept in a fit condition so that it may always be at the service of God. It is not a religion of escapism from the world in the hope of bright thereafter.

The references to the same in the Manipuri Gita are not about the bright thereafter unconnected with the worldly life. To one who has developed self control, his residence is Tapovana. It has no use to go to the forest to seek peace, fleeing away from his duty to humanity.

To the Manipuri Vaishnavas more important than salvation is its devotion. Nothing short of love can give us the pure state of salvation. Love consists in eternally experiencing the love of God. The ultimate aim and purpose of human life is the attainment of the spiritual form of Krishna.

They believe that the individual requires the aid of sacred lore and scriptures on the one hand and the Gurus on the other for realising the liberation. According to pre-Vaishnavite thought one need not necessarily take to ascetic life for salvation. By being a householder he can concentrate on God. This thought has relevance to modern predicament. Some have opted for salvation to apostles and not for God. Some wives attend on their husbands and witness the vision of God even before the husbands could get the divine vision. A warrior or a ruler can maintain the serenity of a sage and can attain salvation through hard work.

Along with the early thought there has developed the Hindu method where introduction is said to be traceable to Hindu missionaries of different periods. It is to be noted that Hindu ideas of karma (action), Jyana (knowledge) and Bhakti (devotion) were accepted with rejoicing after the acceptance of Vaishnavism. The Vaishnavites with their background of Bhagavata have stressed for them the nine modes of Bhakti and Raslila of Lord Krishna in their own way. A Vaishnava would not mind for the life of any being or life in the form of grass, trees or animal provided he is privileged to see the Ras of Nitya Vrindavan.

A conception prevailed that grass, tree and animals have spirits and consequently eligible for salvation on the condition that they are present in the dance. For the general lay believer of Vaishnavism a mere phrase or word of Chaitanya or Hare Krishna might be the means to salvation.

In modern times, i.e. late Twenties a bold Vaishnava called *Prabhupada Bhakti Vedanta Swami* accepted the teaching of Gaudiya method of salvation as the top most Yoga of salvation. The disciplines of Hare Krishna Movement led by Dr. Damodar Swami are propagating this view in Manipur as well as in the west to the masses who being found of its scientific background are encouraging the movement.

Different Paths of God Realisation

The Yogic concept of living including physical health, growth of mental consciousness and ethical fervour has been the foundation of Meitei Philosophical system. The elders drew from their experiences the procedural disciplines for psychological improvement. The secret that teaches the same is called *Punshirol* meaning the science of longivity — a concept of enjoying a full life of 100 years avoiding untimely death. The wise people of yore had formulated these as aids to spiritual and cultural preservation of a high standard of health, vigour and vitality. For spiritual life they began with the body, and the awareness of every pose of the body in sleeping, sitting, eating, exercise, etc. in itself a dharma.

The Meitei adopt a kind of scientific analysis of human body as a means of God-realisation. Lai Haraoba (Merry making of gods) is but an analysis of human anatomy and its underlying scientific principles and a reduction of the scientific principles involved into under the style of Umang Lois. Every family of Manipuri worships the highest God through Umang Lois at the community/national level. They aim at union with the self-evolution and self-realisation of God by the scientific analysis of human constitution. The system does not ignore human body as it is made in the image of the Almighty. To take an instance Lai Eshing Chaiba (anatomical heart) is worshipped and Laikhu rembi (tongue one of them) is pursued. The organs and their functions are the results of dialectical self-evolution of God. The nervous system and the psychic state are the aspect of God's self realisation. Life, conscience and soul are better understood through their physical basis.

Bhakti Marga

Bhakti Marga is considered to protect the human nature against ghastly evils of injustice, immorality and falsehood. The fruits coming from it are thought to be greater than those secured with great difficulty though Chingkherol, Pranyam, etc. The Meiteis are the followers of Bhakti Marga and its forms. It has charmed the devotees and villagers, literate and illiterate, higher classes or lower castes.

None by reason of caste, sex, and creed was denied the gift of god realisation. Vishnava mysticism has become a common property of the Meiteis through different methods such as religious discourses, association of holy Sankirtan in the ceremonies, plays, and dramas. They perform Karma Yoga also in any form which appears in the nation's history. They also perform Mantra Yoga, Yantra Yoga, Tantra Yoga and Jyana Yoga. All Yogas are, however, the means, never the end of Sadhna. The Meiteis have accepted it as initial steps for god realisation and cosmic realisation. Though necessary they should not confound it with the realisation itself according to the Manipuri Vaishnavas. Yoga to the Manipuri was never a negative way of withdrawal, but also cosmic realisation through Bhakti, Karma, Jyana and allied threads and an art of integration of life at all levels.

Art and Architecture

Occupying a prized place in the world of art and handicrafts, Manipur offers a wide range of products. The people of Manipur are highly skilled in crafting amazing handicrafts. The markets of Manipur are the best places to get the glimpses of the rich heritage of Manipur through its wonderful art and handicrafts. Kauna products, cane and bamboo articles, artistic weaving, woodcarving are the favourites of tourists. The women are expert in weaving cotton textiles. Laichamphi (meaning cotton cloth) is the name given to this handicraft. Necessity gave birth to the creation of wonderful wooden items. Block printing is also popular here. Colourful block printed towels or the Khamen Chatpa is a status symbol and is often presented to the village chiefs and warriors. The womenfolk wear colourful block printed dresses on specific religious ceremonies. Kauna mats are one of the specialities of the state. Grown in marshy and wet lands, Kauna are available in two different forms. They are water reeds which are used to make mats and cushions.

Its own art-forms and cultural expressions and ramifications distinctly showcase Manipur to the World. Its famous classical dance remains unique in all Manipuri dance forms whether it's folk, classical or modern and has a different style and gesture of movement.

Love of art and beauty is inherent in the people and it is difficult to find a Manipuri girl who cannot sing or dance. Manipuris are artistic and creative by nature. This has found expression in their handloom and handicraft products, which are world-famous for their designs, ingenuity, colourfulness and usefulness.

Each ethnic group has its own distinct culture and tradition deeply embedded in its dances, music, customary practices and pastimes.

Games and Sports

The women in Manipur have contributed immensely in various events. They won many medals both at national and international levels.

Arts and Crafts

The Indian architecture has a long history spreading over more than five thousand years, but the architecture of Manipur is not very old. Nevertheless, the ancient and medieval architecture of Manipur is closely influenced by the religious belief of its people and rulers. The growth of Buddhism, Jainism and Hinduism (Sivaism, Vaishanvism) gave a great impetus to the progress and development of architecture in Manipur. During the medieval period the shrines of Muslims and the faith and ideas of Muslims made their imprints on the art and architecture of the region.

Manipur has been styled as a kingdom without much of historical relics and monuments. As per the belief of the people, there cannot be secular buildings as the public is not allowed to have brick buildings. Obsessed by the action that private and secular residences must not be compared in grandeur or excellence with the temples of god, the Kings used to destroy the buildings by letting the elephants destroy them. Added to this was the attitude of the ancient monarchs who did not care to leave behind them material palaces and rich treasures through which they could be remembered by the posterity. There have been powerful monarchs but they were not rich enough to build monuments on account of other worldly attitude and socio-economic structure of Manipuri society. Most of the buildings made of bamboo and straw, were of combustible materials. But they had their style of house building and skilful craftmenship in the sacred palatial building locally known as Yamjao.

There were ten temples before the war of 1891. The Buddhists, Burmese motifs are discernible in the ornamentation of the Kyangs or early temples. In the later period, the Hindu style and decorative style have been introduced by the architects and artists from British India. The ruins of the ancient capital of Kangla and temple of General Thangal are the instances in point in showing the combination of Hindu and Chinese styles. The Maharaja's palace on the eastern bank of Imphal river and Shri Govindaji's Golden Temple (1894) are noteworthy.

Building activity has been remarkable in and around the city since 1960. The notable ones include Gandhi Memorial Hall, Imphal Tourist Lodge, R. Medical College, Lamphelpat, New Secretariat Building and a series of Government Quarters, PWD Office, Dance College and Cinema Halls in Khwairamband Bazar and Lamphelpat, Shaheed Minar in Sir Tikendrajit Park, Gurudwara, Jain temple, INA Memorial Hall in Moirang', etc. Gandhi Memorial Hall shows an attempt at evolving an organised relation between the Rath shape of the old and the modern design of architecture. It is a case of combination of contacts.

Tourist lodge is built on modern Indian style. The series of government quarters and churches at Amphelpat and Imphal show a trend towards the western style of architecture. One sees the Muslim, Sikh and Jain architectural styles in the concerned buildings in the main bazar. The INA Memorial Hall has the statue of Netaji Subhash Chandra Bose, a replica of the monolith erected by Netaji at Singapore in 1945. The groves or mounds which were supposed to be the abode of Lai (deity) remained as isolated patches of wooded land in the midst of open area with the passage of time.

After the Second World War, black temples of Umanglais were built throughout the valley where the local committees took charge of them from a particular family. Many Hindu temples were also built in plain villages and hills of the valley of which the Siva Temple at the top of Nongmaiching Hill, as we see in connection with Maharaja Bodhachandra's reign is prominent. Cemetaries and tombs raised over the graves of the forefathers are considered to be of great religious merit to the relatives. But they have fallen into neglect and can now be seen in various stages of dilapidation. The Roman Catholics are the first to introduce their architectural style in church buildings at their centres. Other churches in the hill villages are constructed like Hindu temples by the Meitei workers with little knowledge of the church design. Thus one will see in Manipuri buildings of various styles and varieties.

Painting

Drawing and painting were patronised by the Manipuri Kings. The temples and clothes are decorated by coloured paintings and designs. They had their own system and methods of preparing brilliant colours from the herbs, plants and chemicals. The Paphal (snake form of the first King) design carved on paper/wood revealing Pakhangba form is the unique contribution of the Meiteis. The story goes that Pakhangba was attacked by his brother Sanamahi with revengeful motive when he got the throne of Manipur at the bidding of the Almighty. The supreme power intervened into the constrained affairs and Pakhangba could not come in and hid in this form which is vividly reflected in this sacred emblem.

King Chandrakirti's reign (1850-86) stands as a land mark in the history of Manipuri culture for this period was the first opening of the Karigar Loisang, an institution devoted to the promotion of painting and sculpture. Maharaja Churachand Singh encouraged painting. He maintained a room full of paintings drawn by all the Meitei artists. One of them still hung in the dining room of the Governor of Manipur said to be displayed since the time of Mr. Simpson, I.C.S. the political Agent of Manipur.

Notable artists who flourished between the latter part of the 19th century and the beginning of the 20th century were N. Bhadra Singh (1861-1921) and R. K. Yumjao Singh (1869-1956) who left behind them a whole set of followers. N. Bhadra Singh received his early training in painting under Mangidam Angangmacha Singh, who was a Karigar of Maharaja Chandrakirti Singh. He took to the career of the artist as a painter and traditional sculpture of gods and goddesses. He received favours from Maharaja Churachand Singh and the British Political Agent who sent him to Calcutta for higher training. He was full of admiration for Raja Ravi Verma and the European style of painting in his post-Calcutta period (1913-22). He joined the Kings court as a royal painter whose duty was to look after the needs of the court and the state in matters relating to drawing, modelling and carving.

Even the British officers commissioned him to produce art plates on Khamba and Thoibi (epic of Moirang and on Second World War) some of which have been taken to British Museum and included in the famous book The Meiteis by T. C. Hodson. His major works on art as expression and art as service, include painting on paper and cloth and 52 fresco paintings on the walls of Cheirap Court (now session court) and sculptures of Devi made of wood, mud and straw, etc. To him is attributed the royal insignia of his patron, Maharaja Churachand Singh. His creative genius absorbed new ideas gained from the European style, Raja Ravi Varma and even a little of Rajasthani style which was brought to Manipur. The more important of his works are the stories of Khamba and Thoibi (Meitei Counterpart of Siva and Durga), deities of Hindu pantheon, scenes from the Bengal Vaishnava texts, portrait of a tribal chief with his consort. He produced oil paintings, scenery, impressions, etc. in addition to Manipur's traditions.

He excelled in the treatment of volumes and graded mosaics of colour tones. But he did not make use of European colours and brushes on account of the prevailing circumstances. His works show some local peculiarities in social customs, dresses and socio-political conditions. For instance in the paintings of the epic of Khamba and Thoibi, we find the depiction of Khokkhumba (covering the head with the wrapper by married women), Sai-Kakpa (side lock through cutting the edges by the maidens), use of precious Hooka by the nobles, use of Tilaka marks on the forehead and decoration of the woman's ear by the bunch of flowers, different styles of dressing for both sexes in connection with the scenes of Lai Haraoba of Moirang (festival of merry making of gods) which give us a clue to the conditions in which he lived. A typical example of cultural amalgamation is the drawing of Hindu deities like Siva, Krishna using Nathang (an earring which hung below another earring) and Saraswati as wearing Kyanglikphang (local necklace) around the neck. Apart from these, we find in him a great artist who made paintings of animals. We have as yet to find out the influence of Mughal and Rajasthani schools on his work.

In his personal life he had a great weakness for gambling dice and pigeon fighting on which he spent his earnings. In spite of his association with the King he lived a miserable and poor life. He was also going beyond the established conventions by artistic challenges in the use of colour and models and personal jokes.

The original paintings attributed to him are lying scattered in some families who keep them as a matter of cherishing sentimental feelings. His paintings in colour reproduction in a book (out of print) by T. C. Hodson has been untraceable through negligence. They are not in the second edition of the book.

Of late, he has been the subject of attention among the art circles. The year 1969 being the centenary year of his birth was observed with the exhibition of his works in the State Museum, memorial speeches and culminating in the publication of a small souvenir called Manipuri Painting. Due recognition of his varied contributions to painting, sculpture and design during his lifetime as the artist of the palace was acknowledged by all concerned. Mutuwa Bahadur Singh, a young painter, collected some of original paintings with great effort and arranged an exhibition of them in Gandhi Memorial Hall in April 1975, in the presence of Dr. Mulk Raj Anand, the well-known art critic. He produced a brochure and a litho print copy of his paintings for preservation in his private museum. He has made a serious study of his life and works in the fourth volume of his well-known series A History of Manipuri Arts and Culture which covers the period from 1861-1927. A small volume on him in Manipuri by Bhadra's grand daughter has also been published.

Another artist of the same inclination who worked in a similar style and theme was R. K. Yumjao Singh. He had also earned distinction as a sculptor, painter, architect, drummer and singer but he was better known as a painter and sculptor. He was the son of a monochrome painter R. K. Coura Singh who was at the court of Maharaja Kulachandra Singh. To him goes the credit of introducing what has come to be known as painting for the walls of Kang/Rath, Ihulon and Mandop (Hall of the Hindu Temples).

He painted on Manchester made cloth with modern materials. Among his well-known pieces of paintings are Radha Krishna, Khamba Thoibi, Ananta Sajya, Sakhis (Braj Gopis), Zila Durbar (official meeting of Maharaja Chandrakirti on the yatch on the bank of the Barak river). Most of them have been lost during the Second World War.

Some of the old paintings were thrown into the river or tank by the people when they thought that they would incur the wrath of gods if they were defiled by the touch of their feet. His paintings numbered nearly 5,000, out of which 500 were oil paintings. He had his own style with the use of lines and perspectives. His works speak more of the cerebrum of the heart.

He also executed a large number of bronze images such as of Radha-Krishna, Gopal Deva, Chaitanya, Jagannath, etc. which are still worshipped in the temples in and around Imphal and other places such as Moirang. Thanga and Nagaikhong, Ngangbi Maharani (Queen of Maharaja Churachand) encouraged him and she liked his works. Yumjao Sana Memorial medal is being awarded to the best painter or sculptor by MSP out of the donation made by his son. The two painters have promoted a number of artists such as Maggsidam Kalachand, Lonrembam Kamdeva, Huirem Tol Singh, Hidangamyum Hemchandra Sarma, etc., who by their works could serve as a connecting link between the old and new western styles. They were not so much concerned with the common masses as with those of the religious motifs and the King's Court.

War Paintings

Another distinctive feature is that painters joined the Kheda operation of Maharaja Churachand Singh and worked with the troops in painting the elephants of the same size. After the Second World War greater names of the older generation who are responsible for the great strides in this field are M. K. Priyobarta Singh, Shyamsunder, H. Shyamo Sharma, R. K. Chandrajit (son of R. K. Yumjao Singh), Goure, etc. M. K. Priyobarta Singh was a younger brother of Maharaja Bodhchandra of Manipur, an arts graduate and captain of the army. He received his training at J. J. School of Art, Bombay, and absorbed Western technique during his stay in England.

Though he was a member of the durbar incharge of fine arts and Chief Minister, he has such a knowledge of painting as few possess and he has a hand in all politics and programmes of the states in the field of the fine arts. His early painting is related to peaceful landscapes around local surroundings. His later works reflect the struggle of people against the challenges thrown by realities of life. He boosted the art of painting in the style of Naturalism, English landscape, European realism of the 19th century, French realist, Gusta Kurbe and Onor Domin. He is continuing as a social realist in this field. Mention can be made of his self portrait, Kangla, Govindaji temple, funeral procession and birth of Bangladesh and life of the common man.

H. Shymo Singh (1917) has acquired his knowledge from his grandfather, H. Likhal Khomba Singh, Bhabani Saha of Calcutta (1836-1939) and latter in pottery and ceramics. He is considered to have evolved a style of Western impressionism and sensuous use of colour, form and matter. Originally in the service of the state as Deputy Director incharge of design he has been responsible for art design of emblems of the state. He produced drawing books for school boys and girls.

Shyamo Sharma (1917-79) was a disciple of M. Kalachand Singh, N. Bhadra Singh, and painter of Maharaja Bodhachandra Singh. His works may be divided into two:

- Hindu pantheon in poster colours, and
- Works in the western idiom after the establishment of the school of art.

Life in Manipur has faced the bitter experience of Second World War, its effects, etc. His series of painting Mother Manipur in a Romanticist vein reflects the social disharmony in Manipuri society. It is a personified mother with a broken heart. His mother and child series are expressionistic and he speaks of his cherished desire to have a child. He popularised visual art couched in Western anatomy, perspective and volume.

Imphal School of Art

One of his notable achievements is the establishment of Imphal Art School in 1947 against many odds and problems. The college situated near the Imphal War Cemetery has catered to the needs of the aspirants and produced several young artists of note. Another memorial to him is the annual painting competition for children organised jointly by Imphal Art College and Arts Society in his memory.

H. Goura Singh is another painter of portraits, naturalistic landscape, village life, etc. and makes transitional realism as practised nowadays. The state recognised his merit. R. K. Chandrajit, the second son of R. K. Yumjao Singh, showed his mastery over realistic depiction of Manipur's historic events, naturalistic scenes and anatomy properties. He shows the influence of cinematography, stage lightning dramatic scenes and commercial art designs. His paintings are innumerable in addition to applied and commercial production which present the close coexistence between traditional substance and Western realism. Some of his works have been kept in great cities of India. Major Dayamay is yet another painter who has dealt with the brutalities of war, woes and miseries of women and various aspects of tribal life. Being a military officer in his impressionable years, he was moved by the most bizarre human predicament.

The works of Manipuri artists have been appreciated by the hill-tribes who have utilised their works in portraying Biblical and Christian conceptions and illustrations of tribal music. As a post-war development, a number of princesses and women have taken painting as a favourite pastime. M. K. Binodini Devi, the youngest daughter of Sir Churachand Singh (a great short story writer and a film script writer too) and Rani Khider Devi, wife of late Maharaja Bodhachandra are some names of this period. Smt. M. K. Binodini Devi completed regular training from Kala Bhawan, Shantiniketan and adopted its style in some of her drawings.

Rani Khider Devi took to painting at the instance of her brother-in-law, M. K. Priyabarta. She has produced some works of local realism which have enabled her to receive an award in the state competition.

Contemporary Paintings

The rise of a new generation during the period 1950 to 1970 has produced young enthusiastic painters. It is but natural that modern or contemporary style of painting has had a marked influence on them as it has on the other schools of India. The outstanding names who are working towards the modern style are Prof. Th. Tombi Singh, Phrindra Singh, Brajamani Sharma, R. K. Sanatomba, H. Ibomcha, Rajo Singh, R. K. Saraj Kumar, etc. Possibly some names like Amujao Kamei, Kaiho Mao, along with the young tribal students of the colleges are from the non-Meitei groups.

Most of the Meitei/Manipuri artists are holders of university degrees. Owing to their voluntary efforts, the Manipuris are at present having good works of art from Calcutta, Bombay, and Baroda-returned painters on such art lines as cubism, expressionalism, abstraction, fine realism, and symbolism. Through the efforts of Prof. Th. Tombi Singh and his artist colleagues, an art exhibition of artists was held in Imphal in 1968 and it continued up to 1973 in his capacity as the general secretary of the forum.

But there has been a declining trend on account of patronage, lack of appreciation and public apathy. He has a number of art exhibitions to his credit in Ahmedabad (1882) Baroda (1977), beside participating in a number of All India exhibitions. Since 1972 the state level exhibition of the paintings of selected artists has been annually held under the auspices of Manipur State Kala Akademi with provisions for the best exhibits and purchase of two or three works every year.

It is to be noted that some artists like M. Bahadur, Tena Singh have successfully turned to folk art and themes. In 1982, there were publication of sketches:

- Story of Sati Khongnang in the form of sketches and illustrations from Mangi Devi,
- The Story of Khamba and Thoibi (Kangleirol Classics) in English illustrated by Sanatomba Singh, Designer of Publicity Department, and
- Prince Hirachandra (Dakuningthon during 1819-25).

The result is a great variety in painting style. Interest is, on the whole, increasing all over Manipur and more and more studies and voluntary associations are being opened. In addition to Imphal Art College established by Shyamo Sharma, there is (a) Manipur Art College Naga Mapal, (b) Fine Arts School Society, Uripok, Imphal. Manipur Art College significantly contributed towards the popularity of Manipur paintings in Japan by organising an Indo-Japanese Children Art exhibition in 1976.

Another Voluntary organisation, namely, Arts Society, Manipur was established in 1980 by the painters and art lovers of Greater Imphal for which the ministers and other bodies contributed some amount. The artists centre established by A. Achonba Singh in 1979 organises annual school children art competition and exhibitions. By doing so small boys are given special training in this field. Arts Society organises seminars, art exhibitions and issues souvenirs annually on contemporary art in Manipur.

The art schools and centres came into existence in Imphal for which the painters have been engaged as teachers. They are the employees of the Government Departments such as design Section of Industry Department, Information and Public Relations Department and Regional Medical College, Lamphelpat. Designing of the covers of books, magazines and journals in the order of the day in Manipur and the painters give new designs for improving the quality of the publications, thus we see an outburst of their activities in visual arts. It is the duty of the government and the public to help them and extend the facilities of patronage in all ways. The public should exercise a healthy influence in this aspect.

Sculpture

Judged by the examples of structural works such as Kangla Sa (animal of the sun, personification of divine power symbolising the luck of the state. It is built of masonry to resemble stone installed in front of the gate of the capital), art objects of handicrafts and handloom products (artistry in house roof, leaf plates and cups, ornamental products and other objects of the hill areas) as well as the traditions that have come down to us.

Sculpture must have reached a distinctive place. Drawing, painting and sculpture usually coexist and are inseparable. It is a deep rooted belief that any error in painting/carving will give, him a handicapped child. Carving is connected with a deep knowledge of philosophy and psychology. The artists have accepted the current view of the open environment. The images are made after the human forms showing the intimate relation between human being and god. Sex symbol of a deity is the soul in their belief.

The representation of Urnanglais (Sylvan deities) and Hindu gods in human forms is mostly found in the 17th century. That carving of sculptural work was popular with the people which was established by the worship of idols in individual houses, groves and Hindu Temples. Icons of Hindu pantheon and Buddhism in stone, bronze and clay assignable during period from the 15th to the 19th centuries which have been acquired from different places in the valley and hill areas are now deposited in State Museum, Mutua Museum and Department of Archaeology.

They are displayed and have been studied by the scholars. Hindu deities such as Rama, Hari, Narsimha, Buddha in different poses were carved in accordance with the description of local dress, ornaments and style to be found in the synoptic and formative periods. Idols of wood and Sivalinga commemorate the reign of Maharaja Churuchand Singh and Maharaja Bodhachandra in the Manipur temples and Nabadwip.

Idol Making

Making of idols in clay, bronze and wood was compulsory under the rulers of Manipur. A particular family took to the work of specialising in these artistic products in the past. During the time of Maharaja Churachand Singh, one Leikhom Sana (pet name meaning clay Raj Kumar) made idols from ivory and wax. The Maharaja presented to the viceroy of India folk products made of ivory such as Khamba, Thoibi (the hero and heroine of the epic) scene showing the royal dance. The idols, puppets, Tal Sharnu (elephant made of Hour) prepared by Manipuri women can be compared with the products of British India. Among the Manipuri artists in the royal court of Tripura (beyond the state of Manipur) R. K. Buddhimanta alias Angou Sana was famous for his watch, fan, cane industry, ivory matstick of betelnut, which impressed the British who invited him to Rangoon at the suggestion of his brother Baba Sana and W. L. Leonard (the proprietor of watch company). He was a well known Silpa-cum-artist and was attached as the superintendent of Silpa Ashram Agartala in the Tripura State (Maharaja Virachandra of Tripura).

Artistry in colour of suitable objects caught the eyes of the great people and they became popular in Congress Swadeshi Mela and British exhibitions although the work has declined much since the abolition of the monarchy. The products of today are mainly confined to types of doll-making of wooden, earthen, paper and cloth products at the time of exhibitions. They depict artists such as drum player, fiddle player, Khamba and Thoibi in dance, Radha-Krishna Jugal Milan, swordsman, spearman, etc. The tribal clothes and weapons have a symmetrical and artistic design. Among the Meiteis, the long shield used by as spearman (called *Chung*) is painted in fearful figures. The war sword had floral designs over the handle made of copper and of different colours, and such is the case with Pena tiddle and Pung (drum).

There began the insecurity and lack of patronage consequent on the merger of Manipur with India in 1949. Under the new setup sculptural work has been taken over by the state and placed under the care of the Director of Industries. The Directorate has organised annual exhibitions and instituted a scheme for award to master craftsmen in 1979-80 according to which master craftsmen have been recognised for special honour with cash awards, seals and certificates. The artists have completed advance course in bronze, wood crafts and embroidery works with the aid of the Directorate. They have produced famous creations which can match with any producer of their kind outside Manipur.

Performing Arts

Theatre

Theatre and Jatras: Theatre and Jatras are the main artistic and cultural forms of Manipur. The Meitei people with their concept of the world as the sport of god are particularly fond of the theatre and Jatra. This type of communication through characters has achieved phenomenal success through their Laiharaoba dance, operas and plays of Shri Krishna as far as the form content and expression are concerned.

The contemporary theatre is a continuation of the earlier tradition. The Bengali community living in Imphal has given an impetus to theatre and Jatra. They established in 1903 the Bamancharan Mukhopadhya Bendhab Natya Sala for the purpose of staging Bengali drama, especially on festive occasions. The first drama in the true sense was a Bengali drama Pravas Milan played in the courtyard of Shri Govindaji, adjacent to the royal palace of Maharaja Churachand Singh who was a patron as well. In 1904, the institution was renamed as 'Friends Dramatic Union' with a permanent stage at Babupara under the guidance of a committee.

The first play with a regular plot divided into acts and scenes Pagalini was a comic one written in Manipuri language by Bihari Singh. It was enacted in 1905 at the residence of the author. Subsequently, some of the well-known Bengali plays have been translated into Manipuri and staged. Regular performances were made possible in the permanent hall of the 'Victoria Club' established in 1910. But all the theatres up to this time were confined to Imphal town. Maharaja Churachand gave great patronage to this form of art. It went ahead with the work of giving medals to the talented artists for their roles and performances. In 1931 the Manipur Dramatic Union was established. S. Lalit was the pioneer of Manipuri theatre. Many actors, playwright and able singers came forward from this institution. The theatre institution spread in the suburbs of Imphal as well as rural areas.

The Manipur theatre was, however, shaken by the Second World War. The bombing of Manipur by the Japanese forced the Manipuris to move to the quieter places for life. All the major towns were filled with military people. The institution of theatre was adversely affected. After the Second World War the people reviewed the theatre and the Rup Mahal Theatre Society was established. The writers started reading modern western literature and the effect was seen almost in manifold ways. The composers before the Second World War had a fine command over Bengali and Sanskrit. Devotion of music and dance were considered essential for the plays. The themes were mostly drawn from Hindu religious texts.

The court life of the King was vividly brought out in the dramas. The main roles required gaudy costumes, necklaces of pearls, etc. But such a type of performances were seriously affected when the Congress Government took over the administration of the Kingdom. The Congress movement under the leadership of Gandhiji had the effect of changing costly costumes into local made cloth and simple ornaments. Rupmahal Theatre produced a variety of new literary and popular dramas. Its Director, M. Bir Singh, looked out for heroes who fought against the British and wrote a noted drama called Tikendrajit a Manipuri martyr who was hanged in 1891 for his war with the British. It is a well known historical play.

Manipuri stage became very prosperous through G. C. Tongbra's problem plays, social plays and satirical dramas. He translated the works of G. B. Shaw and Shakespeare's Hamlet into Manipuri life.

The important theatrical personalities of the older generation are Kh. Munal Singh, N. Thanil Singh, S. Lalit, Kh. Nabakishore Singh, Kh. Nongyai, Kh. Madhumangol, Kh. Iboton Singh, K. Amuba, Gokul Chandra Singh, Kh. Dhanachandra, Ng. Jugolchandra, H. Nilarfani Singh, H. Nutachandra Sharma, M. Bira Singh, Ng. Tilak Singh, M. Biramangol Singh, L. Notrajit Singh, Some of them notable and still alive are Gouramani Devi, Tambal Angoubi Devi, Tendon Devi, Bimola Devi, etc.

One Act Play: In the present dramatics, one act play has got considerable importance. Prize distribution competition organised by schools, colleges and state departments have encouraged dramas among the students through one act plays. These short plays were broadcast by the All India Radio, Imphal and some of them are published in the form of collections.

Yatra: The folk play is known by such names as *Phagilila* (farcical play) *Sumanglila* (enactment in the courtyard) and Jatra Wali. The concept of Yatra and ground play is an institution which is as old as the history itself. Sumanglila means a play enacted in front of a house. The courtyard is a miniature *Vrindavan* (abode of god) for the purpose of religious rites. Lila is a term which denotes the deeds of gods as against those of a common people. Jatra is considered to be originated after Manipur's contact with the mainstream of Indian culture. *Phagilila* (comic play) is in some respect similar to the Jatra of Assam and Bengal and has remained as the medium of mass communication and education among the lower strata of Manipur society. It is inseparable from its sociocultural ethos. It is a theatre of the people. At present it has almost eclipsed modern theatre in view of its association with the wide public popularity. The Jatra, unlike its fate in the rest of India, can compete favourably with the modern films in respect of income and popularity.

Evolution of Manipuri Sumanglila: The music and dances which are widely cultured in Manipur may be stated to be the precursor of Jatra type. Abhinava is expressed in various Rasalilas, Nata Sankirtan and religious Lilas. The more important Jatra of the present day are: (i) Female Jatras, (ii) Children Jatras, (iii) Ishei Lila.

Female Jatra: The patriarchal society has been influential in determining the position of women in their life. The position was traditional, women being a housewife did not take much interest in Jatras. But now females have about two dozens of female associations who perform Jatras. The Jatras performed by females are mostly of the episodes of immortal epic of Khamba and Thoibi. The group consists of female performers only. It was during the drama, Jatra festivals in 1976 that the females groups began to contest in the Jatra competition. The All India Radio, Imphal has immensely contributed to the popularisation of Jatra female as a monthly programme.

Children Jatra: There is no organised body for the children Jatra. Some small boys and girls have, at times, applied their talents to the performances by joining the Jatra groups from their early career at the suggestion of the concerned directors. The Jatra programme of this group is held from time to time by the All India Radio, Imphal.

Ishei Lila (Music Jatra): It was in 1975 that a new type of Sumanglila with plenty of music and orchestra and modern instruments as an item was introduced to enliven entertainment of the audience. With it are connected modern singers like Suren Goswami, Y. Suren, etc. The performers have commissioned the work of several playwrights for acting. Legitimate occasions are enacted for music and the relationship between words and music. At present, there are fourteen permanent associations which have so far produced such Lilas. The direction, acting and problems are different from those of dialogue types. The song-plays in spite of public, support are not recognised by the state.

Ipom (One Man's Jatra): In one man show an actor performs all the characters of a play through his voice modulation and song (sometimes with a slight change in dress). Among the artists of this category, the names of B. Achau Sharma who play the entire Lila of Gouranga (Saint Chaitanya of Bengal) by himself in Satya Chant, G. Gourahari Sharma in his role as Shish (disciple) plays all the characters of Krishna, Radhika, and Gopis by himself, and Gandhar Singh who plays the role of an aged man, aged woman, main singer and drummer through his voice training.

Ipom is a form of entertainment where two or three Jatra personalities take part and discuss something. The themes are social political in nature which evoke the laughter of the audience. The All India Radio, Imphal is providing regular programme of leading jokers of the Jatra.

The production style of popular Sumanglila is simple with the action area being the courtyard (Mandap), street, a place on the bank of a river, etc. in the centre and the spectators around the place. The instrumentalists and the chorus singers of about two or three sit in a suitable place close to the circular play of the actors. The green room is at a distance of a few yards and a narrow path is left for the actor's entrance and exist. This passage also serves as an additional shouting and acting area.

A particular actor by advancing a few steps from the place where he stood, used to describe another scene as if he actually traversed all the distance. Artists of not less than 10 in number, formed a troupe normally, coacting with three or four females were at first seen in some Jatras. Nowadays there is no dearth of the young to appear in female roles with artistry and grace. Sometimes they are found to throw away their dresses and dress themselves as women in full view of the public, while playing the serious part of women of high rank. Some of them might be observed to wear on their face and body some left over mark that had adorned their previous part.

The performances up to recently (1971) were usually done in the night and lasted three hours. The first ten minutes are spent in singing the glory of Meitei Leima (goddess of

Manipur), and of a presiding deity of the play with Dholak and cymbals. All Jatras are concluded with a closing song to the accompaniment of Dholak and cymbals and clapping.

The audience compressed people of all ranks though it was very popular among the village women and children. It was a free entertainment to which the cultured persons Muslims, Naga tribals were allowed to see. As per the convention, early comers occupied the front places, irrespective of their position, and late comers had to take back seats. People however did not miss them. The people stood for hours together without minding the trouble of seating arrangement and courtesy.

In spite of the want of aesthetic perception the notable Jatras can charm the audience. The people used to throw stones or pieces of earth if the performers failed in their work. The comedian/singers come frequently into the midst of performers, making a little commentary and thereby drawing the public attention to the scene. The Jatra without any secrecy and story and proper costumes can arouse emotion which are nowadays seen in film and dramas.

Some of the Merits and Demerits of Jatras are as under: The Lila Mis (actors of yesteryears) had inborn qualities which dominated the scene. So high was their acting of their roles that the audience under a sort of spell made gifts to them on their Abhinaya and their acting earned appreciation. The present phase of society has placed the Jatra actors/script writers in the literary field along with actors and dancers.

The present make up technique and dress are completely different from what we found before the war. The aged artists make use of Chandan, Tiki. Now the actors/actresses have managed them at their own cost. All extraneous elements of the drama and films have been introduced to win over the growing spectators to the Lilas.

It was customary for the common roles to display their feats and skill before the King or nobles in early performances. They used to perform feats such as magic, acrobatics, wrestling, sword play, spear play and to lay a body on the top of six bayonets. The points of the bayonet cannot pierce the flesh of the person when he lays down along the upward tops of the bayonet. Enthusiastic spectators were allowed to participate in the display of skill. Nobody could object to such feats. The modem Jatras have to discard such feats in their performances.

A word of caution is required in the performance of folk plays in the present context. The modern artists are apt to use improper dress, ornaments and make up without any dignity. According to Meitei codes, an unmarried maiden has to wear her lower garment round the loin, the upper part of the body being kept bare. A married woman has to cover herself from the calf to the top of the breasts.

The two ends are folded round the body under the armpit and over the breasts. The ultramodern person in informal roles does not observe this decorum. A King in the Lila is shown to wear Ajmeri turban, a practice which is lot approved by the community. A folk Meitei lady is shown to paint vermilion mark and wear Sari dress. The folk dresses are a unique feature of Manipur and provide a lively contrast to the modern dress.

The Jatra troupes have not so far arranged their auditorium a central stage and seats, pandals. Arrangement are made for a mobile stage and a courtyard. The circular acting area in the centre is supposed to be the temple of Hari Krishna. No Jatra artists can dare to put on shoes when he enters the central area. No spectator is permitted to do so although we can multiply such instances of using shoes in the dramas. The performers cannot dispense with the sentiment and therefore though modern fashion can come in the politeness has been retained.

The money payable to Jatra troupe for their show is technically termed *Dakshma* (gift for play) in Manipur society. In pre-War period the charge per show was Rs. 27. Now it is raised up to Rs. 300 or more. Despite the high rates the Jatras are in great demand in connection with state celebrations and festivals performed by the girls in the season after Doijatra. The money making boys and girls are still fond of them. After long hard work, domestic activities they forget their worries by enjoying the Jatras at proper time. The early tradition continues successfully till today.

In the pre-War period the veteran and experienced persons joined the Jatra with the object of reforming the society. At present there are enough of art loving and style oriented young-men. They are not behind in modulating, in inflicting voices in several ways. Young persons who represent females have become enemy to the real females. In the pre-war times Jatras were extemporised and were taught to the artists through rehearsals over a long period. 'But they were more or less durable in the mind of the audience. Now many scripts have been written though they were not preserved in print.

Over forty Sumanglila troupes are touring the length and breadth of Imphal Valley in order to satisfy the creative needs of the Meiteis. Selected Jatra groups are sent for tours in different parts of India. It is a very good item of inter-state cultural exchange. They arrange performances on social themes as also folk themes. The number of Jatras taken up by the groups can be fixed at more than one thousand. A number of offices have been opened in Imphal with paid staff and employees. The Jatras have enriched the cultural life of Meiteis and Manipuris in their own way. The artists are recognised by the Sang W Natak Akademi for suitable awards at the national level.

Music

Manipur is a region of India. Some varieties of folk music from the area include the rural love songs khullang ishei, the rhythmic Lai Haraoba ishei, which contain lyrics with veiled references to erotic mysticism and pena ishei, which is accompanied by a pena, an instrument made from a bamboo rod and the shell of a gourd or coconut. The pena is an ancient instrument that is a sort of national symbol for Manipuris.

Other songs include the religious thabal chongba, the classical music performed at various special occasions, the women's devotional nupi pala songs, Gaur Padas, sung in praise of Chaitanya Mahaprabhu and dhob, sung accompanied by the jhal, a large cymbal. Manohar Sai is another important class of songs, devoted to a 19th century man of the same name. Khubaishei is a kind of song accompanied entirely by clapping.

- *Gaur Padas:* This is a kind of devotional music of Manipur which is sung to uphold the greatness of Chaitanya Mahaprabhu, a religious preacher.

- *Manohar Sai:* Named after Manor Sai, this music of Manipur is sung along with the music of Ramkartal, or cymbals and Khol or drums.

- *Lai Haraoba ishei:* Full of erotic mysticism, this music of Manipur is based on dual meanings where there real meaning is camouflaged by innocent words. The tune and the rhythm is the main asset of this music.

- *Thoubal Chongba:* This song is sung with the Thoubal chongba dance and has a religious theme.

- *Pena ishei:* The Pena, a musical instrument, is an integral part of the music in Manipur. The Pena ishei is a kind of song that is sung is accompaniment of the Pena.

- *Khullang ishei:* This music of Manipur is sung mostly by the Meiteis while they are working in the fields. This music usually has love as its theme and the singer can uses words at his will and adjusts it to the tune.

Folk Songs: In Manipuri folk song is known as Khunning lshei or Khutlang lshei which covers the entire range of human activity. Most of the Manipuri population is in villages and village folks have evolved different types of songs to suit their vocations, geographical positions, beliefs and practices. The ancient Yek/Salais and the different groups of the tribals have their distinct variety of folk music. They are the precursors of modern sankirtan variety. *Bangdesh* (old form of kirtan), Nat Kirtan, etc. owe their origin to folk tunes. The folk songs have a direct and spontaneous appeal and have a way of touching the innermost chords of the heart, they symbolise the hopes, aspirations, the joys and sorrows of the people.

There are several songs relating to craft of occupation such as *Loutarol* (ploughing at the time of spring), *phisa ishei* (weaving) and *Hijin Hirao* (wood cutting, etc. There are also ritualistic types of songs such as Augri, Khemco, Ahonglon, *Yakaib* (awakening the King), etc., which are to be found on the ceremonial and religious occasions of the royal family. There are songs of rain as well as songs of vernal rain. The underlying idea of these folk songs teaches us the philosophy of life and principles of conducting oneself in society. There are songs of mythological or importance which through their simple tunes can enlighten the listeners with the stories of creation and the tough subjects in easy methods. Such songs narrating the deeds of heroes, especially the warrior rulers and patriots convey the true sentiments and feelings to the young generations.

The folklores expressing sorrow, lamentation and sympathy were expressed in Savara Madhyama where as moods expressing joy and devotional prayers to gods were expressed in Swara Panchame. Khongjom Parva style is the result of influence of Hindu Raja and Tala systems. Folk music however, suffered eclipse for many years. Oral tradition is one of the characteristic features.

Attention is not bestowed on it although the youths prompt it through voluntary subscriptions. It was H. Anganghal Singh the great poet of Manipur, who presented the folk story of Khamba and Toibi after collecting material for Ch. Manikchand Singh, the foremost Pena singer. Notation of these songs with the help of Ragas and Talas has been attempted by the renowned artists of the All India Radio, Imphal. With the help of teachers and scholars it is possible to collect from the different corners of Manipur Valley and the 29 groups of tribals, varieties of folk music instruments, etc. of which some are fast fading out. Mere collection is not enough unless they are made use of in education and culture of the masses. The effort of Manipur Folklore Society, Imphal ought to be encouraged although it is as yet in its infant stage.

Sat Sankirtan: Prayers and songs are the favourite practices of Bengal Vaishnavas. This cult is vital among the Manipuri Vaishnavas of today. They were taught the doctrine of the efficacy of Hannama as the best method of salvation by the preachers. With this object in view they practise Sankirtan and dances in their own ways. King Jayasimha is said to have initiated the present form of Nata Kirtan style, its stages, stage decoration, design, dimension, auditorium, arrangement of fruit, flowers and the detailed code in this connection. He with the help of learned and dedicated Gurus and scholars adopted the Bengali devotional songs. As he was not wholly influenced by Bengali ways he set his own composition in the Nata style to which he gave original form which is quite distinctive. Judged by its formal contexts, it is not found anywhere. Raga, Ala pa, etc. have grafted their impact on Manipuri movements, methods of worshipping, etc.

It is par-excellence, the expression of Vaishnavite culture in Meitei soil. It is a form of collective worship, service and devotional prayers expressed through a series of songs movements on the part of the Pala Singers with lig cymbal in their hands and the players of the Pung. Nata Kirtan is an invariable item for the life cycle of the Meitei and religious festivals. Nothing from birth to death is complete without it. It is usual for the Kings and the high class people to participate in it.

Holi: Singing during the Dol Yatra has added a new chapter to the history of dance and music of Manipur. By the time of Maharaja Churachand, this style had come in use for singing at the temple at Shri Govindaji on the Pichkari day and at the temple of Vijay Govindaji on Halankar day (6th day) and was just an instrument of devotional entertainment. The parties consisting of singers, drummers (Dholak) and instrumental musicians sing the Krishna themes is Basant Raga. Even today Holi songs are as much alive in the important temples as they were some sixty years ago. In spite of opposition from the followers of Apokpa Marup, and secular nature of the government, it has not lost its place in the new mass culture that is gaining ground in the state.

Dance

Manipur is known to the world through its dance. Its most important feature in the close association of religion with music and dance. The distinctive approach to culture is best seen in the fact that dance is religious and its aim is spiritual experience. Development of music and dance has been through religious festivals and daily activities of lives. Not only dance is a medium of worship and enjoyment, a door to door divine, but indispensable for ceremonies like the birth of a child, marriage, Shraadh, etc.

Dancing in all its pre-Vaishnavite or Vaishnavite varieties was performed before the ruling deities with strict humanity and surrender. The Meities are ignorant about the use of dance for the sake of dancing and contract system. Some of the salient characteristics of Manipuri dancing are as under.

- The places where dances are performed are sacred. It is considered to be a crime or sin to violate the decorum of the sacred texts, conventions, etc. Any time, any place is not good enough for dancing.

- Dances are devotional or ritualistic rather than entertainment of the eyes. It is a Sadhan-Bhakhti a kind of devotion to God for both dancers and the lookers. The second of the nine forms of Bhakti is felt by the dancers, that production of religions ecstasy of Bhakti Rasa (Prema Bhakti Rasa). The first of the nine forms is felt by the onlookers. It establishes relation between them and the close attendants of the Lord, who are superior to them. Being responsible to the suggestion of the movement, the spectators feel a tendency to identify themselves with the dancers. The theme relates to the dancers and the onlookers to have access to the company of the close associates of the lord and then to join this play.

- With its grace and sweetness, devoid of any adulteration, sensuality and communication between the dancers and the audience by words or through gestures of any part of the body, it is a thing of joy, and beauty, supremacy adaptable to group dancing.

It is the dance of all men, women, the old and the young, the rich and the poor, of all Manipuris in spite of their sophisticated developments in choreography and intricate Talas. Dancing as a profession for few classes of people is unknown to them. Every Manipuri can dance without additional effort and for considerable time. The movements of the participants are restrained and graceful with exquisite customs it produce a great impact on devotees. Manipuri dance is soft and graceful, resembling nature in her kinder aspect. The dancers appears like corn stirring in the breeze, or waves rippling in soft undulations."

Early Period: A copper plate inscription credits King Khuoyi Tompok (c. 2nd century CE) with introducing drums and cymbals into Manipuri dance. However, it is unlikely that the style resembled the form known today before the introduction of Krishna bhakti in the 15th century CCE. Maharaja Bhagyachandra (r. 1759-98 CE) codified the style, composed three of the five types of Ras Lilas, the *Maha Ras*, the *Basanta Ras* and the *Kunja Ras*, performed at the Sri Sri Govindaji temple in Imphal during his reign and also the *Achouba Bhangi Pareng* dance. He designed an elaborate costume known as *Kumil*. The *Govindasangeet Lila Vilasa*, an important text detailing the fundamentals of the dance, is also attributed to him.

Maharaja Gambhir Singh (r. 1825-34 CE) composed two parengs of the tandava type, the *Goshtha Bhangi Pareng* and the *Goshtha Vrindaban Pareng*. Maharaja Chandra Kirti Singh (r. 1849-86 CE), a gifted drummer, composed at least 64 Pung choloms (drum dances) and two parengs of the *Lasya* type, the *Vrindaban Bhangi Pareng* and *Khrumba Bhangi Pareng*. The composition of the *Nitya Ras* is also attributed to him.

Modern Times: This genre of dance became better known outside the region through the efforts of Rabindranath Tagore. In 1919, he was so impressed after seeing a dance composition, the *Goshtha Lila* in Sylhet (in present day Bangladesh) that he invited Guru Budhimantra Singh to Shantiniketan. In 1926, Guru Naba Kumar joined the faculty to teach the *Ras Lila*. Other celebrated Gurus, Senarik Singh Rajkumar, Nileshwar Mukherji and Atomba Singh were also invited to teach there and assisted Tagore with the choreography of several of his dance-dramas.

Guru Naba Kumar went to Ahmedabad to teach Manipuri dance in 1928. Soon, Guru Bipin Singh popularised it in Mumbai. Amongst his pupils, most well known are the Jhaveri sisters, Nayana, Suverna, Darshana and Ranjana.

Traditional Dance: The traditional Manipuri dance style embodies delicate, lyrical and graceful movements. The aim is to make rounded movements and avoid any jerks, sharp edges or straight lines. It is this which gives Manipuri dance its undulating and soft appearance. The foot movements are viewed as part of a composite movement of the whole body. The dancer puts his or her feet down, even during vigorous steps, with the front part touching the ground first. The ankle and knee joints are effectively used as shock absorbers. The dancer's feet are neither put down nor lifted up at the precise rhythmic points of the music but rather slightly earlier or later to express the same rhythmic points most effectively.

The musical accompaniment for Manipuri dance comes from a percussion instrument called the Pung, a singer, small cymbals, a stringed instrument called the *pena* and wind instrument such as a flute. The drummers are always male artistes and, after learning to play the pung, students are trained to dance with it while drumming. This dance is known as Pung cholom. The lyrics used in Manipuri are usually from the classical poetry of Jayadeva, Vidyapati, Chandidas, Govindadas or Gyandas and may be in Sanskrit, Maithili, Brij Bhasha or others.

The Manipuri dances may be classified into two categories:

- Pre-Vaishnavite forms, and
- Those connected with the Hindu cult in the 18th century.

The two types are associated with religious motifs and mutually involve each other as we find them today. We do not have evidence of sculpture, temple architecture and inscriptions of pre-Vaishnavite form of dances apart from the living traditions and manuscripts in Meitei script. The Palace Loisang (Royal Archives on Imphal) and the various texts in the possession of Pandits and Gurus throw valuable light on the two divisions of dance.

Laiharaoba: The ancient people have developed a little comprehensive form of dance popularly known as Laiharaoba which reflects the pre-Vaishnavite culture and other types of solo, duet, group, etc. within its body. It is performed generally between the spring and the rainy season. Sometimes during March and April before the temples of Umanglais (sylvan gods and goddesses) of the valley in strict accordance with the early Manipuri tradition.

It has been in vogue since the creation of the earth by God Ashiba, 9-Lai Pakhang (male god in the prime of youth) and 7-Lainuras (female goddesses in their virginity). As mentioned in the sacred texts, the Kings arranged this dance of (merry making of the deities) annually for imitating the play of gods and chanting actions Hoirrou Haya (songs sung by Guru Sidava and God' Ashiba) while receiving the things given from the Guru's body.

The Laiharaoba is an important festival giving us a glimpse of life and art of small Kingdoms. The Kings, members of the royal family, little holders and the common people participate in it under the direction of high priests and priestesses (Ma ibas and Maibas). It is customary for them that the Kings danced with their Queens, unmarried princes with the girls of their choice, princes with prospective youths as their partners. Husband and wives, boys and girls take part in it for peace and prosperity of the country. Thousands of villagers, both males and females of all ages, way in a group dance. A sort of 'undeclared competition for the presentation in dance and costumes exist among them. In this way Manipuri society acts as a medium for the promotion of its distinctive culture.

Laiharaoba has several types, the most typical of which are:

- Kanglei Haraoba in springs includes all Manipuri rites connected with the romantic life of Nongpok Ningthon (Siva) and Nongpok Panthoibi (Parvati),
- Mairang Haraoba in autumn depicts the rites connected with the life of god Thangjing, and

- Chakpa Haraoba in summer, describing the rites connected with the human efforts to please the Highest God the Laiharaoba of Moirang. Thangjing in the grave of lake Loktak is attractive. People flock there to witness the beauty of their past glory.

It consists of several rituals and dance themes. In the initial part called *Maibi* dance, the Maibi holds such items as breath, ceremony of the God on the bank of a river or pond, summoning its spirit in an earthen pot through nine threads and seven threads for gods and goddesses, dance of the Ma ibis holding the leaves of the sacred plant called *Langthroi* between the fingers, trance revealing the God's message and the *Laipou* dance (the creation and evolution of earth).

In the most important stage is the circular dance of the mass participation of the villagers under the leadership of the Ma ibis experts where ought to dance together in the same there are the dances of the love story of Nongpok Ningthou and Panthoibi, sowing of the human seed in the womb, birth of the child, attainment of maturity, problem of housing, weaving, cultivation, etc. one by one through the movement of the fingers, hands, etc. There are many taboos to be observed strictly by all during the dance. They sing songs and pray in archaic Manipuri and express through them the welfare and prosperity of the King and the subjects of the country.

This dance last for about 10 to 12 days or more and ends with some old games and sports such as *Sagol Kangjei* (polo), *Khong Kangjei* (foot-hockey), *Thouri Chin gnaba* (tug of war), *Hiyang Tanaba* (boat-race), spear dance, sword dance and races that the gods and goddesses are supposed to have played. The *Lairen Mathek* (curve of the python), *Paphan Taret* (complicated diagrams of the serpent coil representing different aims and objects) and Augrihangel dance depicting the Tangkhul Naga in the role of a farmer are performed on the night of the last day as variable items of the festival. It is believed that any slight error on the part of performers will imply the wrath of gods in the form of epidemics, war, evil consequences and natural calamities. The ruling deities of this dance are said to be Nongpok Ningthou and Panthoiki.

A big Dholak and flutes, Pena (a string instrument) and balls (for the Maibis) are invariably used in this dance. Lyrics are sung by Pena Sakpa. Tight Dhoties and Turbans for the males, stripped *Phanek* (lower garment), *Inaphis* (scarf) for the women participants, long loose hair of the virgin and the hair in a bun for the elderly women, flowers and necklaces look colourful and elegant.

The Ma ibis put on special costumes such as tight fitting white uniform, Sarong Phi (a' sheet of cloth with special skirt), Reshan Phurit for this performance. The Maibis donning female costume appear in this ritual whether they are men or women. The male Ma ibis (males playing the role of priestness) are allowed to use Chamar to avoid the movement by order of Maharaj Bodhachandra.

On the day of *Lamthokpa* (going out of the enclosure) all interested persons dress as they like in the form of fancy dress. Some of the youths are seen wearing the dress of Khamba. Girls are seen to wear the dress of Princes Thoibi. Persons playing the role of Naga tribes are frequently seen in those dresses. The dress or uniform is not confined to any class.

The Laitharaoba dance as it stands at present does not exist in its pure form that prevailed in the past. The world famous Raslila has developed form and content of Laiharaoba by the Manipuri mind. Para Keeya Rasa and Lila of Nongpokningthou (Siva) and Panthoibi (Durga) of Laiharaoba provide scope for the same themes which are integral to Bengal Vaishnavism.

The underlying ideas, Takas, Mudras employed in different parts of Laiharaoba have certain affinities with those of Indian dance texts. Manipur under the able rulers has evolved a new form of dance in its own form with Vaishnava and Hindu touches. Laiharaoba flourished in the groves of the Umanglais where it became an annual feature for the Meiteis. It spread to Meitei inhabited areas in Burma, Assam, Bengal and Tripura. They were performed under the direction of high priests and priestesses. Of late, however, it has ceased to function as a standard of high philosophy. It is in the process of gradual liquidation on account of the following:

- Irresistible in roads of band music into an otherwise sanctified atmosphere of traditional fiddle and song,

- Deterioration in the use of Swars, careless innovation of allied body movement,

- Arbitrary performance without knowing the nature and attribute of the concerned deity,

- Entry into the fold of Laiharaoba dance by persons representing the role of the Punjabis, Muslims, Fishermen, Pathans and their performance of dances during the sacred festival, and

- Dressing of the male Maibi as a pure woman for playing as a practical joke.

The palace Loisang for Ma ibis and scholars served as the centre of this dance under the Kings. Successive heads of these departments were responsible for the innumerable compositions elaborate rites and leaving a considerable number of formalities for each god and goddess.

Nupa Pala: Nupa Pala which is otherwise known as Kartal Cholom or Cymbal Dance is a characteristic of the Manipuri style of dance and music. The initial movements of this dance are soft and serene, gradually gathering momentum. It is a group performance of male partners, using cymbals and wearing snow white ball-shaped large turbans, who sing and dance to the accompaniment of Mridanga, an ancient classical drum "Pung" as it is called in Manipuri. The Nupa Pala acts as a prologue to the Ras Lila dances, besides an independent performance too, in connection with religious rites.

Dance in Temples: Management of the temples of Umanglais (forest deities) and Laiharaoba festival. The temples of about 480 Umanglais in whose worship the Haraoba festival takes place can be divided into the following:

- Umanglais for the whole country such as Pakhangba, Nongpokn-ingthou, Thangjing, Wang-baron, etc.,

- Umanglais for all the Manipuris but their seva is done by a particular clan being Laikhurembi (Durga) worshipped by Taibungjam, Soraren (Indira) by Sorensamgbam, and

- Umangalais for the Sageis, viz., Hijam Lairema of Hijam, Lainingthou Ishingchaiba of Paonam, etc.

These temples alongwith household deities in a house form the backbone of pre-Vaishnavite culture in Manipur. The Maharaja being the religious head visits all the temples and gives timely directions and instructions with the help of his Pandit Loisang, Maiba and Maibi Loisang on matters of Laiharaoba and connected items.

Some of the important deities have rent-free land for their maintenance. The concerned people or village with the help of the local people raise funds for the festival. It is believed that they would incur divine displeasure if they neglect the service. The spiritual service is carried on through the persons who have the authority and proficiency in Meitei lore and dance.

The temples which were managed by the Maharajas through their Laisang are now under the control of Shri Govindji Temple Board of the Government of Manipur, since 1976. The Loisang as affiliated body of the Board has survived almost in name. All the Umanglais in spite of the pro-Hindu character do not come under any control, either of Sanamabi Temple Board or a separate Board. But many voluntary organisations at different places have been established due largely to the revivalist interest. An institution called All Manipur Haraoba Committee was set up in 1968.

Scholars interested in Meitei script and lore have identified themselves with it. It projects its works through the observance of *Maichou* day (day of scholars) and publications of a quarterly journal namely, Umang Lai Khunda. Some publications on Laiharaoba and Umanglais are brought out from time to time. It confers degrees on the persons dedicated to Manipuri script, culture and literature. It promotes awareness about wealth of Manipur's heritage. Its activities are linked with other organisations.

New brick temples and good grounds are constructed and improvements effected out of donations and endowments from the pro-revivalist members of the Meiteis. In the past the festival in most villages was purely parochial as only the inhabitants of the concerned village were allowed to be present. The organisers were instructed to take proper care of the shrine, and not to allow any Rajkumar to approach it for should one of the royal family contrived to worship there and offer gold and silver, he would certainly try for the throne and might cause endless trouble.

The palace which once used to produce well qualified Maibas, Maibis and singers and dancers now remain defunct and almost came to a stop by 1960. In the changing conditions such practices adversely affect the public sympathy and effort on which the success of this festival rest mostly.

It is the moral responsibility of every Meitei to organise, this festival and maintain temples of the locality. Many of the fine arts such as mark-making of the deities, preparation of several designs of cloth, dances and music are also fast disappearing. A successful organisation of this festival would naturally mean the promotion of those fine arts.

Devadasi System: The Maibas and Maibis are remarkable as they are the indispensable characters from the beginning to the end of this ritual dance. They are either male or female living like Devadasis. They dress themselves in white uniforms in spiritual works. According to local convention the entry into Maibihood is preceded by certain mode of thinking and action.

The men or women who would be Maibis had a call which is evidenced by the suffering of an unidentified disease for a long time, incoherent speech and peculiar accent and tragic call for fate. After purification of their body by the Teiren leaves (sacred plant) and clean clothes they require training under a Mama Gun (Mother Guru) of the same temperament and inclination. Though they are illiterate they get *Leinunglol* (God's Words) by heart.

They become possessed by the spirit of gods and goddesses like Pakhangba, Mahadeva, Durga, or the three Gurus in utterances. They abstain from eating fish with thorns, food cooked by other man and use of coloured or dyed cloth. They are under obligation to use only the fire produced by the friction of woods. They are enjoined to sleep alone and to perform divination or oracles with the help of bells, Coins of the country or sticks. They take fixed rates of fees for fortune telling, the customers stand in queue to get the reading of the Maibis. There was the belief that the Ma ibis fail to get the correct prediction if some one violates the due order.

The spiritual partners of the Ma ibis are Maibas who conduct the festival with their knowledge of ancient lores, scripts, incantations and psychoanalytic methods. He has to receive training in the Loisang which was attached to the court for a period for five or six years. After schooling himself long enough in this field, he is qualified to be ordained as a recognised Maiba. The main difference between the Maibi and the Maiba is that the former is god-gifted and ordained completely while the latter is made and trained through his labour and research.

Raslilas: When the entire state adopted Gaudiya Vishnavism as the official religion, the Manipuris produced the beautiful Raslila under the patronage of Rajarshi Bhagyachandra (1768-1798). The first Ras strictly after the classical tradition was dedicated to Sir Govindaji at the Ras Man-dat at Langthabal (now Kanchipur) on Mera Purnima (full-Moon day of Sept.-Oct.). The present Ras varieties are the sum total of the contributions made by different teachers of the succeeding generations who were convinced that the Pre-Vaishnavite traditions of dance as in Laiharaoba, sword and spear dances and the Vaishanvite expression are complementary and not contradictory.

The old tradition provided plenty of basis for the proper estimate. The foundation of Ras, techniques, the costumes, ornaments, and makeup, etc. are said to be revealed to Rajarshi Bhagya Chandra in his dream. In the sphere of religions history, Rajarshi occupies the same place as Constantine in European History. He and his daughter Vimbabati were ardent devotees of Shri Govindaji Dance is the medium of Bhakti Marga. It represents the finest flowering of Vaishnavite culture as an extension of Sankirtan tradition. Ras is not for showing to the onlookers but it is a meditation of God who plays in Vrindavan in human form. The eye glances are kept on the two sides of the nose. In fact, one never says that he is going to witness the Ras but he says that he is bowing down before the Ras.

It is considered sinful to talk of the Ras in the mundane or material plane. The place is thought to be the Ras Mandal in Vrindavan where nobody can enter and touch Shri Krishna, Radha and the Gopis during the Ras performance. The pious Meiteis hold that no one witnessed the Ras in the material world prior to its exhibition in Manipur, the second Vaikuntha. Nobody except Siva, the gatekeeper sees the Ras as their mind was deeply engrossed in meditation of Shri Krishna.

Description of Ras Nartan: An ardent devotee should possess necessary stamina to observe vows, penance and perform the necessary rituals such as worship of Shri Govindaji, Sanamahi, Tulsi plant, abstaining from fish and worship of earthen pot and sanctification of the dance arena. The male Nata Pala Kirtan which begins in the night must serve as a sort of prologue to Ras in which they sing songs of Chaitanya, King Bhagyachandra and personages for the proposed dance.

After this, the Sutradharas (mostly females) in the northwest corner of the hall sing the songs of Krishna's divine love play as described in the Bhagavata. According to the song, the Gopis along with Krishna performed the dance on the bank of the Yamuna. The plays such as the arrival of Krishna, Radha and the Gopis at the appointed place, Krishna's disappearance from the company of Gapis and Radha searching for the Lord through song on the bank of Prema Seva of the Gopis towards Him, questioning Him by the Gopis His answers to the questions, His Raslila with the Gopis, Jalakeli wandering in the forest and Gopis return to their homes at the end of the night are performed in due order. It ends with the Arati Nritya in which the whole audience stands up and takes part.

It was the policy of the Vaishnava Kings to allow the people in using a foreign language in their vehicle of expression. By doing so the audience is induced to believe that the dialogues and songs which were of the deities were really the words of the deities and not of the ordinary people. The Vaishnava songs can arouse the awe, reverence, etc., in the minds of people. They were made to appeal to the rulers, audience, etc. because of their culture in those days. It is worthy to note that Vishanava Kings of Manipur composed devotional songs in Brajavali which is an artificial language containing Maithili, Bengali and Sanskrit words.

Important Types: There are four main types of Ras, namely, Maharas (on the full-moon day of Hiyangei in November), Kunjaras (on the full-moon of Mera in October), Vasantaras on the night of the full-moon of Hiyangei in November) and Nitya Ras (no specific time). The palace held Raslilas of the first three categories. They can be performed locally only after the performances in the palace or selected temples with care and extreme orthodoxy. The departure in new composition and reasonable alterations is allowed in Nitya Rasa. It revolves around Krishna's play with Radha and Gopis without separation, fear, anger, etc. in presentation. Late Guru Amubi is of the opinion that Diva Ras was introduced by Maharaja Churachand Singh.

Emphasis on a particular episode, songs, Ragas, Ragini are found to differ from category to category. Certain episode in one Ras is excluded in other categories. Abir Khel (sprinkling of coloured water) and appearance of Chandravli as Radha's rival is found only in Vasantras. Some of the solo and duet dances presentation of Krishna, Radha, Chandravali, etc. which figure prominently in other Ras do not apply to Govindaji Temple where the wooden images of Rajeswan and Shri Govindaji were placed at the centre of the pavilion. Palace Raslilas consist of the gopis only. Music provided by the voice in the background with the Man jiras has different Ragas and Raginis for different Rasas.

There are Parengs (series) which are performed at the beginning of a Ras. The more common ones among them being Vrindavana Pareng, Khurumba Pareng Bhagi Pareng, etc. which are classical compositions of dedicated Gurus. They are presented in the form of group dances. While presenting them the members of the audience cannot leave the place till its presentation is complete. It is now held that the period covering a night is too inadequate for a dance consisting of several themes, performances and many Parengs. It creates a world of phantasy by its music and dance acting and speech dress and background orchestra.

The Guru! Ojha Purel in his capacity as the leader of orchestra party and structure of Ras must exercise his discretion in editing them to suit the performance. Unlike other dances, Manipuri feature lies mainly in *Chali* (steps) *Uplei* (Bhramari) Longlei and soft and effortless movements.

The Talas employed for songs are Teen tal, Mel, Tanchep and Menkup (three beats and one stress) and Rajmel (in the Vilamvita Laya according to the Mridanga players of Manipuri Nata Sankirtana. We have innumerable Talas of dance and Pung (Drum) playing as set forth in the texts such as Shri Krishna Rasa Sangeet Sangraha of Thukur Bhakti Siddhanta, Padamrita Samudra, etc. The Talas and rhythm pattern range from 4 to 54 beats. There are as many as 120 Talas in all in a treatise called *Govinda Sangit Lila Vilas*.

Almost all the scientific treatises on the Talas of Manipuri music and dance have been discovered and are being edited and published with translations in modern Manipuri. For technique Trital, Rupak, Ihaptal, Chowtal, Dashkush are in common use. The Bhangimas are done in Lofatal followed by Dadra and Kannwara.

Dance Costumes and Ornaments: So far as the costumes and ornaments are concerned, there are many Potloi Set pas (those who keep these costumes and ornaments) who rent them for the performance at same rates. The costumes part for 50 or 60 years and earn them a good deal of money. The costume makers as well as the participants are guided by the spirit of production and use of new costumes and design within the accepted norms. They are good instances of Manipuri workmanship.

The Potloi Set pas enter into a contract with the participant (except the professional) on some fixed charges, part of which has to be spent for the costume and ornaments. It is the cherished ambition of every Manipuri girl and the aged woman to participate in the Ras by putting on costumes and ornaments. The costume for Krishna consists of a blue silk Dhoti, crown of flowers topped with fan like piece embossed with silver Jan and peacock feather, a silver flute with flowers, rings, bangles, bracelets, armbands for the hand and silver Jan beads and ornaments for the foot.

The costume and ornaments of Radha and other Gopis consist of an embroidered brightly coloured silk skirt called *Kumin*, a blouse called *Rasham Phurit* (green colour for Radha and red colour for all gopis), a short flair of silver gause over the silk skirt a girdle round the waist, and a veil thrown over the head with various ornaments on different parts of the body. They do their hair high up with flowers round the coiffure (Buddha Jata style). Mask is generally put on in connection with Gostha Lila and Kaliya Daman. The dressing is so designed as to free them from any stimulus, excitement to the opposite sex. Dance is but the rhythmic expression of actions and activities of life on the upper part of the body. The parts below the neck to the feet are covered with cloth. The women hide the movements of the lower position of the body while dancing.

Diba Ras: Diba Ras is performed by the gopis by wearing sari. The theme is drawn from the Bhajan Lila of Thakur Mahasy by the Ojhas during the reign of Maharaja Bodhachandra. The Nitya Ras belongs to village, and its another form is called *Nartta* which is dedicated to Shri Govinda on any day of the year. This has been in existence since the time of Sir Churachand Maharaj. When the British became the rulers of Manipur, they wanted to see Ras by divesting it of time factors.

They took it from the main temple to Hapta Bangla (British Residency) of Major Maxwell the Political Agent, where his wife, Princess Sanatonbi Devi played the role of Makok Chingbi. The Gurus recast its dress and name to meet the need of the British officials and call it Natta or Nartta Rasa. *Beni* (braid of hair) of the Bai is used in this dance which has become a recognised fashion for all dance dresses. *Koktumbi* (coiffure) which was used for the Ras in the villages is being replaced by it. But the traditional Nitya Ras is restricted to the Asta Kala Seva of Shri Govinda and does not go out of the temple.

Today as a result of modern pressures and internal reflections the Gurus in spite of orthodoxy have worked on new productions on the stage, compressed one whole night Raslila to a 10 or 15 minute piece, the lyrics of which are in Manipuri translation. With movies TV cameras the film producers have started to use Ras dance in some films. The organisation of palace category is different from that of the villages. During the reign of the Hindu Maharajas funds were set apart for celebration of festivals including the Rasas. Now the management has been entrusted to Shri Govindaji Temple Board with the ex-ruler as the chairman and laying down policies which are executed by the D.C. of Imphal Central.

The Vaishnava Kings made the ruling that they should send their children to play the main roles of the Ras of the palace. The circumstances leading to the organisation are fulfilment of a promise to god on the eve of the birth of a son or daughter, promotion or prosperity in life. By playing such roles in the sacred dance children are thought the counter the evil effects of their Karma, bad Dasha and evil eye.

As per the convention, willing people contact the person in charge of the dance for permission to enable their children to play the role of Lai or Gopi. Children of the royal family or top ranking officials are normally given the chance in the temple of Shri Govindaji, Vijoya Govindaji or famous temples which had royal sanction. The young girls selected for participation in the Rasa dance of the palace receive their training from the Rasdhari (approved Guru) for a period of two or three months.

The children can show talents for this dance since they live with the devoted people in the environment of a sacred land. The professionals are also requisitioned for their contribution on the final day of the performance. The full-time dancers, other members like Sutradharis, flute players and instrumentalists are handsomely rewarded. The rates of charges are relative to their position efficiency and performance. They have maintained their own glorious tradition. They enjoy an enviable position in society as teachers of culture.

As for the Rasas in the village or cities they are conducted by the well to do families voluntarily. The parents of children acting main roles raise higher subscription to the same. There is a marked tendency towards collective patronage of Ras and Nata performance. Friends and relatives in great number of the persons whose children play the leading roles come and offer in cash or kind or a garland of Rupee notes to the solo performance of the leading roles in the dance arena. Such presents are collected by the concerned parents after the dance.

A man with considerable influence may receive in cash or kind the value which can meet the expenses. Thus the age-old method of sacred tradition continues to this day, supported by an enthusiastic public including the high dignitaries and admirers.

Udukhol: Krishna's Valya Lila and Vatsalya Ras is enacted through dance and devotional music. Maharaja Churachand encouraged it with his appreciation and he himself visited and paid his respect to his appreciation and he himself visited and paid his respect to his brother-in-law Thomchou Singh who first hosted this performance.

Sansenva/Gosthalila (Cowtending Dance): This is a kind of religious dance, where in the story of Krishana and his Gopa friends is performed by the small children dressed as Krishna with sticks and flutes. Shri Krishna's game, association with the pastoral boys Yashoda's love for her son, the coming of sage Narada to the palace of Nanda and teaching Krishna and Balram how to milch and graze the cattle are invariably shown. Then the Gopas go for tending cattle with the permission of the parents. Every year on the Gostasami, 8th day of Kartika (Hiyangei), this dance in its due order takes place at the temples of Shri Govindaji (palace), Shri Vijoya Govindaji (Sagolband) and Gopinath at Nigthouskhong.

Gouralila: It is performed by boys of the age group of 8 to 10 years in different areas of the rich people. Some parts are meant for the professionals who have attained popularity in their roles. The Lila orchestra is constituted by the director/teacher of the boys, other noted people and instrumentalists which provide explanations, announcements and timings.

Pung Cholomg/Mridanga Kirtan (Dance of Manipuri Maridanga): This drum dance may be performed either as an integral part of Nat Sankirtan or independently. As a part of Nata, it is performed by two players but as an independent dance at least 14 players follow the sequence of Nat Sankirtan with about 40 complicated Talas and Sanchars (particular compositions of complicated rhythms). The rulers patronised and organised 4 distinct types in connection with Hindu religious festivals like Durga Puja. The number of players may go up to 100. Various types of bodily movements are executed with great artistry and excitement. It articulates the sound of thunder, voice of birds and animals. The movements are initially soft, but become momentous and vigorous. They have a special type of turban which they drop by their flicking of head and movements.

Khamba and Jhoibi Dance: It is performed as a part of Laiharaoba or independently. In this dance men pick up their partners, girls all dressed gaily, dance is a duet dance which tells the story of Khamba, or poor brave lad of the Khuman clan who fell in love with Thoibi, a Princess of Moirang. They succeeded in love affair after a series of heroic deeds on the part of the hero and the exile of Thoibi by her father for defying his will.

They are fabled to dance so nicely in the Haraoba of god Thangjing that they came to be regarded as the incarnation of Shiva and Parvati respectively, who were responsible for the famous Ras of Manipur. This dance typically represents the Tandva and Lasya aspect of Laiharaoba movements.

Thabal Chongbi means jumping in the moonlit night by the youths and girls in a courtyard. The Meiteis have been performing this dance since the pre-Hindu period in the name of Keiyen (a dance encircling Pakhangba) by joining hands of nine gods and seven goddesses) and jumping anti-clockwise so that Sanamali (as tiger) cannot break the circle or Ke-Krchongba. The youth and girls form a circle with hands joined to each other. If the number is great they may form two or three rows so that everybody and anybody can participate in the dance of its special interest is the dance of the legs and of the mind by the side of the girl on the part of the males and also by the side of youth on the part of the females and hand in hand dancing. They wear no makeup and special costume for the same.

During the old days a main singer or a well trained' artist with *Haribola* (Hail to god) sang religious songs, historical ballad, epics of Moirang, etc. The participants echoed his words in a chorus. The Dholak beating supplied the tempo and rhythm of the dancers. When the dance progressed, the singing ceases, they continued swift jumping. Its peculiarity lay in the fact that they exhibited their skill of legs with some success without any formal training as if they born with its talent.

Augrihangel and Thengkou are sacred and secret dances performed by capable persons with swords and a shield of spear, the purpose of which is creation, preservation and destruction. Augrihangel is a part of Kanglei rhythmic dance in circle singing a hymn for the ruin of an occupied territory, at least for a short time if not forever. Nine (some say 10) Thengkourols are symbolic movement which are coordinated either with the steps of dancing or with the skilled movements of a sword or spear, nine kinds of diagrams of the snake god (Pakhangba) are technically called *Paphals*, which are said to be supporting the earth. Figures of the leg movements for sword and spear then gkou are related to the hood of the snake Pakhangba Ananta. All the 35 letters are interwoven with this science. After a sacred text gkourol tells us that God Ashiba started to make the earth with the performance of Jhengkon dance. The teaching or performance takes place with the approval of the King in one of the following places:

Lalambung, Heibok Hill, Takyel Lake and Lamphel Lake. A lucky day, hour and star according to Meitei belief are always chosen on (which to do all these works. They are absolutely obliged to spread the flour over the dancing arena, above the flour, Kokan leaves, after which the place is pure. Out of these nine forms, two namely, Athou Achouba and Athou Macha were performed by Maharaja Bhagyachandra and his son Maharaja Gambhir Singh during the Burmese devastation of Manipur at Khebu Hill and Lamangdong (Visnupur).

They were so successful in spear dances that the people of Manipur thought then to be the liberators of the country and restores of normal life against the Burmese devastations. Instances can be muiltiplied. After the abolition of the monarchy, the above dance forms have become stale and lifeless.

There are also dances normally at the social structure and social system under these categories:

- Women in domestic affairs,
- Rice pounding dance,
- Harvest dance, and
- Weaving dance. Numerous dance drama and ballet are developing out of these forms.

Games and Sports Dances: As a fighting race in defence of freedom and independence of the country Manipuris are well versed in the use of swords, spears, Yubi Lakpi (game of one vs. many), arrows, hockey, polo, and Manipuri style of wrestling. There are unavoidable items of Laiharaoba and Kwak Jatra festival (Vijai Dashmi Day of Durga Puja) before the distinguished gathering which include the title holders, dignitaries and prominent members.

Mukha (wrestling or breaking the balance of a man with special tricks of legs), use of arrow and Arambal, foot hockey in combination with wrestling polo (hockey on horseback) and various items of physical culture are coloured by religious beliefs and are dedicated to different presiding deities of different seasons.

Martial arts particularly in the use of spear and sword and use of horses and the names of their own constructions have been practised in their own ways. Sword constitutes the body and spear, the soul, so goes the saying of the Meities. One can find much similarities between the movements of Thang Ta (sword and spear dance) on the one hand and those of the movements of Laiharaoba, Raslila, Pung and Pala choloms on the other.

These dances which had been relegated to the background due to the use of modern weapons, bombs and guns have of late prospered and made rapid strides. Manipuri martial acts like Thang Yannaba showing the skill of self defence by swords in hand in a continuous series of aggressive and defensive gestures and artistic movements of body, throwing spear and catching it by other, Ta Khousaba (skill and experience in the use of spear against the wild animals like wild bear and tiger) has won the applause of foreign observers and these are included as a variety in the National School of Drama (Delhi).

Polo was resuscitated by the All Manipuri Polo Club/Riding and Training and Horse through their simplification of rules (removing of dangerous practices, polo tournaments both in old Pana style and new style and uplift of its standard. In the past it had the support of the rules and nobles. The women of Manipur as is customary among them turn up in their best to witness it and offer garlands, sweets, fruits, Pan to the players to encourage them. This is known as Potlamba.

Voluntary associations such as Hurla Under the initiative of Birjit Ngangomba, the Huyen Lalong Tha Cultural Association under the Directorship of G. C. Sharma (HLMTHTA) Kanglei Nat Sindam Sang under the inspiring leadership of L. Heramot Meitei (Kongpal) attempted to impart training and study in this field of sword and spear.

These centres are imparting training in different methods of pre-Hindu and post-Hindu styles of training through books, seminar papers and regular demonstrations. This variety has become a world art by its inherent technique and greatness. It can be favourably compared with Karate, Judo (zendo), etc. After independence and particularly after the attainment of Manipur's statehood, honours have gone to the Gurus of the Thang Ta from the state and the Government of India. Manipur Sahitya Parishad honoured P. Tharango Singh for his service in the field of Thang Ta. Then followed the Padmashri award for Damo Singh in 1983.

Along with the different dances of the Meiteis, a number of folk dances have developed among the Naga-Kuki tribals, like Kabui Naga, Thangkhul Naga, Mao Maram Naga dances. Bamboo dance of the Thadou Kukuis, etc. The non-Naga tribal group perform fourteen different types of dances on different festivals. The folk dance festival has become an integral part of the Annual Republic Day celebrations of the State and the Centre.

Kathak: Kathak dance was introduced by Kunjo Mishtri and Gopi Mohan in Maharaja Chandrakirti's palace which the Meitei called *Marbak Jagoi* (foreign dance). After the Manipuri war of 1891 this form came to be associated with loose moral character and the girls branded as women of easy virtue got interested in extracting money from the low class people of Manipur.

Under the British regime and the influence of western civilization, the younger generation hated the dance itself. It degenerated so badly that the sacred religious dance of Raslila became the exclusive monopoly of some sections of the society. The people frowned and looked down upon erotic dance of Laiharaoba as a relic of folk culture and less civilized past. The period of the Second World War also witnessed the declining trend in the values of religious dances.

The witness of the Raslila and sacred dances by the non-Hindu Manipuris and non-Meiteis is indiscriminately prohibited by the Maharaja and the orthodox community. Dances had been in the hands of Gurus as there was neither the public nor private schools. Any composition was ensured by the Maharaja.

For the first time Raslila in Virandavan was dedicated by Maharaja Churachand Singh and a small portion of Bhangi Pareng (Krishna in Tribhanga pose) was shown before the

Prince of Wales in Calcutta in 1921. The wise and capable Maharaja could control the social uproar that must risen over the decision to admit forth into the audience including the Europeans.

The Preliminary work of popularising Raslila outside Manipur has been followed by other steps which include the opening of Manipuri dance in Vishwabharti by Tagore with the help of teachers from Tripura and Manipur, the founding of institutions such as Jawaharlal Nehru Dance Academy, Shri Shri Govindaji Nartalaya, Manipur, Nartalaya (Bombay, Calcutta and Imphal), Parimal Academy (Bombay), Jagoi Marup, Kala Kendra, etc. Great exponents of this style were M. Amubi, Amudon Sharma, H. Tomba, R. K. Priyagepal, Bepin, A. Amubi, R. K. Shinghajit, etc. Females who have devoted their life to performance and research are Savita N. Mehta, Zhabheri sister of Bombay, Dr. Kapila Vatsayayan, Devajani Chaliha, Thambal Anganbi Devi, Tondon Devi, Ibetombi Devi, Nangni Devi, Nayani Devi, etc. Some of them were lucky enough to receive awards and official patronage. Many of them are handing over this art to their children and students.

Typical Instruments

Drum: The drum is a member of the percussion group of music instruments, technically classified as the membranous. Drums consist of at least one membrane, called a drumhead or drum skin, that is stretched over a shell and struck, either directly with the player's hands, or with a drumstick, to produce sound. Other techniques have been used to cause drums to make sound, such as the "Thumb roll". Drums are the world's oldest and most ubiquitous musical instruments, and the basic design has remained virtually unchanged for thousands of years. Most drums are considered "untuned instruments", however many modern musicians are beginning to tune drums to songs; Terry Bozzio has constructed a kit using diatonic and chromatically tuned drums. A few types of drums such as timpani are always tuned to a certain pitch. Often, several drums are arranged together to create a drum kit.

Cymba: Cymbals are a common percussion instrument. Cymbals consist of thin, normally round plates of various alloys; see cymbal making for a discussion of their manufacture. The greater majority of cymbals are of indefinite pitch, although small disc-shaped cymbals based on ancient designs sound a definite note. Cymbals are used in many ensembles ranging from the orchestra, percussion ensembles, jazz bands, heavy metal bands, and marching groups. Drum kits usually incorporate at least one suspended cymbal and a pair of hi-hat cymbals.

Flute: The flute is a musical instrument of the woodwind family. Unlike woodwind instruments with reeds, a flute is an aerophone or reedless wind instrument that produces its sound from the flow of air across an opening. According to the instrument classification of Hornbostel-Sachs, flutes are categorised as Edge-blown aerophones.

A musician who plays the flute can be referred to as a *flute player*, a *flautist*, a *flutist*, or less commonly a *fluter*.

Flutes are the earliest known musical instruments. A number of flutes dating to about 40,000 to 35,000 years ago have been found in the Swabian Alb region of Germany. These flutes demonstrate that a developed musical tradition existed from the earliest period of modern human presence in Europe.

Harmonium: A harmonium is a free-standing keyboard instrument similar to a reed organ. Sound is produced by air, supplied by foot-operated or hand-operated bellows, being blown through sets of free reeds, resulting in a sound similar to that of an accordion.

The harmonium is very popular in India.

6

Education

Education in Manipur today is at par with the rest of the country. Earlier, education in the state was meant for the elites of the Manipuri society. The tribes and the poor were not allowed in many places to take higher education. However, with the advancement of time, the modern outlook of the people and the efforts of the State Government have changed this outlook.

The arrival of the British missionaries in Manipur brought a change in the educational scenario of the state. Reverend Pattigrew became the first Inspector of Schools of the state in 1903 and brought many reforms strengthening the educational structure of the state. The introduction of a separate education department in 1950 was a step forward towards improved educational conditions in Manipur.

Today top of the line schools, colleges, technical institutions, universities and training establishments have made Manipur one of the leading educational hubs of the north east. Some of the well known schools in Manipur are:

- Adimjati Little English School.
- Amusana Girls' High School, Keinou.
- Anallon Christian Institute, Charongching.
- Agape Jr. High School, Sangaikot.
- Ajad English School, Meitram Awang Leikai.
- Alice Christian High School, Ukhrul.
- Amuba High School.

Some of the leading colleges in Manipur are:

- D. M. College of Arts.
- D. M. College of Commerce.
- D. M. College of Science.
- Bethany Christian College, Churachandpur.
- Biramangol College, Saombaong.
- Canchipur College, Kyamgei.
- Churachanpur College, Churachanpur.
- C. I. College, Bishnnpur.
- Damdei Christan College, Kanglatombi.

Education System

Manipur, "the jewel of India", is famous for its art and rich traditions apart from its scenic natural beauty. Being a part of North East India, great steps have been taken by both central and State Government to elevate the education system here and they have yielded positive results.

The education of Manipur is today at par with any part of the country. Though earlier education in this state was considered to be a prerogative of the elite class, times and thinking of people have changed. In fact the people of this state have a very enthusiastic approach towards education. Only because of this approach, the government is making efforts to raise the quality of education being imparted in schools and colleges.

There are a lot of excellent schools and colleges. Apart from graduate colleges, the state also houses some of the best medical colleges and law colleges. These colleges have state of the art facilities and are capable of giving competition to any world class institute. All these institutes have made the state an educational hub of the north east.

The best proof of the quality of education being provided in the state are the students of this state. Students of Manipur have made a name for themselves in the whole world.

Elementary Education

The ancient educational system of Manipur embodied the method of oral teaching and memorising the text by heart. The teaching and learning was effected through oral transmission of knowledge from generation to generation, before it was transcribed in the manuscripts.

Historically, until 1872, there was no primary school for formal education in Manipur. Efforts of Captain Gordon and Major General W. F. Nuthal, the political agents to open vernacular schools failed due to negative attitude of the people towards formal education which was exogenous to their cultural system and social structure. As a result, growth of primary education was very slow. In course of time, Maharaj Chandra Kirti gave his consent to Sir James Johnstone for establishing an English School in 1885 at Imphal. Later on the school was known as Johnstone Middle English School. During 1893-95, four Lower Primary Schools, three in Imphal and one in the hill area (at Mao) were opened. The enrolment at that time was confined to boys only as the parents were unwilling to send their daughters to these schools. In spite of such prejudice against female education, a separate Girls' Primary school was established in 1899 at Imphal. Only 12 girls came forward to join the school.

In order to cope with the expansion in all stages, the Department of Education was established in 1910. It is on record that the first batch of students appeared in Matric examination at Sylhet in 1909 as there were no high schools in Manipur in those days. In 1921 Johnstone M. E. School was upgraded to High School level and it was affiliated to Calcutta University. During 1931-41 many more High Schools came up as there was increasing demand of schools. In 1914, for the first time, Manipur produced a Doctor and in the subsequent years more and more students became Engineers, Doctors and other Graduates.

During 1939-43, education in Manipur was greatly effected because of the outbreak of the World War II. It was only after 1944 that few schools started functioning in Manipur. In 1946, a college was established at Imphal in the name of Maharani Dhanamanjuri who donated a large sum of money, i.e. Rupees ten thousand for the cause of higher education. After the World War-II, there has been a sharp increase both in the number of schools and enrolment in Manipur. In the year 2005-06 the enrolment in class (I-V) was 3,62,999 in 2521 primary schools and that of class VI-VIII became 1,17,370 in 807 upper primary schools.

School Education

There are a number of schools in Manipur and all of them operate with the sole intention of enlightening the young minds. There are different kinds of schools in Manipur which include:

- Montessori Schools.
- Day Schools.
- Residential Schools.
- Convent or Anglo Schools.
- Government Schools.
- Public Schools.

Most of the secondary level schools in Manipur follow the curriculum of the CBSE and also abide by the textbook lists provided by them. Besides providing textual education, the schools in Manipur provide physical education and aim towards the all round development of the students. The most popular schools in Manipur include:

- Gurukul High School, Thangmeiband.
- Bashikhong High School, B.P.O. Kitna Panung.
- Bengali High School, Imphal.
- Jawaharlal Nehru Model High School, Churachandpur.
- H.M. English High School, Keithelmanbi.
- Bethel High School, Behiang, B.P.O. Singngat.
- Hamei English High School, Tamei.
- Jamdal Memorial Model High School, Churachandpur.
- Hanship High School, Churachandpur.
- Bengoon High Madrassa, Mayang Imphal.
- Islamic Baby English School, Lilong.
- Bethany Christian Hr. Sec. School, Churachandpur.
- Don Bosco High School, Imphal.
- Bethany English High School, Senapati.
- Guru Nanak Public School, Imphal.
- Ithai Junior High School, Ithai.

Different Kinds of Schools

Both government and private schools provide elementary and secondary education in Manipur. The state-run schools in Manipur are affiliated to the state education board. However, most of the private schools in Manipur are affiliated to the Central Board of Secondary Education (CBSE) or the Council for the Indian School Certificate Examinations (CISCE).

Medium of Teaching

Students studying in any Manipur School may choose their first language from any of the following-Manipuri, Bengali, Mizo, Paite, Nepali, Thadou-Kuki, Hindi, Assamese, Tangkhul, Hmar and Zou. The CBSE and ICSE schools also use English as their medium of instruction.

Drop Outs

The school dropout rate in Manipur is higher than many other states in India. Lack of infrastructure and social culture of the people are the major factors behind the high rate of drop outs from the schools in the state.

Famous Schools

Some of the best schools in Manipur are Bengoon High Madrassa, Mayang Imphal Chingkham Makha High School in Thoubal, A. Rudra High School in Tronglaobi, Chingtam High School in Salungpham, A. Jalil High School in Khergao, Azad Hr. Sec. School, B.P.O. Yairipok, and Adimjati Little English School in Imphal.

Students can also look for admission in other schools like Bal Vidya Mandir in Kongpal, Chinkham Modern High School in Churachandpur, Agape Jr. High School in Sangaikot, Churachandpur, Bal Vidya Mandir in Palace Compound, Christian Model English School in Tamenglong and Adimjati High School in Imphal.

Higher Education

Education in ancient times was discriminatory. It was the privilege of the few elites of the society, the children of the aristocrats as well as those of the nobles. Selection of the pupil was based on the status of the parents, who would only take part in the affairs and administration of the state. However, education at present is open as well as encouraged to all. Everyone having desire to learn can enrol themselves in an educational institution provided he or she has the skill and talent. The change in the structure is based on the dictum that "education for all is the key to the progress of the society" and "every citizen is responsible and should play an important role in the affairs of the state". Thus, the 'right to education' has become a fundamental right of every citizen'.

The modern-day education system is the legacy of the education system that imparted enough skills to the colony to serve in the clerical jobs of the British Colonial Administration. No doubt, times have changed, we have become our own masters (in theory), and since then many changes have been introduced in the education system too, but how far? What are the aims of our education system? Has it been able to keep up its promises? If education is for the progress for all then, education can be taken as a means to progress, if it is a means then it should show an end or a goal. But can the present system of education deliver the goal for all? If not then, to me, the question of education system itself is the primary problem of higher education in Manipur and for the country as a whole.

The problems and prospects of education cannot be discussed in isolation. And in Manipur, the problem of higher education is the fallout of a larger problem of social and cultural upheaval, political unrest, and economic stagnation of the day. This in turn has compounded into tentacles of problems that has gripped the education system. Some of them are high level corruption in public places, bandhs and strikes, a very flexible academic calendar, insincerity of teachers and students, etc.

Fundamentally universities are instrumental to changes in the society but such changes come through the products of the universities and not through universities themselves. Paradoxically they change very slowly often enduring the stereotype ideas and modes of thought for years. A debated issue is how far it meets the fast changing needs of the society. Rather the unprecedented economic pressure forced the universities all over the world for change in their outlook to the concept of education as against what was reared in the minds of the masses. Higher education in India is state funded and State funding is shrinking to frighteningly low levels because of financial stringency and increasing cost of quality higher education. The pressure to reduce the expenditure and the common impression of a failed education system led to an overall changed attitude towards higher education. The reason is thus socio-economic.

The mad rush of students out of the state after the declaration of 10+2 Examination Result and the vacant seats lying in some of the M.A. Departments in Manipur University is a clear indication of the failure of higher education in Manipur. This flight has become a necessity. The reason, a Three Years Degree Course (TDC) of Manipur University is misnomer, for it takes about five years to complete it. A Master's (MA) degree that is supposed to complete in two years takes more than three years. Thus the course that is supposed to complete in five years takes more than seven years. We have successfully robbed and wasted those crucial years in the life of a student. Now the problem we need to address; what's wrong with the system? Who is responsible and why? And of course who pays the price.

The price obviously, is on the students. They have to leave the state to avoid this inhospitable system of higher education. But it should be more of a concern to the policy-makers who run the education system of Manipur – the political masters and their servants, the bureaucrats. Those who run the show are interested more on their individual glory and self-promotion. Politicians, bureaucrats, social workers are above all concerned with appointment of teachers irrespective of merits and norms and availability of posts. This includes sending out their children out of the state for a better and focused education, whereas the masses that are caught in the education system of Manipur are condemned. It is not that those who get their education in Manipur are inferior or in anyway substandard. But except for few students, they fail to compete with those products of students that had better system of education, exposure to the cut-throat competitions, who were better taught and those who are aware of what is happening around.

The government would be tempted to say that the circumstances of the state along with bandhs and strikes are a hindrance to the conduct of a proper academic calendar of higher education. Because of bandhs and strikes the students themselves wants their examination postponed, for their syllabus have not been covered, and other reasons too. Though there are some elements of truth in their statement they cannot clean off their hands easily of their responsibility which they are employed for and responsible too.

Then the students and their organisations on their part should also take up the responsibility of being a student. Pockets of student organisations have been targeted by influential groups, who clearly understand the strength of the students, to serve their own vested interests. Students' agitations have unbelievably polluted the serene atmosphere of education. They have become more mercenary and politically motivated. Career and character building have little relevance for them.

Participation of teachers in politics, in doing so, they have not only politicised education, but have also disrupted the education scenario. Apart from these, academia on their part should also play an active role in providing directions to the governments and students to initiate and formulate programmes for a better education system. And the civil societies too can play a positive role. All said and done what we require urgently now is to leave aside the blame game, trying to find mistakes on the other and capitalising on that mistake, for a while. What we require urgently now is an honest approach for the improvement of education in Manipur.

The students can come up with their problems in colleges and in university and for that matter anything that concerns with education, leaving aside their vested interest. They can consult with the academia. And the academia on their part can formulate practical and practicable set of ideas that can help the government to formulate a purposeful programme. And above all the government should be sincere enough to earnestly implement those programmes. If one approach another with sincerity and the other listen with equal honesty, then why should be there any gap and room for a blame game. This up to a certain extent can reduce the problems arising out of the flaws in the education system.

Another problem is of the educated unemployed, which up to a major extent should be the responsibility of the state. Education falls under the concurrent list. But, for a country with such diverse environment the central government can give only certain guidelines. The State Government should be given more freedom to initiate their own educational policies. Achieving full autonomy by the institution is a *sine qua non* for efficient functioning in the 21st century.

This must be based on the equation of demand and supply. Students seeking tertiary education clamour for joining professional course of study than course in general education. Unlike the professional education courses, general education courses remain inflexible and students often complain that they are not able to exercise choice in selecting what they want to study. Students no longer have the confidence in its ability to prepare to enter the world of work as the nature of jobs has been changing and their curricula practically unchanged. Higher education must be need-based and self-reliant. The curriculum must be up to certain standard keeping along side with the changing world and its requirements. This would greatly reduce the mismanagement between what is required and what is produced.

Education to most of the prospective students in Manipur means 'white-collared' jobs. This problem is a symptom of an underdeveloped economy and also partly, the failure of the education system itself. Prospective job-seekers find security in the government jobs. However, government cannot employ all the hopefuls. Now the state is no longer the principal employer of the educated youth in the country. The hard reality is that majority of the employment opportunities now are in the private sectors – which changes to keep pace with its global competitors.

But in Manipur, besides government jobs, there are no private undertakings that can substantially employ a noticeable section of these educated people. This is due to lack of entrepreneurship among the people. The failure of the education system to expose and provide the skill necessary to encourage such private undertaking is one of the causes for this lack of entrepreneurships. Education now has to be tailor made to meet the requirements of the present scenario. Another reason is due to the socio-economic and political situation of the state. When there is no political stability, where there is social unrest and economic degradation, who on this earth would want and come forward to take up such undertakings.

The education system is unimaginative. It has never encouraged creativity. Education is textbook based. Instead of imparting vales of truth, justice and equity, integrity, discipline and dedication, the system has encouraged cut-throat competition. It has encouraged cheating in examination. Value of education is based on the marking system. The students are given marks referring to a certain level of standard answers that they have copiously prepared which they vomited out during the examination. The examination system has become not an examination of the education that the students have received but just a test of memory. This problem is up to a great level, due to the insincerity of the teachers and students.

The propensity of the students to understand the issue, to analyse it and express it creatively in their own has been restrained. The teachers seldom encouraged their students in such endeavours lest that would take time to correct the papers and extra time to teach the students the art and skill to express themselves imaginatively. Besides the duty to lecture the students, they need to improve the students and take them nearer to their goals. Tutorial classes should be compulsory for a teacher. It should be included in the curriculum of the academic calendar. With that a teacher can analyse the standard of the student and show him or her, the ways they can improve their understanding of the topic. The way it should be analysed and reproduce in their own way, innovatively. This is part of education. Education should not be just another memory test. Besides the teachers, the students must also take the initiative. However, they can take the initiative only when they are given the opportunity. And it is the system that should provide the opportunity.

Education should not be confined to the class room and its related laboratories. It should be a broad base institution that encompasses the society as well as the outside world. Students should not be alienated from their environment. Otherwise they end up being literate in their subjects rather than educated. In recent times there is much ado about 'quality education' in Manipur. Whatever the result and progress it might have achieved, but one thing is for sure, education cannot be tackled in isolation.

It has to be tackled along with the socio-economic and political problems of the state. It has been a step forward when people began to talk about exempting educational institution from bandhs and strikes, like those of electricity, medical, etc. Subjectively, education must be regarded as an essential service. Because without it, we would be moving backward rather than forward. But the irony of exempting education would be contradictory to the purpose of the strike. If educational institutions are to function, public transport system should also ply on the road. They should be exempted too. But just for education related passengers, the transporters won't run their vehicles at loss. Then to make the public transport ply, people should be allowed to move freely. Then where is the bandh and strike?

In this age of information technology, where do we stand and most importantly where do our students stand? The isolation and position of our state affected a lot on the education of Manipur. But with the changing technology of World Wide Web, the gap has been minimised. There is a free flow on information on almost any topic and every subject, for free. And if you are willing to pay you have it. This has revolutionised the information and knowledge worldwide. The students must be made aware of this changing world of information that would immensely enrich their knowledge which itself is a part of education.

The gap between the students and teachers, and students to students' relation is immense in Manipur. Except in the class room there is hardly any academic interaction between teachers and students. This is where you require the enthusiasm of the teacher to teach their students and to bring out the inner potential of the students chiselling their mental faculties and, the students' dedication to learn, in return. What is required is a combination of qualified and dedicated teachers with students eager to learn. Besides this, interaction between students in academics is very poor.

Practically there are no study circles among the students. This is the crucial area where they can freely express their ideas and share with others alike. And the students should be given the opportunity to interact with the teachers and among themselves by organising seminars and discussions. At the outset, it is the responsibility of the authorities to provide such platforms and it is the duty of the students to participate. And later the students can initiate themselves with the advice and help from the authorities. Education is also sharing knowledge that automatically opens up the doors that lead to more knowledge.

Absence of a counselling cell for students is another hindrance in the education of Manipur. Guidance and counselling to individual students through the involvement of faculty and senior teacher, departmental orientation and stay-in-orientation is a must. This should be one of the most important organs of the educational institutions. This is the map in a student's journey to their destination. Besides the problem of students in general, they can come up with their personal problems. Most of the students go about their study without any fixed aim or purpose. They just follow a trend, regardless of their skill, capability and creativity.

This has led to the alienation of the student form what they are learning. After they finish their study they are nowhere. Naturally they get frustrated and are lured into many undesirable professions. The first mistake they committed was not choosing the right direction, where to go, which course to take up and for what. But without proper guidance they are not to be blamed. Here the counselling cell can provide immense help to the students, for a bright and successful future.

Undeniably, a dispassionate assessment would tell us that the system has its success and failures – few success shrouded in silence but failures spotlighted in nasty reputation. It must be rejuvenated to meet the challenges of the 21st century so that it becomes alive to the needs and to improve continuous improvement in quality. And for a meaningful survival, lots of changes are but sine-qua-non. Education must be meaningful, realistic and should appeal to the mind, body and spirit of a person, and then only we can visualise the prospect of a fruitful education.

Women Education

Girls Education is essential for the progress of the society. Through education girls can improve and enhance their personalities and contribute towards the progress of the Society.

The Sarva Shiksha Abhiyan recognises the need for special efforts to bring the out-of-school girls, especially from disadvantaged sections, to school. This would require a proper identification of girls who are out of school in the course of micro planning. It also calls for involving women through participatory processes in the effective management of schools. The provision for girls' education would have to be designed to address learning needs of girls and relating education to their life. The Sarva Shiksha Abhiyan is committed to making these interventions possible.

It is said that Manipuri women is far better then their counterparts elsewhere, both socially as well as economically. The history of Manipur has proved that Manipuri women can take important roles in any situation at the individual level as well as in groups. Manipuri women are playing different roles at their best.

Domestic Aspects

Women irrespective of their profession have their priorities in the domestic chores, whether they are working women, women leader, labourer.

Economic Aspects

Women in Manipur are economically independent by engaging themselves in handloom and handicrafts, kitchen gardening, silk rearing and yarn making, farming, pottery, fishing, animal husbandry, pan shop, tea and snack stall, etc. Ima Market, is the women markets where the buyer and seller are mostly women.

Social and Cultural Aspects

Manipuri women are actively involved in fighting against violation of human rights and other social evils. Customs of Manipuri women varied different occasions reflecting the cultural heritage of the state.

However, gender inequality is also in Manipur. In the table, we have seen the District wise population and literacy percentage of Manipur and the state literacy percentage is 68.87 per cent where male literacy is 77.87 and female literacy is 59.70. It shows that, there is about 20 per cent literacy gap between male and female in all districts.

Women are considered as weaker sex requiring social and economic protection. This attitude has led to a limitation on their mobility and consequent lack of opportunities for development of their personalities.

Women have, therefore, lagged behind in the field of education and skill development. Women have less time for education, preference is given to the male child, girl child helps mother in domestic works.

Women are primarily seen in their roles as mother and wives and not as women in their own right. The status of women is identified by their parents, husband and children. Widow of drug addict or alcoholic or HIV/AIDS, patients is outcast by the society for no fault of theirs. Due to various reasons such as deteriorating law and order situation, poverty, unemployment, low rate of education, lack of infrastructure for development and lack of awareness women are facing problems.

In order to empower women we need to focus more on education, health, income generating facilities and women welfare programme in particular.

With this concept, Residential camps were organised for girls of different communities with the resource persons of different items/activities. Demonstration, practical activities and exercise were held in the following during 2006-07:

- Health and Hygiene.

- Food and Nutrition.

- Some vocational based activities like needle works, flower making, inscent stick making.

- Participation, Interaction, News reading, singing and other cultural programmes, etc.

At present, there is no much difference among the boys and girls in the schooling scenario. However, more than 50 per cent are out of the school at Upper Primary level. In order to retain these children in school at least up to elementary level Education programme may be of such option.

Work Education Programme in Formale Schools and in AIE Centres: Most of the girls are engaged in household works and other income generating activities at home as the women takes a major roles in the family economy. In order to enhance the children, short-term vocational training course on local based activities may be given along with the education.

Incentives Like Textbooks, Exercise Books and Materials for Works Education: At present, children in Government and aided schools are of under privilege/ poverty families. To retained them in school system at least up to class VIII and to achieve minimum level of learning, learning materials may be provided to encourage the children in education.

ECCE Centre in the School Premise: Girls are absence from school due to the siblings care, they will be attend school if the ECCE centre is open in the school premise as well as the working women.

Income Generating Programme: The vocational training imparted to the students should be a local suit and the products are of the day to day life of the community, family and student like basketry, weaving, tailoring, knitting, needle works, pottery, plantation and other handicrafts, etc.

Manual and Practical Activities: School is the centre of activities of the community. The activity of the community is reflected to the school. Along with the classroom teaching other activities like social service, sports, painting, cultural and educational programmes, etc. It will helped in discipline, integrity, friendship, physical fitness, participation and interaction.

Teacher Education

As early as in 1906, the need for giving training to the teachers was felt in Manipur. During that time, the Department of Education organised a training course for teachers which was of 4 months duration for the improvement of the method of teaching. Twenty primary school teachers attended the course. This was the beginning of teacher education in Manipur. Imparting training to secondary school teacher began in the year 1928, when one of the teachers of Johnstone High School, Imphal was deputed to undergo B.T. Training outside the state. This marked the beginning of training programme for secondary school teachers. After 1947, the State Government took a keen interest in teacher training programmes. A humble beginning of training the primary and middle school teachers in Manipur was made in 1952-53 by starting Normal Institute at Imphal. The Normal Training School was substituted by Basic Training Institute in 1956. Since then, the Basic Training Institute (BTI) was giving training to elementary school teachers in the state. By 1958-59, there were one Junior Basic Training Institute and one Hindi Training Institute in the state with 80 enrolments in Basic Training and 10 in Hindi Training Institute. Training of Secondary School teacher was done by opening a BT Section in the D.M. College in 1959.

The B.T. course was intended for graduate teacher and Certificate in Teaching (CT) course was for the undergraduate teachers. The B.T section at D.M. College was converted into full-fledged training college and named as P.G.T. (Post-graduate Training College) which was affiliated to Guwahati University on 15th September 1972. Subsequently in 17th January 1997 the P.G.T. College is converted as D.M. College of Teacher Education as a member College of Dhanamanjuri Group of Colleges which is affiliated to Manipur University. After the implementation of National Policy of Education 1986, District Institutes of Educational Training (DIET) has been established in every district of the state to provide pre-service and in-service training to primary school teachers.

Secondary Teacher Education

Secondary Teacher Education programmes (B.Ed. Courses) are provided by 5 colleges of teacher education. The course pattern is as follows: Part A consists of core papers: I: Teacher in Emerging Indian Society; II: Development of Learner and Teaching-Learning Process; III: Development of Education in India; and IV: Educational Technology and Management. Part B consists of Optional Papers V & VI, any two method subjects out of: English, Social Sciences, Mathematics, and Physical and Biological Science. Part C is Elective Group: Additional Specialisation, Paper VIII: Any one special paper — Educational and Mental Measurement; and Educational Management and Administration. Part D. consists of Field Based Experience: Classroom Teaching and Practical Work.

Elementary School Teacher Education

Elementary School Teacher Education is done in District Institute Education and Training (DIET). There are as many as 8 (eight) DIETs in Manipur. These DIETs play a very important role in providing quality teacher's education. District Institute of Education and Training (DIETs) are under the control of SCERT. Primary Schools teacher working in the institutions in different districts of Manipur can join the in-service teacher training programmes conducted by DIETs. The aim of DIET is to provide the latest methods of teaching and learning. Since information technology is included in the new syllabus and textbooks for class I-V have been introduced from the session in 2004-05 and the teachers are to be oriented to acquaint them the knowledge of teaching new textbooks.

Some of the common problems faced by the DIETs are related to: Manpower, finance, non-availability of teacher educators. Many employees are under contract basis. Another problem is non-payment of Salaries regularly to the employees of DIETs working on contract basis. There are 154 Block Resource Centres (RBCs), 156 Cluster Resources Centres (CRCs) functioning under the direct control of SCERT, SSA and DIETs respectively.

Pre-primary School Teacher Education

Pre-Primary Teacher Education programme in Manipur is at the initial stage. The training centres run by the State Government and NGOs give on-job training courses to Anganwadi workers and helpers. The Central Social Welfare Board also organises Orientation courses at regular intervals for the benefit of Anganwadi helpers. There are more than 7 (seven) pre-primary teacher training institute in Manipur which are under the control of private agency. These institutions are developing day by day and contributing a lot in the field of pre-primary education.

Summary

Preparation of well equipped and qualified teachers is must for brighter future of Manipur. In the context of present society, peace is the most important objectives of the human beings. It is a must for all the developmental activities in any society. Thus it seems pertinent that peace education be incorporated in the teacher education curriculum to train the would be teachers to teach school students about peace. Again for promoting the principles of 'Inclusive education' special education should also be added in the curriculum of Teacher Education Programme. Moreover, in order to develop professionalism among teacher trainees the duration of B.Ed. training programme may be enhanced to two academic sessions.

Tribal Education

Every social groups have their own interest to bellows and claims for, even sometimes counter claims for social fair dealing and educational rights by the people, and therefore our generation can rightly be called as claim-generation for a simple reason that every individuals, groups, and tribes or communities, have several claims to make. Claims and assertion by and for particular social groups or by all such social groups are indeed encouraging and they are politically a part of meaningful awakening in a country like ours that is the largest and may be, sometime in the near future, the greatest developed democratic country.

It is fundamental in governance of the country and is the duty of the state to direct its policy in such a manner as to make effective provision for securing the right to education for children up to the age of 14; and to promote educational interest of Scheduled Castes and Scheduled Tribe. The Constitution's Eighty Sixth Amendment Act 2002 has brought free and compulsory education to all children of the age of six to fourteen years into the realm of fundamental rights under a new article- Article 21 A: 'Right to Education'. This is a benchmark strive of India to bringing up its tenure citizen who can able to read and write.

Moreover the fundamental rights that relates to the education of scheduled castes and scheduled tribes that can be read with the directive principles of state policy mentioned above is also Article 30 (1), which envisages that minority section of the citizens can conserve their... 'language or script'. Clause (1) of Art 30 also implies that the state has the power to determine the medium of instruction if such power does not infringe the right of a minority community to impart instruction in their own language. The most important insertion in the records of the Constitution in this subject matter is that of Article 46.

It states: "The State shall promote, with 'special care', the education and economic interest of the weaker section of the people, and, in particular of the scheduled castes and scheduled tribes, and shall protect them from social injustices and all form of social exploitation." It is glaringly comprehensible that Articles 330, 332, 335, 338 to 342 and the entire Fifth and Sixth Schedules of the Constitution deal with special provisions for implementation of the objectives set forth in Article 46.

If the Union Government in the Centre and the State Government are serious to solve the current socio-economic and political problems of most of the tribes in Manipur, they could have translated these provisions into action in letter and spirit. More important is the fact that it is never too late to start at this earnest opportunity. The State Government of Manipur has taken up a few commendable steps to recuperating education of the tribes of our State.

Nevertheless, how much such rights, provisions and directives contain in the Constitution of India for the scheduled castes and scheduled tribes have been concretised in Manipur is held in reserve for anyone's computation. But the government also ought to see into the future social feasibility and lasting good while taking not only such decisions carrying the translations of rights so claimed but also while fulfilling the aspirations of the people. Social justice and education can be a good other half and companion as long as it's translated significance are meant for a common importance and lasting social synchronisation.

The education system in Manipur with its entailing fact like the introduction of vernaculars subjects of almost all the tribes and communities is hard to think of as hard-earned achievements. This introduction of vernacular subjects in schools of the state is purely in fulfilment of the 'Three-Language Formula' following the expressed view of the Secondary Education commission in 1952-53 and as devised by the Central Advisory Board of Education in 1956 and again as subsequently modified by the Kothari Education Commission.

This 'Three-language-Formula' is only the outcome of the apparently imposition of Hindi language as the national language. The southern States have no objection in Hindi being the National language but opposed tooth and nail on the imposition of Hindi learning. Thus came the three-language formula to solve language problem in independent India. Thus, this introduction of three-language formula, especially in the context of Manipur, has nothing to accomplish in the development of tribal dialects and cultures.

As long as it does not cater holistically to an approach of formulating and creativeness of tribal dialects to suit the needs in bringing about changes in the retention and understanding aptitude of the tribal learners by way of introducing novel approaches and methods, no much remarkable achievement would be seen in the education system of the tribes. For example, the government can rather bolster tribal scholars through an institutionalised system to work in research and production of books in our mother tongues that are badly needed like, to name a few, definitional dictionaries and terminologies in different disciplines written in tribal dialects in order to equip the learners with better understanding of subjects like mathematics, sciences, etc.

Without much hectic social and political bargaining, such a department or an institute can be magically put in place provided our State Government is serious about solving socio-political problems, including education of the tribal.

In view of the rich ethnic cultural heritage and diversity of languages in the northeast, special packages of grant under non-Lapsable Central pool of resources have been sanctioned year after year. Nevertheless, sadly, a little of these resources are actually spent for the advantage of tribes' education backwardness.

In the present standard of learning of mother tongue, I find a little good quality if the government's concern is to somehow change the perceptive attitudes of these tribes on the subjects of various disciplines. There is no span of knowledge for improving the educational backwardness of them in such endeavour.

Again, putting the present trend and pattern of such introduction in to reflection, it has become something like an old story that goes into a hoary trail. It is too far yet to gauge it as a stroke to bridge the gap of educational backwardness of the tribes with that of another section of the society. If we subscribe that using mother tongue is the best medium of instruction; and as textbooks by considering it and at the same time it is the best means of imparting quality education, something further steps need to be taken.

We are talking about quality education through process of one's mother tongue.

Then how much quality education is expected of our present trend of importance given to inferior educational group of people? The State is, to a greater extend, responsible for changing the old life pattern into modernisation of the so-called tribal. In and through those simple importance the government is giving attention to this group of people, there could hardly be any fulfilment of objectives of education like — Increasing productivity; Social and National integration; Accelerating the process of modernisation, and lastly, Developing social, moral and spiritual values. In those tribal subjects of today in Manipur, there might be just a little tinge of realisation of only the last objective in doubtful calculation.

We need to understand the rational as to why there is tribal reservation in employment and educational institutions. It is believed that this came about firstly because tribals lack the perceptive capability of things taught. By their long absence in the domination of modernisation and development, the minds have become dormant thereby causing in them a dominant retardation of intelligence in their understanding of things there, which are beyond their vision. In this situation, they could not go along with the people who had seen development earlier than the so-called tribal had.

Secondly, both the State and Union Government do not really want to give to the tribes in India, in general, and those of Manipur in particular, the knowledge required to catching fish save for providing us only one-fourth of our day to day need. Is introduction of tribal dialects in schools the beginning of such changes the government wants to effect in the educational system of the tribes? If it is so, we wish it went well. If not, tribal problems in economic, social and political shall continue to alloy with problems of all on the whole that will be costly in terms of their solutions.

However, another questionable thing is kept suspending in the air. After more than fifty years of freedom from repression, the government is putting a section of that freed people in dungeon without letting them see the light of the day. Simply knowing that the education of its citizens is one of the yardsticks to measure the development of a country and thereby enacting a numbers of laws to that effect will help the educationally backward tribes a little unless accompanied by actions in the right perspective?

How long India chooses to remain in the back stage of world standard. Also to put very straight, the state as well as the Union Government have done nothing-commendable service to the tribal, especially, of Manipur as far as their educational backwardness is concerned. The tribal research wing Department of tribal development can be made use of in the contour opined here. It shall be a very good thing to upgrade the Tribal Research Wing of Tribal Development Department of Manipur into a fully functional Tribal Research Institute/Institute of Tribal language. Most of our sister States in north east have moved ahead of our state in this matter.

Manipur being a unique mixture of tribes and languages shall be befitting place to have an exclusive social and political approach in solving its varied interest.

Unless an institute of learning and research that should specifically indenture with the socio-economic and political problems of them is established, it shall be a blunt mistake giving way to persistency of problems. As already pointed out before, many educated tribal youths, who are frustrated and hopeless due to absence of employment opportunities, can be given not only meaningful employment but also productive work in such institute.

The institute shall be a research institute engaging in works that are to produce educational books in tribal dialects. Such tribal institute should also be entrusted to find significant ways of augmenting the competency of tribal learners to open the cosset of their lack of knowledge and thus leap up from it into the world of development and edifying freedom.

Why an educational endeavour with little prospect in terms of its achievability in the common competitive world should be pursued and precious time and husbanded exchequer should be diminished, it is not because of the fact that such a venture should be kept in abeyance but it is rather because it fails to address the mainstay of the required.

Parents, educationists or academicians and alike institutions have been working and discoursing since the later part of the 20th century in India on the paramount importance of choosing the right streams or subject for students of the present generation that could be readily suitable in the present cutthroat world or novel level of education credence.

Be that as it may, our mother-tongue-instruction and textbooks are thus far unable to afford us any of our educational objective. So, we are emphasising on the point of what fruitful result our first language textbooks that are introduced in schools of Manipur can equip us with. In the competitive sphere as well as in our struggle to survive in the changing economic structure we are neither enlighten nor given the expertise by our mother tongue textbooks. It is not about being critical of the general significance of First languages-tribal textbooks.

Some of the first tribal dialects introduced by the State Government in school curriculum and syllabus in the 1950s were Thadou, Tangkhul, Paite, Hmar and Mao. These dialects were studied initially only up to class V. In later stages, these subjects were again introduced into class IX and X under Board of Secondary Education, Manipur. Some of them earned 100 marks while some carried only 50 marks, depending on the requisite standard and norms expected of each textbook. Since then, all other tribes in one way or the other have been trying to have the same social and educational privileges.

Such tribes who are still on the limit of justice may be politically, and more importantly, socially, feeling neglected and that they could be thus on the trot to grasp the opportunity. Very recently, the State Government accorded new recognition to some tribal dialects and that are indeed a welcome state. Moreover, some have earned a niche in the university. In an order dated 22nd March 1977, the education department notified that the medium of instruction in primary schools having 90 per cent of pupils on its rolls belonging to any of the tribes, viz. Tangkhul, Thadou, Paite, Hmar, and Lushei, within the state of Manipur shall be the respective tribal dialects with effect from the current academic session, i.e. 1977. Undoubtedly, there must be certain such norm and guidelines of the Board of Secondary Education under which tribal dialects should be taught in recognised schools of Manipur, especially in Classes IX & X. In case of the medium of instruction being that of the dialect of the 90 per cent constituent, it is vividly understood that the interest and rights of the remaining 10 per cent has to be sacrificed at the altar of the larger interest of the majority. On the other hand, this 10 per cent constituent either has to go with the majority or opts out of that social class-group under what is called compelling situation. It is here wherein experts, Government agencies, and policy-makers should empty m their wisdom and resonance so that education and justice is not a cause of its own destruction.

Secondly, our young learners always have the inclination to think that studying the books of their own dialect, especially in Class IX & X as of now, is something out of choice. They are not certainly aware of the fact that offering such textbooks as the first language subject is neither under compulsion or of good prospect as far as their future career is concern. They would basically opted it simply on the ground that it is scoring that can fetch them high marks to pass out in good division. For a time, schools do also have the tendency to arrange a particular dialect-textbook to be offered by its students in devoid of rooms for choice and change. The logic follows in such situation is the democratic principle of 'majority' and '90 per cent'. Under such prevailing situation, schools and teachers have easier-said-than-done time. There are schools where many and different tribes studied together. In such school, it is an annoyance for the school authorities to arrange teachers required to teach all the dialect subjects.

Moreover, should only a particular dialect-subject be arranged, would not it be a breech of rights of the rest of the tribal students studying in that school? The alternative one may move forwards in this circumstance is to make the rest of the students offer Additional English and Alternative English, as is in the present practice. Then the students still have the rights to demand for the introduction of such First Language-tribal dialects that may undoubtedly override the standing rules and regulations of our schools. In such ambiguous situation, another thrilling fact that is undeniable in the end compounded the matter. Partition will be emerging, predominantly in primary and lower secondary educational institutions on lines of tribes and communities which shall be the counter-productive educational fruition effecting not only our education system but also education itself as a means of spreading social harmony. Moreover, the meaning of social harmony and national integration as a cherish goal of our education will be slowly but surely fading out. Out of love and attachment to one's dialect/language, seeking admission in school that offers subjects of their choice becomes very important.

7

Language and Literature

Manipuri and English are the languages of the state. Hindi is spoken and understood by most of the people. Manipuri language has been the court language of Manipur since time immemorial. It has also a separate script of its own which is found in old manuscripts and began to evolve about the 17th century. The Meitei language and the script under the able Kings brought about a great unification. Under the influence of Bengal Vaishnavism and the British rule, the people accepted the Bengali script for their language though the number of books reached its height in the 19th century. The modern Manipuri literature starts from the beginning of the 19th century after English pattern of administration had found a share among the people. The establishment of a first High School, i.e. Johnstone and its reorganisation in 1891 and affiliation to Calcutta University, are important steps. Important works had been done by English officials and Meitei educationists who started writing about Manipur.

In the beginning of the 20th century men like Rev. W. Pettigrew, Mr. Wince, Bengali teachers like Babu Ramsundar Roy and the educated Manipuris like H. Maker Singh, Munal Singh, Jatiswar Singh and Haodijam Chaitanya began to print Manipuri books is Bengali. Maharaja Sir Churachand Singh was a great patron of Manipuri literature and culture. At first the Manipuri literature was confined to writing textbooks for the beginners. New books were later written and published on a variety of subjects. A steady output of books on Bengali model also appeared.

The Meitei language, which is the official state language is basically the language of the valley people and other dialects spoken by the tribes in the hills are classified under Tibeto-Burman family. Meitei language has been borrowed by the Naga and Kuki people of the hills. Manipuri was recognised as a national language in 1992.

The official languages of the state are Manipuri and English.

Manipuri Language (Meiteilon)

Meiteilon, the official language of Manipur, has a long history. Courses on Manipuri Language and Literature are offered as a subject up to M. A. level in both Central and State Universities. It is the main language of communication among all different tribes and people inhabiting the state. English Language is also slowly gaining ground as a common language of communication here. Meithei (Meiteilon) has been recognised as the Manipuri language by the Indian Union and has been included in the list of scheduled languages (included in the 8th schedule by the 71st amendment of the Constitution in 1992). Meithei is taught as a subject up to the post-graduate level (Ph.D.) in universities of India, apart from being a medium of instruction up to the undergraduate level in Manipur.

Meitei Mayek (Manipuri Script)

Meitei Mayek is a script, commonly referred as Mayek, which is being used since the ancient times. Though it was not in vogue for a certain period, its revival in recent past has gained popularity.

Tribal Languages

There are 29 different dialects spoken in Manipur. Six main tribal dialects recognised by the State Government for medium of instruction and examination up to class V are:

- Tangkhul, language of Tangkhul people;
- Hmar, language of Hmar people;
- Paite, language of Paite people;
- Lushai, language of Lushai people;
- Thadou/Kuki, language of Kuki people;
- Mao, language of Mao People.

Manipuri literature bears the imprint of the state's encounter with three civilizational paradigms-conversion into Hinduism in 18th century, annexation by the British in 1891, and its merger with India in 1949. These encounters produced the rejection/acceptance syndrome in literature, reflecting the people's struggle to come to terms with itself.

Peculiar Keepers of the Oral Tradition

Manipuri literature till the 17th century has been said to constitute its early period. Ritual songs and hymns composed before the advent of the Manipuri script form part of the corpus of the literature of the early period. These songs and hymns are not treated as folk songs or part of folklore as they were not widespread amongst the people. Neither were they handed orally through successive generations. They were confined to a certain erudite section of performers whose performances were limited to 'particular ceremonial functions, ritual observance and festive occasions.'

The manuscript Panthoibi-Khongkul gives an account of the religious and social festival known as the 'Lai Haraoba' where the Khaba community paid homage to the deity Nongpok Ningthou and his consort Panthoibi. This festival, believed by scholars to be part of the cosmological theory of creation in Meitei myth, is a repository of numerous songs. Significant among these Lai Haraoba songs found in Panthoibi Khongkul are the 'Ougri', 'Khencho', 'Anoirol' and 'Lairemma Paosa'. 'Ougri' and 'Khencho' are much more archaic in diction and steep in historical allusions. 'Ougri' is also mentioned in the manuscript Laisra Pham as a coronation song on the occasion of the accession of Nongda Lairen Pakhangba in AD 33.

The royal chronicle known as Cheitharol Kumbaba begins with Nongda Lairen Pakhangba's accession to the throne in AD 33. Another manuscript titled Naothingkhong Phambal Kaba refers to the 'Ougri' as an important aspect of Meitei culture and tradition. The lines of the first part of 'Ougri' comprise six syllables each while those in the second part comprise eight syllables. Noted for its cadentic quality, 'Khencho' remains as an obscure and unintelligible literary piece to the modern generation. Still considered as one of the most important components of the Lai Haraoba festival, this immensely rhythmic song is characterised by its archaic diction.

It consists of lines of six syllables each. 'Lairemma Paosa' and 'Anoirol' are based on the theme of love. Diction appears to be comparatively simple in these songs with a lyrical flow created through alliteration and rhythm. Another song associated with the festival is the 'Hijan Hirao', a long narrative poem extremely lyrical and sentimental. Some other prominent songs associated with rituals are 'Ahonglon', 'Yakeiba', 'Pakhangba Langyensei', 'Langmailon' and 'Kumdamsei'. 'Ahonglon' is important as it is mentioned in the manuscript Loyumba Sinyen, a written codification of laws and customs dating back to the twelfth century.

Another important aspect of the literature of the early period was the treatment of heroism. Rivalry and clashes between the clans resulted in the development of martial skills. Bravery and courage remained central to the numerous conflicts that created a martial culture. It dominated the spirit of the society till the late-19th century. Anonymous writers of the early period dealt with the saga of heroism in numerous works like Chengleiron, Tutenglon, Numit Kappa, Thawanthaba Hiran, Chainarol and Nongsamei. Chengleiron stands as one of the earliest known text in Manipuri literature whose style has been widely followed. Opening with a dedication to the patron King, the lyrics are meant to be recited or sung. It is a narrative that spans three generations of Kings of the Chenglei clan. Interesting narrations are found in Numit Kappa, an allegory with a strong political overtone which still commands a wide practicality in today's Manipur where there are inter and intra-ethnic clashes overpower.

Language

Manipuri Language is originally known as Meitei. It is the official language of the south eastern Himalayan state of Manipur in India. There are about 1,500,000 people in the world which speak Manipuri. The major chunk of this population resides in North East India mostly in Manipur. The rest of the Manipuri speaking population can be found in some parts of Bangladesh and Myanmar. This is also the language used by the offices and government institutions in the state of Manipur. It has been recognised as a scheduled language by the Indian Union and is taught up to Ph.D. level in the Indian universities. It is also the medium of education in Manipuri Schools. This language has been a major adhesive in the integration of all ethnic groups of Manipur.

The Manipuri Language belongs to Kuki-Chin group of Sino-Tibetan family of languages. As per the earliest written evidence on the history of Manipuri, the language dates back to the 11th century. It had an independent script that was in use until 18th century. This script was derived from the Tibetan group of scripts. With the arrival of the British rule, the script was modified and came to be known and used as the Bengali script. This script is being used till date. Efforts are being made to restore the original script and renew it. This will give it further recognition and importance among the current generation. In Manipur, more than 60 per cent of the people converse in Manipuri and there is an urgent need to revive its original script before it completely fades away from the memories of the people.

The Manipuri Literature can be divided into three phases-the old phase, the medieval phase and the modern phase. The period from the eighth century to 1074 AD is the old phase of the Manipuri Literature. It is the period when the dialect of the Ningthoujas gradually attained the status of the standard norm. Early Manipuri Literature consists of only folk and poetries. The early medieval phase ranges from 1074 to 1709 AD. It was the time when Shans (Pong) migrated to Manipur from Burma.

In the later years, from about 1074 AD to 1469 AD, Shans who called themselves the Tais outnumbered Mnaiiouris and exerted considerable influence on the culture and literature of the state. During the late medieval period, i.e. after the 1709 AD, the Manipuri literature went through a new phase with the arrival of Burmese in the area. Later after the British invasion, a new phase, i.e. the beginning of the modern period in Manipuri literature began with British influence. Quite later the short stories and novels also became popular in the Manipuri Literature. H. Guno Singh and Pacha Meiti are the popular names in Manipuri Literature in contemporary times.

Meitei had its original script named Meitei-mayek which was in use up to the 18th century. However, later the Eastern Nagari or Bengali script adopted for scripting Manipuri. It is also the script used till now. However, efforts to revive the Meitei-mayek are still on. The Grammar of the Manipuri Language is interesting yet simple; the phonological system of the Manipuri language can be basically divided into three levels — Vowels, Consonants and Tones. In Manipuri Grammar, there are two types of roots — the free roots and bound roots. All nouns, in Manipuri, are free roots. There is also no grammatical gender in Manipuri, the human and animate nouns are addressed according to the masculine or feminine on the basis of the natural sex.

Bishnupriya Manipuri Language

The Bishnupriya or Bishnupriya Manipuri (BPM) is an Indo-Aryan language spoken in parts of the Indian states of Assam, Tripura, Manipur and others, as well as in Bangladesh, Burma, and other countries.

History and Development: Bishnupriya Manipuri is spoken in parts of Assam, Tripura and Manipur in India, as well as in Bangladesh, Myanmar, and in several other countries. It is different from many Indo-Aryan languages like Bengali, Assamese, Oriya, etc. The language originated and developed in Manipur and was originally confined to the surroundings of the Loktak Lake. Other authorities such as An account of the valley of Manipore by Col. McCullock, Descriptive Ethnology of Bengal by E. T. Dalton and the Linguistic Survey of India by Dr. G. A. Grierson mention that the language was in existence in Manipur before the 19th century. Dr. Grierson calls the language as "Bishnupuriya Manipuri", while some other writers call it simply "Bishnupriya". The principal localities where this language was spoken are now known as Khangabok, Heirok, Mayang Yamphal, Bishnupur, Khunan, Ningthankhong, Ngaikhong, Thamnapoxpi.

A great majority of speakers of BPM fled from Manipur and took refuge in Assam, Tripura, Sylhet and Cachar during the eighteenth and nineteenth centuries due to internal conflicts among the princes of Manipur and due to Burmese attack. Consequently, it was difficult for the small number of Bishnupriyas who remained in Manipur to retain their language in the face of the impact of Meitei, although in 1891 Dr. G. A. Grierson found the existence of a considerable number of speakers in two or three villages near Bishnupur, locally known as Lamangdong. The language slowly started losing its ground in Manipur against a vast majority of Meiteis and is slowly facing its decay in Cachar and Bangladesh against a vast majority of Bengali-speakers. This language is still being spoken in Jiribam (a subdivision of Manipur), Cachar (a district of Assam) and in some pockets in Bangladesh and Tripura.

Source and Origin: The language is known to its speakers as Imar Thar meaning "Language of my Mother". They call themselves and their language "manipuri", and use the term "Bishnupriya" to distinguish them from other ethnic races of Manipur. The term "Bishnupriya" is most probably derived from "Bishnupur" along with the suffix "-iya", meaning "people of Bishnupur", the old capital of Manipur. Orthodox Bishnupriyas hold that the language was carried over to Manipur by some immigrants from Dvaraka and Hastinapurajust after the Mahabharata war. It is further said that these immigrants were led by Babhruvahana, the son of Chitrangada and Arjuna, the third Pandava. Some scholars and history writers came to support the Mahabharata origin from observation of the morphology, the vocables and the phonology of the Bishnupriya Manipuri language. They hold that BPM is highly influenced by Sanskrit and Maharastri as well as Sauraseni Prakrits. Sauraseni Prakrit was the colloquial language of the soldiers and the people of Kuru Panchal and Matsyadesa including Hastinapura Indraprastha etc. Dr. K. P. Sinha, who has done considerable researches on Bishnupriya Manipuri, disagrees with the theory and is of the opinion that the language was originated through Magadhi Prakrita.

The Bishnupriyas were a group of people who settled in present-day Manipur state in early time when they were captured as war prisoners by the then King of Kangleipak. They are therefore, outsiders, i.e., mayangs. However, the Bishnupriya Manipuri language is certainly not one of the Tibeto-Burman languages, but is closer to the Indo-Aryan group of languages with remarkable influence from Meitei both grammatically and phonetically. At a different stage of development of the language the Sauraseni, Maharastri and Magadhi languages and the Tibeto-Burman languages exerted influence on it as well. It was probably developed from Sanskrit, Sauraseni and Maharastri Prakrita, making it comparable to Hindi, Bengali, Oriya and Assamese.

The Sauraseni-Maharastri relation is evident from the fact that it has retained the dominant characteristics of the Sauraseni and Maharastri pronouns (declensional and conjugational endings are the most stable elements of a language; they undergo changes very slowly). A study of the pronouns and the conjugational and declensional endings of Bishnupriya shows that most of these forms are the same, as they are closely related to those of the languages which are derived from Sanskrit. The Magadhi attachment is also remarkable as the language retains many characteristics of Magadhi. It can further be noted that Bishnupriya Manipuri retains much of the old (15th century to 17th century AD) Meitei sound vocabulary, as the majority of speakers of the language left Manipur during the first part of the 19th century.

Dialects: Bishnupriyas have two dialects, namely Rajar Gang (King's village) and Madai Gang (Queen's village). Unlike the dialects of other tribes, these dialects of Bishnupriya are not confined to distinct geographical areas; they rather exist side by side in the same localities. In Manipur, however, these two dialects were confined to well-defined territories. From the viewpoint of phonetics, Madai Gang is more akin to Assamese and Meitei, whereas Rajar Gang is more akin to Bengali. In vocabulary Madai Gang is more influenced by Meitei while Rajar Gang is more akin to Bengali and Assamese. The morphological differences between the two dialects are negligible.

Vocabulary: Like other Indic languages, the core vocabulary of Bishnupriya Manipuri is made up of tadbhava words (i.e. words inherited over time from older Indic languages, including Sanskrit, including many historical changes in grammar and pronunciation), although thousands of tatsama words (i.e. words that were re-borrowed directly from Sanskrit with little phonetic or grammatical change) augment the vocabulary greatly. In addition, many other words were borrowed from languages spoken in the region either natively or as a colonial language, including Meitei, English, and Perso-Arabic.

- Inherited/native Indic words (*tadbhava*): 10,000 (Of these, 2,000 are only found in Bishnupriya Manipuri, and have not been inherited by other Indic languages).

- Words re-borrowed from Sanskrit (*tatsama*): 10,000.

- Words re-borrowed from Sanskrit, partially modified (*ardhatatsama*): 1,500.

- Words borrowed from Meitei: 3,500.

- Words borrowed from other indigenous non-Indic languages (*desi*): 1,500.

- Words borrowed from Perso-Arabic: 2,000.

- Words borrowed from English: 700.

- Hybrid words: 1,000.

- Words of obscure origin: 1,300.

Bishnupriya Manipuri Script: The orthodox Bishnupriyas claim that they have their own script, that is, the Devanagari script, which was used to write in the Bishnupriya language in its early years. However, on introduction of modern education during the British period through the Bengali language the Bishnupriya Manipuri writers began to use the Eastern Nagari script. The alphabet has consonant letters with dependent vowel signs (matras) as well as independent vowel letters. Punctuation marks and numerals are also used. Bishnupriya Manipuri is written from left to right and top to bottom, in the same manner as in English. Some of the consonants can combine with one another to make orthographic clusters.

Places where Bishnupriya Manipuri is Spoken: In Manipur the language is still spoken in the Jiribam subdivision. A large number of Bishnupriya Manipuri people settled in Assam ages ago, particularly in the districts of Cachar, Karimganj andHailakandi. These people are counted as one of the major groups of people in the Cachar and Karimganj districts. In Tripura, the Bishnupriya Manipuri population localities may be divided into a Dharmanagar sub-area, a Kailasahar sub-area, a Kamaipur sub-area and a West Tripura sub-area. In Meghalaya, Arunachal Pradesh and Mizoram, there is a scattered Bishnupriya Manipuri population.

Outside of India, Bangladesh has the largest Bishnupriya Manipuri population. The main localities are Sylhet, Moulbivazar, Habiganj and the Sunamganj district. There are also a considerable number of the Bishnupriyas Manipuris living in local cities like Mymensingh, Rangamati of the Chittagong Hill Tracts and also at Tezgaon, Manipuri-para in Dhaka, the capital city of Bangladesh.

In Myanmar Tbangdut, Mawa Kalewa and Bumnuk, etc. are the Bishnupriya Manipuri areas. And in case of the United States of America, Canada, Germany, Middle East and Austria, there are a considerable number of Bishnupriya Manipuris settled there.

Not a Dialect of Bengali or Assamese: Though there is a relation between the denotative words of BPM and those of Bengali and Assamese for regional and periodical reasons, it does not mean that the original language is lost by the influence of the surrounding languages nor it reasonable to think that the BPM language is the formative language of the plain people of Assam, Bengal and Manipur as unwisely viewed by certain phoneticians. The phonological and syntactical mainstream of the BPM language was never hampered and still has its distinct identity. Moreover, the plain people of Assam, Bengal and Manipur were not culturally, linguistically and politically united; nor conscious that they mutually might have formed a language like Bishnupriya Manipuri, in the Valley of Manipur.

Dr. Suniti Kumar Chatterjee, a recognised Bengali phonetician, listed the BPM language to be a dialect of Bengali, whereas Dr. Maheswer Neog and Dr. Banikanta Kakti claimed it as a dialect of Assamese. Their assumptions later caused contradiction about the origin of Bishnupriya Manipuri language. But the assumptions were proven incorrect by scientific research and observation of morphology, vocabulary and phonology of BPM.

Firstly, mere similarities of a few elements are not sufficient to prove that BPM is a dialect of another language. Secondly, Dr. Chatterjee, in his phonetic analysis, had used a peculiar version of Bishnupriya Manipuri, which is much different from the original BPM that is spoken in the Bishnupriya Manipuri localities in Assam, Tripura, Manipur or Bangladesh. For example, "Manu agor Puto Dugo asil...." is neither syntactically nor grammatically the correct form of BPM. Thirdly, there are numerous dissimilarities between Bengali/Assamese and BPM in the context of syntax, semantics and morphology. In fact, Bishnupriya Manipuri is a complete language itself and cannot be called a dialect of any other language.

Literature

Written documents of Bishnupriya Manipuri literatures of older periods are unavailable, because records and historical books including literatures had been destroyed and efforts had been made to destroy the history of Manipur and Manipuris. There are, however some rudiments of folk-literatures of Bishnupriya Manipuri which are of elder origin and are handed down to this day through oral traditions. These elements originated during the period from the 16th century to the beginning of this century. Thus the history of Bishnupriya Manipuri literature can be broadly divided into two periods namely ancient Folk-Bishnupriya Manipuri literature and modern Bishnupriya Manipuri literature.

The general trend of writings was spiritual rather than secular and creative. The post-modern writers have given up many time-honoured conventions. They have come to contact with English, French and German literature with are rich in all respects. There is also the influence of contemporary Bangla, Hindi, Assamese and Manipuri Meitei literature of Bangladesh, West-bengal, Assam, Tripura and Manipur.

Varieties of Bishnupriya Manipuri literature began to be produced very rapidly in a different and changed atmosphere. The Modernism has its manifold effects giving rise to a complete shape of the literature in prose, viz. dramas, stories, novels, travelogues, essays and criticisms, biography, etc. and in poetry, viz. lyrical and modern.

Translation of a number of classical works of Sanskrit and world literature was done successfully by Bishnupriya Manipuri writers. Of them *Srimadbhagabat Gita, Ishoponisad, Meghodutom* and *Ritu Samahar* of Kalidas, *Rubayaate-Umar-Khayam*, Greek drama *Anigone*, Eliot's *The waste Land*, Japanese Haiku, Poems of Rabindrnath are worthy to be mentioned.

Bishnupriya Manipuri literature developed a lot within a very short period and it has become possible only due to the sacrifice of the writers, who invites endless sufferings due to economical, social problems and also due to the disturbance from government authorities and other antagonistic forces on the mother language issue of Bishnupriya Manipuris.

Ancient Literature: A good stock of folk literatures of Bishnupriya Manipuri, which are older in origin, are handed down to this day through oral tradition. The ancient literature of Bishnupriya Manipuri is represented by folk stories, folk-songs, folk-poems, rhymes and proverbs. A rain-invoking song called *Boron-dahanir Ela* (1450-1600 AD) and a song relating to the conjugal life of Madai and Soralel known as Madai Soralel Ela (1500-1600 AD) are sometimes considered the most important. The language of the songs are archaic and are replete with words of Tibeto-Burman origin. These two songs are very important for the study of the cultural and linguistic history of Bishnupriya Manipuri. Besides these, there are songs which are sung by women who work in the fields. Proverbs form another important part of BPM folk literature.

Modern Literature: The Bishnupriya Manipuris have established Bishnupriya Manipuri Sahitya Parishad, Bishnupriya Manipuri Sahitya Sabha, Bishnupriya Manipuri Sahitya Singlup, Pouri, Manipuri Theatre and many other organisations to encourage literary activities among the people. Serious literary culture of the BPM language began during the 2nd quarter of 20th century. In fact, the history of Manipuri literature began in 1925 with the literary magazine Jagaran edited by Falguni Singha who was a Bishnupriya Social worker; this magazine published articles both in Bishnupriya and Meitei. The Manipuris of Surma valley formed their first formal association, Surma Valley Manipuri Society (later called Surma Valley Manipuri Association) in 1934. The members included the Meiteis, the Bishnupriyas and the Pangals (Manipuri Muslims). From 1933 a number of journals, e.g. Manipuri (1933), Mekhali (1938) and Kshatryajyoti (1944), fostered nationalism as well literary and cultural activities.

Bishnupriya Manipuri Society: Like any Indian family, the Bishnupriya Manipuri society according to the place of residence of newly-wedded husband and wife is patrilocal which means newly married wife leaves her parents' house and goes to reside with her husband's parents in their house.

From the point of view of authority in the Bishnupriya Manipuri family, it is patriarchal. The father is the formal head and takes decisions on behalf of the family.

Bishnupriya Manipuri poetry: A branch of modern BPM poetic literature, namely Vaishnava Padavali, based on Vaishnava philosophy, deserves special mention.

Great Personalities:

- LT MAHRNDRA SINGHA from Rajargoan (Assam) became the first Bishnupriya Manipuri to pursue Bachelor degree from Calcutta university and then completed B.Ed. He worked a lot through his pen for the enrolment of the caste in the Indian OBC. He was the founder of NIKHIL BISHNUPRIYA MANIPURI MAHASABHA (NBMM).

- LT GOKULANANDA GITISWAMY was the first innovative and highly sounded poet, ever born in Bishnupriya Manipuri caste. His poetry and dialogues became so popular that he was crowned with a title "GITISWAMY" added before his name.

Manipuri Literature

Manipuri literature is the literature written in the Manipuri Language (Meeteilon), including literature composed in Manipuri Language by writers from Manipur, Assam, Tripura, Myanmar and Bangladesh. The history of Manipuri literature trace back to thousands of years with flourish of its civilization. The survival of Manipuri literature after passing through the massive devastation, the terror event of history, by burning of Meetei Scriptures, which is known as Puya Meithaba, was a miracle. The resilience that Meeteis could acquire in the event of devastation proved her ability to survive in history. Most of the early literary works found in Manipuri Literature were in Poetry and Prose. Some of the books were written with combination of both the Prose and Poetry.

Manipuri Literature in History

Manipuri literature bears the imprint of the state's encounter with three civilizational paradigms-conversion into Hinduism in 18th century, annexation by the British in 1891, and its merger with India in 1949. These encounters produced the rejection/acceptance syndrome in literature, reflecting the people's struggle to come to terms with itself.

Over centuries, the people inhabiting what is presently called Manipur experienced numerous upheavals as a result of clashes with different cultures and powers. Known as Kathe to the Burmese, Meklee to the Assamese, Mooglie to the Cacharies, Cassey to the Shans, the people of this ancient Asiatic Kingdom, have witnessed three major epoch-making encounters in the vicissitudes of its history. Based on these encounters, the paper seeks to scrutinise certain aspects of Manipuri literature as it unfolds during the travails of its growth and development, and its engagements with the changing realities.

Even though signs of Manipur's contact with Hinduism can be traced to King Charairongba's reign in the 17th century, it was King Pamheiba's ascension to the throne in 1709 that saw the brutal imposition of Hinduism. The ensuing clash between the indigenous Meetei faith and the alien Hindu faith was essentially an encounter between two traditional cultures and worldviews. The second has been the encounter with the Western civilization vis-à-vis the British conquest of Manipur in 1891 though its contact with the British was established much earlier. The impact of the encounter with the British immediately followed by the two World Wars brought about a massive change in the collective experience and consciousness reflected in terms of cultural values being rendered more open, liberal, equalitarian and humanistic.

The second encounter also brought far-reaching political changes in the wake of the swelling tide of decolonisation that swept Asia, Africa and Latin America. Manipur eventually became free from British control in 1947 and remained a sovereign democratic state till its 'integration' with the newly independent State of India on the 15th October 1949. The third encounter comes with this contact with India. It presents a queer picture of an encounter with another not too dissimilar entity. With its own logic, the society and culture of this ancient Asiatic land has experienced the dynamics of these encounters.

Peculiar Keepers of the Oral Tradition: Manipuri literature till the 17th century has been said to constitute its early period. Ritual songs and hymns composed before the advent of the Manipuri script form part of the corpus of the literature of the early period. These songs and hymns are not treated as folk songs or part of folklore as they were not widespread amongst the people. Neither were they handed orally through successive generations. They were confined to a certain erudite section of performers whose performances were limited to 'particular ceremonial functions, ritual observance and festive occasions.'

The manuscript Panthoibi-Khongkul gives an account of the religious and social festival known as the 'Lai Haraoba' where the Khaba community paid homage to the deity Nongpok Ningthou and his consort Panthoibi. This festival, believed by scholars to be part of the cosmological theory of creation in Meetei myth, is a repository of numerous songs. Significant among these Lai Haraoba songs found in Panthoibi Khongkul are the 'Ougri', 'Khencho', 'Anoirol' and 'Lairemma Paosa'. 'Ougri' and 'Khencho' are much more archaic in diction and steep in historical allusions. 'Ougri' is also mentioned in the manuscript Laisra Pham as a coronation song on the occasion of the ascension of Nongda Lairen Pakhangba in AD 33.

The royal chronicle known as Cheitharol Kumbaba begins with Nongda Lairen Pakhangba's ascension to the throne in AD 33. Another manuscript titled Naothingkhong Phambal Kaba refers to the 'Ougri' as an important aspect of Meetei culture and tradition. The lines of the first part of 'Ougri' comprise of six syllables each while those in the second part comprise of eight syllables. Noted for its cadentic quality, 'Khencho' remains as an obscure and unintelligible literary piece to the modern generation. Still considered as one of the most important components of the Lai Haraoba festival, this immensely rhythmic song is characterised by its archaic diction. It consists of lines of six syllables each. 'Lairemma Paosa' and 'Anoirol' are based on the theme of love. Diction appears to be comparatively simple in these songs with a lyrical flow created through alliteration and rhythm. Another song associated with the festival is the 'Hijan Hirao', a long narrative poem extremely lyrical and sentimental. Some other prominent songs associated with rituals are 'Ahonglon', 'Yakeiba', 'Pakhangba Langyensei', 'Langmailon' and 'Kumdamsei'. 'Ahonglon' is important as it is mentioned in the manuscript Loyumba Sinyen, a written codification of laws and customs dating back to the twelfth century.

Another important aspect of the literature of the early period was the treatment of heroism. Rivalry and clashes between the clans resulted in the development of martial skills. Bravery and courage remained central to the numerous conflicts that created a martial culture. It dominated the spirit of the society till the late 19th century. Anonymous writers of the early period dealt with the saga of heroism in numerous works like Chengleiron, Tutenglon, Numit Kappa, Thawanthaba Hiran, Chainarol and Nongsamei. Chengleiron stands as one of the earliest known text in Manipuri literature whose style has been widely followed. Opening with a dedication to the patron King, the lyrics are meant to be recited or sung. It is a narrative that spans three generations of Kings of the Chenglei clan. Interesting narrations are found in Numit Kappa, an allegory with a strong political overtone which still commands a wide practicality in today's Manipur where there are inter and intra ethnic clashes over power.

The First Note of Realism: However, the first work to register the note of realism is Thawanthaba Hiran, a tragedy based on a crime story. Departing drastically from the legendary nature of stories in the other works, it was based on historical events. Closely aligned with history, it grapples with the violent and bloody conflicts between the Khuman and the Meetei clans. The horrific violence that characterised the work makes it distinct. Chainarol is an account of combats based on the feuds of the clans. There are twenty-seven stories based on real life incidents.

Besides the numerous literary tracts on the cult of heroism and bravery, the theme of romance and love found abundant expression in the literature of this period. We find works, which can be classified as pure fiction in clear distinction from those fictions based on historical realities. Many of these fictions were based on mythical legends. Nungpan Ponpi Luwaopa narrates the romantic saga of Luwang Prince Luwaopa and Koubru

Namoinee, the adopted daughter of the Koubru King. Myth and legend fuse together with divine intervention playing an important role in the narrative. After a series of mishaps and ordeals, the two lovers are finally united. Fate emerges as the overarching power dominating human lives in the tragic story of Naothingkhong Phambal Kaba. Human actions and human characters are helpless in the sweeping changes brought by the elements of fate and destiny.

Panthoibi Khongkul is one of the most valued literary works in Manipuri. It is, perhaps, the most, critically assessed work of Manipuri literature of the early period. As the title suggests, the story deals with the trail or foot prints left by Panthoibi after she leaves the house of her husband. As per this text, Panthoibi is the epitome of freedom which makes her distinct and ahead of her time. Panthoibi, the Meetei Princess, is described as a maiden of rare beauty. Eagerly sought by many powerful Kings and princes, she is portrayed as an extremely independent character. Her spirit is symbolic of a natural zest for life. Spurning many proposals for marriage, she was finally persuaded to marry Taram Khoinucha, the Khaba Prince born of Khaba Sokchrongba, King of the Khaba dynasty and the Queen Teknga. With great pomp and grandeur, the bride was received in her new household. However, Panthoibi still retained her zest for freedom and independence. She never took to married life as a married woman was meant to. Instead of keeping indoors, she roamed the countryside alone. It was fate that took her by chance to Angoupa Kainou Chingsompa, the Lord of the Langmai hills. Instantly, they were attracted to each other. The love-struck couple decided to break all traditional social barriers by running away. Angoupa wanted to take her to his land. After some dramatic twists and turns, the lovers finally managed to elope. The Khaba warriors led by their King pursued the fleeing couple but eventually failed to capture them. Thus united, the two lovers were received by the Langmai people with dance and music.

The Epics of the Seven Incarnations: Apart from several other works based on the theme of love, literature from the Moirang region of Manipur stands at a height. A civilization situated on the magnificent Loktak Lake, the culture of the Moirang clan has been noted. Numerous manuscripts of the Moirang region dwell on the theme of love. One of the most popular stories refers to the seven pairs of lovers who are regarded as incarnations of the same souls in different generations or ages. The seven cycles are: Akongjamba (hero) and Phouoibi (heroine); Henjunaha (hero) and Leima Lairuklembi (heroine); Khuyol Haoba (hero) and Yaithing Konu (heroine); Kadeng Thangjahanba (hero) and Tonu Laijinglembi (heroine); Ura Naha Khongjomba (hero) and Pidonnu (heroine); Wanglen Pungdingheiba (hero) and Sappa Chanu Silheibi (heroine); Khamba (hero) and Thoibi (heroine).

Even though the development of this literature in its written form may be traced to the twelfth century, the oral tradition had existed much earlier as indicated clearly by the chronicles. The literary tradition that prevailed till the encounter with Hinduism was rooted in the indigenous script, language, culture and social milieu. A pertinent aspect of this literature of the early period is its distinct character unmarked by any traces of outside influence. This remained a characteristic feature till the dawn of the eighteenth century.

Culture by Dictate: The close of the 17th century and the beginning of the 18th century mark a turning point in the history of Manipur. The year 1709 witnessed the ascension of Pamheiba to the throne after the death of his father King Charairongba. Rechristening himself as Maharaja Garibniwaz, he issued a dictate pronouncing Hinduism as the new religion of Manipur under the influence of the proselytising Bengali Vaishnavite, Shantidas Goswami. This act engendered an upheaval with colossal implications for a society's identity. Opposition and resistance to this autocratic move to obliterate the traditional faith and culture were brutally repressed. The King and his Bengali mentor left no stone unturned to erase traces of the indigenous faith. Places of worship were destroyed, worship of traditional and local ancestral deities, traditional rituals and rites, including Lai Haraoba festivals, were immediately banned. Burial of the dead was replaced by cremation. Along with the imposition of Hinduism, the manuscripts and texts in the indigenous script were confiscated and burnt in full public view. Universal use of the indigenous script was replaced by the Bengali script.

Shantidas Goswami composed an entirely different chronicle in Bengali known as Vijay Panchali, which was a deliberate attempt to efface the history of the people. It projected the land as Manipur of (the Hindu epic) Mahabharata and traced the lineage and genealogy of the first King of Manipur to Chandrabhanu whose daughter Chitrangada was married to Arjuna, the great Pandava archer. Brabrubahana was the son born of this wedlock. His son Yavistha was then identified with Nongda Lairen Pakhangba who first ascended the throne in Kangla in AD 33. Imported art forms like the Natya Sankirtan actively encouraged by the royal power gained popularity. Corruption in language became the order of the day as the elite and aristocratic class got increasing exposure to Indo-Aryan languages like Sanskrit and Bengali. Manipuri vocabulary witnessed introduction of many new words from these languages.

The Great Translation Enterprise: Literature as a social entity conditioned by historico-political, material circumstances naturally did not remain unaffected by these drastic changes. Restrictions on the practice of the indigenous faith and widespread patronage of the newly imported alien faith saw a marked rise in the influence of literatures of Indo-Aryan languages, especially Sanskrit and Bengali. Apart from the changes that can be seen in the formalistic domain of writing, thematic engagements were heavily influenced by the new religion. The two Hindu epics, the Ramayana and Mahabharata, came to assume a central space in the Manipuri literature of the period.

Garibniwaz patronised one Kshema Singh Moiramba to compose the Ramayana in Manipuri. Five young scholars were engaged in the project, viz. Pramananda Nongyai

Khumanthem, Mukundaram Khoisnam, Laxmi Narayan Soiba, Ramcharan Nongthomba and Lakhmi Narayan Saikhuba. Parikshit, a part of the Mahabharata was translated by one of the King's Vaishnavite teachers, Gopaldas. Virat Santhuplon was another work from the Mahabharata produced by crown Prince Nabananda. He engaged two eminent writers, Wahengbam Madhabram and Mayengbam Brindavan, to produce this work.

In the sphere of fiction, contact with Indian culture brought about new trends in terms of theme and narration. Mention can be made of Wahengbam Madhabram's Sanamanik, Dhruba Charit, Ananda Pukhrambam's Dhananjoy Laibu Ningba, the anonymous Rupaban and Lalananda Das' Bhakta Gunamrita. Translation of the Bhagavad Gita is also a notable feature of this period. Repressed and marginalised writers who retained the traditional indigenous faith also worked hard, in the face of severe constraints, to produce remarkable literary works anonymously. Several manuscripts written during the period extolled the need to protect and nurture the indigenous faith and culture of the pre-Hindu period. A text known as Sanamahi Laikan stands out distinctly with its rich historical, legendary and mythological references woven in an intricate narrative pattern. Many critics have noted the poetic quality of this work. The other great works of this strand are Khagemba Langjei, Sanamahi Laihui and Chingoiron.

The close of the 19th century marks another significant turning point in the history of Manipur. British victory in the Anglo-Manipuri War of 1891 brought the land under British control. This marked a long chapter of foreign rule, the second in Manipur's history since the Burmese occupied it during 1819-26 in what has come to be known as Chahi Taret Khuntakpa (Seven Years' Devastation). The British were not only responsible for introducing a new administrative system but also other things like new roads, new judicial system, new modes of trade, schools based on Western system of education, etc. Apart from the technological changes, the British also made inroads in the social landscape of the land with their religion. Christian missionaries played a crucial role in proselytising the non-Meetei people living in the hills.

It seems that the literary domain has not been able to fully capture the long British colonial interlude. Instead, mainstream Manipuri consciousness continued to be steeped in Vaishnavite Hinduism and the rhapsodical art forms it spawned like Sankirtan and Raslila. There was a lull in creative and critical efforts in the field of writing as dance and music enthralled and captivated the collective mindset. An important literary personality of this transition period, Haodijamba Chaitanya, published four significant works — Khamba Thoibigi Warini (1899); Khagi Ngamba (1900); Takhel Ngamba (1902); and Chingthangkhomba (1902). But these works are traditional in essence. Except for the first one, which is based on the romantic saga of Khamba, the orphan, and Thoibi, the Princess of Moirang, the remaining three are based on three great Kings of Manipur. Engagement with the changing realities generated by the thrust of modernity did not take long to emerge.

The Triumvirate Usher in Modernity: The literary landscape witnessed a dramatic upheaval in the early part of the 20th century with the entry of three overarching figures-Khwairakpam Chaoba, Lamabam Kamal and Hijam Anganghal. New consciousness shaped by forces of modernity, imprinted clearly in their works, heralded the advent of modern Manipuri literature. Their works made a lasting impact on the collective Manipuri consciousness by interrogating many assumptions and notions of received ideas and practices. Their literary works celebrated the richness of their culture, language and history as well as passionately foreshadowed a resurgent literature written in the grass-root Manipuri language with an explicit attempt to foreground its strength and vitality. Their versatility made them foray into different genres-poetry, drama, novel, short story, essay, epic and criticism. Rightly called the founding fathers of modern Manipuri literature they paved the path of modern sensibility in literary expression.

A serious poet, Chaoba never fails to use a word with optimum effect. His collection of poems Thainagi Leirang (The Flower of the Ancient Time) (1933) bears the hallmark of powerful use of language. In prose, too, he was equally prolific. His prose work Chhatra Macha was prescribed by Calcutta University in 1924. The historical novel Labanga Lata (1940) also remains as a work of distinction.

As a poet, Kamal laments the debility and neglect of our rich heritage. He calls forth a vision to reinvigorate the rich traditional culture. Influenced by Western Romanticism, his appeal for nature's beauty and harmony is striking. As a novelist, Kamal is credited for giving Manipuri literature one of its great classics, Madhabi (1930), a story of love and sacrifice.

Anganghal, in spite of poverty compelling him to drop out of school at an early age, gave Manipuri literature some of its most remarkable poems and novels. Of his works, Shingel Indu stands out along with Khamba Thoibi Seireng (Khamba Thoibi Poem), his magnum opus. His lone novel Jahera has continued to exercise a grip on the minds of the people till today. Based on a love story between a Muslim girl and a Meetei boy, it has remained popular. This is a reflection of the existing cultural distance in terms of conjugal relationship between the Meeteis and the Meetei Pangals (Muslims). This is the sociotextual reading of a tradition in the literature. His plays Thabal Chongbi, Nimai Sanyas, Ibemma and Poktabi performed by the Manipur Dramatic Union made him a rare genius gifted with great literary skill and imagination. Other literary figures like Hawaibam Nabadwipchandra, Asangbam Minaketan and R. K. Shitaljit made significant impact on the Manipuri literary landscape.

The Unsung Giant of Manipuri Literature: Hijam Irabot emerged as a towering personality whose overarching presence was felt in almost all aspects of life and consciousness in contemporary Manipur. His radical vision and activities left an indelible mark in the collective psyche of the Manipuris. Apart from being the most charismatic and visionary leader in contemporary political history of Manipur, his contribution to

Manipuri literature has been immense. A pervasive legacy of marginalising and obscuring this great personality from the Manipuri mainstream consciousness in the interest of the prevailing power structures-from the colonial and feudal period till today-can be seen clearly. Hailed as the first truly modern poet of Manipur, many of his works were published posthumously. Some have not been published till today.

A pioneer in different spheres of life, Irabot was the first to start a literary journal in Manipuri. Titled Meitei Chanu (Meitei woman), the first volume appeared in 1922 with contributions from great poets like Kamal. His early work titled Seidam Seireng (1924), a collection of poems, was prescribed as a text for schools in Manipur. He wrote the first travelogue in Manipuri titled Mandalay Khongchat (A journey to Mandalay). As a radical revolutionary leader spearheading organised resistance against feudalism and the British imperialism, he steadfastly refused to be daunted by imprisonment, deportation, banishment and exile.

An interface between Irabot and history took place during his imprisonment in Sylhet Jail (now in Bangladesh) in 1941.8 It resulted in the production of some of the finest poems in Manipuri literature. Titled Imagi Pujah (The Worship of Mother), the poems Irabot wrote during his imprisonment in Sylhet were published posthumously only in 1987. A first glance at these poems immediately strikes the reader with its profound engagement with varied themes like identity, nationhood, patriotism, struggle against injustice, emancipation of the exploited, etc. His poems in this collection (Imagi Pujah) attempt to capture a historical picture of Manipur since the pre-colonial era to the grim realities of contemporary Manipur. A commonly held view amongst critics of Manipuri literature is that if Irabot's poetry were published during the colonial period, those would have made substantive impact on the revolutionary politics of the day.

Post World War II Manipuri literature saw a new trend with playwrights like Haobam Tomba and Sarangthem Bormani drawing deeply on the rich ballads and legends of Moirang. Tama Salon Saphaba, Pidonnu, Thainagi Leirang, Sajik Thaba and Thaja Thaba by Tomba, and Kege Lamja, Tonnu Laijinglembi, Nura Santhalembi and Haorang Leisang Saphabi by Bormani are notable works. G. C. Tongbra's plays created ripples in the literary landscape. With his first published work Mani Mamou, he went on depicting the ironies of life in its various shades and colours. A. Minaketan and R. K. Shitaljit are the new voices of post-war sensibilities in Manipuri poetry.

The rapidly changing political configurations in the post-Second World War era vis-à-vis the swelling tide of decolonisation marks a new signpost in Manipur's history, too. The British Union Jack was replaced with the Manipuri national flag in 1947 at Kangla, the historical seat of power in Manipur, marking the end of colonial rule and the beginning of a free independent Manipur. But this ancient Asiatic Kingdom newly transformed into a democratic political structure in the post-colonial period was 'merged' with the newly independent State of India on the 15th October, 1949 in pursuance of the Treaty of

Accession. This crucial encounter with India has produced highly conflicting tendencies in terms of explicit moves to impose a homogenising framework operating at every level of existence-social, political, cultural, legal, economic, etc.

New Theme Song: Hegemony and Resistance: Contest at the political level with the emergence of armed resistance movements fighting against the 'merger' with India has created the articulation of a conflict at various levels of existence. Elangbam Nilakanta's first published poem 'Manipur' (1949) raises fundamental questions that foretell the shape of things to come:

> O Mother Manipur, one day your children will trace you

> Like Dushyanta with eyes bathed in tears,

> But by that time where shall they find you?

> *Where shall they find you?*

Intensification of armed struggle in Manipur has made profound impact on contemporary literature. Poetry has plunged deep into this conflict and notable poets like Laishram Samarendra, Yumlembam Ibomcha, Thangjam Ibopishak, and Shri Biren explore the sordid reality, informed, shaped and distorted by the conflict. Ibopishak's collection of poems Apaiba Thawai (The Wandering Soul) (1969) has been hailed by critics as a trendsetter for a new wave of poetry that grapples with the rising tide of conflicts emerging from the crucial encounter in 1949. A growing sense of dissent and anger at the degeneration in society can be discerned clearly. Shri Biren's Asibagi Lamdamda (In the Land of Death) aptly captures the decadence that has eroded the social fabric. Yumlembam Ibomcha's Shingnaba (The Challenge) (1974) documents the extreme note of anger in contemporary Manipuri society. R. K. Bhubhansana's 'Marup Ani' (Two friends) in his collection titled Mei Mamgera Budhi Mamgera (Whether the Light is out or the Mind is) expresses the stark and sordid reality of life under the draconian laws like the Armed Forces (Special Powers) Act, 1958.

Women poets have attempted to scrutinise contemporary life and society in a radical tone. Questions of identity, freedom and status figure prominently in many of these poets whose female sensibilities offer another dimension of social analysis and critique. Memchoubi's Androgi Mei (The Fire of Andro), Borkanya's Mongphamgi Meenok (Laughter of the Grave) and Pukhrambam Urmila's Ashibagi Marakta (In the Midst of the Dead) are notable works that capture the stark social realities. Different genres like drama, novel and short story share similar concerns. In theatre, mention can be made of writers like Arambam Somorendra, Brajachand Khundrakpam, and Kanhailal, whose literary engagements are shot through with stark social realities. In novels, mention can be made of writers like M. K. Binodini, Aribam Chitreshwar, Elangbam Sonamani, Aramban Biren, Loitongbam Pacha Meitei, B. M. Maishnamba, Hijam Guna and M. Borkanya. The short story has emerged as a powerful mode of literary expression with writers like M. K. Binodini, N. Kunjamohon, Khumanthem Prakash, Shri Biren, Hijam Guno and others.

A more detailed study and analysis of Manipuri literature can provide crucial insights of the several shifts in the socio-political history of Manipur. Assuaging as analytical framework through the contours of Manipuri literature through the ages, one indeed feels the need to address crucial debates on the society's attempt to come to terms with the new changes that we witness today.

Contemporary Literature

The pre-war literature was composed in metrical form which restricted the poets' choice of words and rhythm. They depended for their themes and sources upon the lores of Manipur, glory of the rulers and Hindu epics. There was a deep faith among them in Vaishnava philosophy and aesthetics as practised in Manipur. Their writings have points in common with traditional Sanskrit culture. The general trend was spiritual rather than secular. On the other hand, the modern writers have given up many time honoured conventions. They came in contact with the varied stands of English literature which is rich in all respect.

They have learnt new forms with pleasure and zeal. Modern writers are well equipped with the art of painting. Varieties of Manipuri literature began to be produced very rapidly in a different atmosphere. Post-independence literature is becoming regional in form and content rather than national. They are not so much concerned with their problems of community literally cut off from the rest of the world by a difficult communication system and of their small number.

Manipuri Sahitya Parishad which has completed its 49 years of active existence is trying to make Manipuri literature up-to-date through collection of old books, publishing books, organising annual sessions in different places and conferring suitable titles on the artists of traditional Manipuri School. Among other institutions are Naharol Sahitya Sabga, Naharol Sahitya Samiti, Premi Samiti, Cultural Forum, Astrological Society, Universal Literary Association, etc., all of them have rendered significant service to the Manipuri language and literature.

The Manipur Students Union is an association of Manipuri young students who live in the state. The tradition of heroic deeds, chivalry and distinctive culture has developed strong regional consciousness in them. The sacred land and its history remain a source of inspiration to the young Meitei mind. The members have taken up arms against any humiliation, to do within their power by strikes, agitations and propaganda, to restore.

Manipur's ancient glory, to include Manipuri language in the 8th Schedule of Indian Constitution, to recognise it as a subject in Manipur Public Service Examination and to continue research work in this language. They impress in the mind of Manipuris an interest in treating Manipur as the land of the ancient people and expelling new comers by an Act of the State. The resultant effects of their efforts have been the measures adopted by the state in these demands.

Manipuri literature has the credit of receiving recognition of the Sahitya Akademy almost every year. Some of the Manipuri writers have been awarded the Akademy's prizes though the traditions of pre-War output have not been kept in the same spirit in there fields.

Prose

The post-independence era has given a brilliant batch of young essayist and critics. Most of them are college and university lecturers, who are in touch with Manipuri modern literature. But none of them has made a critical and serious study of old manuscripts and texts. They have yet to write books and submit research papers on different aspects of literary progress and essays.

Journalism in Manipuri language is popular. There are thirty daily papers, two English weekly papers, numerous fortnightly and monthly papers/magazines. Manipuri language, at given at the outset, is the state language. Its script is also recognised by the government for teaching.

The publication of Manipuri magazine has considerably increased. Publication of Manipuri Government's Angangsingi Numit (Children day on November 14), Manipur (fortnightly) from the Director of Information and Public Relations, Bulletins of different Government Departments and souvenirs of many literary organisations are noteworthy. The important names in all these magazines include Matarngi Khongt hang published by the United Literary Association, Lamlong Bazar, Yeningtha published by Young Writers' Forum, Imphal. They have been successful in creating taste for Manipuri magazines in the intelligentsia.

As far as the prospect of Manipuri literature is concerned, there are better hopes. With the spread of literacy, production of research degree holders, study of old Meitei Puranas through the culture of Meitei script by different sections, better conditions for writers and scholars through the patronage and cooperation of ministers will put Manipuri literature on the path of progress.

Poetry

Post independent Manipuri poetry is negligible. The poets and writers have no Sadhna. There have been Manipuri translations of Meghanad Bodh Kavya, Gitanjali, Meghaduta, Raghuvamsa, Rape of Lucreces, Kumar Sambhava, etc. Daily papers with their supplements, magazines of different types in Manipur encourage new creative writers and accelerate the new course of literature.

In the realm of novels, it may be mentioned that the first and foremost Dr. Kamal's Madhabi, a romantic realistic social novel in the Thirties of the present century is a commendable piece of literature. It depicts the sacrifice of an unsophisticated girl, Madhabi, who inspired the people by the ideals of self negation. The author becomes more prolific in the novel than in the poems. Kh. Chaoba's La-ban ga-Lata gives a picture of the romantic love themes of Labanga, a young soldier and Kunjalata, the princes. It gives the pomp and grandeur of the court in the time of Khagemba (1597-1652).

Jahera by H. Anganghal is on the theme of the love between a Manipuri Hindu youngman called *Kunjo* and a Muslim girl called *Jahera*. Short story as a distinct literary form is hardly fifty years old in Manipur. Rajkumar shitaljit Singh is regarded as the pioneer of short-story writer in Manipuri literature. In the Forties of this century two volumes, namely Leikonungda and Leinun gshi were published by him. He has also to his credit a number of novels like Thadokpa, and Ima Rohini. Now we 'have the numerous important novelists and short-story writers but they have not achieved a degree of success. Attempts are being made to introduce English, Bengali, Hindi and Russian works to Manipuri readers of the present generation.

Drama

The dramatists came out as drama writers first and actors afterwards. Dramas which need particular mention are Nar Singh written by L. Ibungohal, Sati Khongnang and Sh. Areppa Marup of S. Lalit, Mairang Thoibi of A. Dorendrajit, Sh. Mainu Pemcha of A. Shyamsundar, Kege Lamia of S. Bormani Singh, Bir Tikendrajit of M. Bir Singh and Kabai Keioiba by A. Jai Singh. The most respected contemporary playwright writer is G. C. Tongbra with his thirty one plays and some one act plays.

With the development of radio plays, theatre-Yatra competition and film industry scripts for new types of creations have been written or rewritten. It is obvious to name a few of them to the exclusion of others.

8

Economy

- -

In the absence of basic minerals, the economy and society of Manipur is agrarian in character. While the people of the plain area are practising intensive-subsistence agriculture, those of the hills and mountains have a primitive economic base. Their economic activity is primitive subsistence activity which entails a quality of life at its most basic level and provides for only primary human needs, i.e., food, clothing and shelter. The hill-men are largely dependent on primitive gathering, primitive hunting, primitive herding and primitive agriculture.

The *Jhumias* (shifting cultivators) consume most of the food they harvest and surplus if any is taken to the nearby villages where small markets are held at given time intervals. The Jhumias barter or sell their limited produce in order to obtain other items they need. Thus the economic life and in order to obtain other items they need. Thus, the economic life and the life style of the people of the hills of Manipur is very simple and least affected by modernism and urban mode of life. These people dependent on primary activities are living at a poor standard of nutrition and poor standard of living. The growing number of these people is accentuating the problem of unemployment, poverty, undernourishment and malnutrition.

Industry

Manipur is underdeveloped so far as the industries are concerned. Industries provide employment to about 10 per cent of the total workforce. Industries in Manipur are not growing at a faster pace owing to lack of finance and infrastructural facilities. The lack of entrepreneurship is also a barrier in the development of industries in the state.

A majority of the urban population take up small scale and household industries. The age old industries in Manipur which deserve emphasis are: (i) weaving and dyeing, (ii) work in cane, (iii) work in wood, (iv) blacksmithy and (v) pottery.

- *Weaving and Dyeing:* The Manipur Spinning Mills in Imphal are the modern factories. Apart from this there are numerous handloom units. Handloom is the dominant industry in Manipur. There are about three lakh looms and equal number of persons, especially females are employed on it. Manipuris have traditional skill is weaving. The weaving specimen from the plain areas and the hilly tracts comprise a wide range and number which display themselves as pieces of precious art treasures showing in respect of designing and processing, an accomplishment of great measure. The distinctive costumes, dresses, scarfs and apparels comprise wrappers, skirts, aprons, Lungis and bed-sheets resplendent with skilful colour combination in their own fashion and design. In the weaving practices and processing, variations are noted from region to region.

Weaving is still the dominant undertaking as the Meities Kukis and Nagas rely for a great portion of their daily dress upon their own weaving works, particularly womenfolk. In the plain areas of Manipur, the dress materials have further been supplemented by factory made fabrics. The Manipuri Shawls, bags, aprons and bed-sheets with especial textures and designs are highly valued and have found great demand in the large cities like Calcutta, Delhi, Bombay and Kanpur. The Manipuri cloths are however, slightly expensive owing to the laborious processing and the difficulties caused by the shortage of yarn.

The superior Meitei and Naga shawls are woven of yarn. The shawls have soothing colours and designs. Weaving in the villages is entirely confined to the womenfolk who, besides shouldering the domestic and cultivation works, weave their apparels and cloths. The tradition of weaving is being handed from mother to daughter. Cotton, silk, and jute-fibres are woven into cloths. Superior yarn is imported for finer textures of cloths. In the urban areas, especially that of the Valley of Manipur weaving has been modernised by the efforts of the State Government and professional weavers. Consequently, they are producing modern designs of shawls, skirts, bags, neckties, table cloths, bed-covers, curtains, and handbags which have had a great deal of demand outside the state.

Manipuri weavers have great aesthetic sense for colour combinations. They have several traditional and modern techniques of dyeing. Dyes are generally, prepared from indigo, cultivated, especially in their homestead gardens, but also from tubers, sappers, leaves and plants. At present chemical dyes have supplemented those procured locally. In dyeing process, the common system is boiling the yarn or cloth or hair/wool meant for dyeing which gives lasting colouring but variation in the process occur from place to place.

Sericulture is becoming increasingly popular in the state of Manipur. The development of sericulture will help in promoting the silk-textiles which is traditionally weaved in Manipur. The Department of Agriculture of the state of Manipur has established research centres of sericulture in the vicinity of Imphal.

Wood Work

The Meities, Kukis, Nagas and all the other hill tribes are pretty skilful in woodwork. Bamboo and cane are plentiful in Manipur especially on the undulating slopes and mountainous areas. The cane and bamboo are used as the raw materials in woodwork. Picturesque cane crafts comprising bowls, mugs and containers with multi-coloured engravings on them are made by the Manipur people. Other varieties such as fillets as part of ornamentation have elaborately have worked out design. Cane helmets and hat frames are prepared in numerous shapes and designs. Mats woven of cane strings with fine textures have decorative value.

Numerous varieties of baskets with different shapes and sizes, used for different purposes — as containers for crops and other household goods are prepared. Baskets are also made to carry luggage and merchandise. Cane ornaments such as head-bands, bangles, leg-guards, and table-pads constitute another model of workmanship.

A large number of articles are also made with wood. Timber has multifarious use. Tree trunks serve as poles, pillars, battens and cross-beams for house construction. The most exquisite manufactures out of wood are dishes, sancers, platters, cups and other utensils which exhibit in their own fashion a splendid workmanship. A wooden cup may have cane-hanks. Mortars for pounding rice are scopped out.

In Manipur, wood carving has more artistic than commercial value. Dolls, statues and tobacco pipes of different shapes and size are prepared from special woods. Various types of furniture are also prepared for the domestic and commercial use.

Smithery and Ironwork

Manipur is deficient in iron-ore and coal. Consequently, development of iron and steel industry is not possible in the state. The local ironsmiths have small scale smitheries from the time immemorial to prepare tools and equipments for the hunters and cultivators. Local forages where certain agricultural tools and ceremonial weapons made are found in almost each village of Manipur. The ironsmiths manufacture tools like spears, axe, knives, Dacs with primitive and indigenous techniques. Now the cultivators and villagers have started purchasing of their tools from outside of the state which are much cheap. It is, however, interesting to note that at present even the village blacksmiths have started making use of springs and other mechanical devices in place of the old piston bellows for supply of air to the forges.

Pottery

Making of pots from clay and especially prepared silts is widely practised in most of the villages of the plains of Manipur. The clay found around the Lake Loktake is soft and smooth which is used for pottery. It is believed that with some especial treatment this clay may be used for ceramics.

Pots are made in different sizes and shapes. Some of the handmade wares which serve as containers of are especially designed. The potters prefer red and black colours for their pots. Looking at the resource bare of Manipur, the major thrust of the industrial development of Manipur might be on the following industries:

Mineral based Industries

Small scale mining of chromite, limestone, evaporate and asbestos in this area needs to be encouraged for making available commodities which are rather scare in the region. Small scale mining may be the only practicable way of exploiting there deposits by virtue of their shape, size and mode of occurrence. There deposits may be worked as open cart, quarries.

In the case of chromite deposits, prospecting at deeper level is necessary to prove actual and total reserves of the ore. Field evidences such as, mode of occurrence of the deposit indicated the possibility of huge chromite deposits at deeper level which would be proved only by deep exploratory drilling and, therefore, there is scope of underground development and open cast mining of this deposit simultaneously, thus increasing the production figure. The opening and development of small mines will lead to a better understanding of the geology of the area, leading to the development of larger mines.

The correct evaluation of quality and quantity of limestone and asbestos deposits of the area is further necessary which is vital far mining and quality control within reasonable cost and time.

Mineral Benefication and Smelting

The low output from small scale mines will not justify the cost of installation of a concentrator or smelter until they are transformed into large mines in due course of time through subsequent discovery of larger deposits and larger mining output.

Cement Industry

The limestone contains very low magnesia (less than 1 per cent) and is suitable for manufacture of cement. All limestone deposits of the area taken together will be able to sustain a cement plant of modest capacity of 400 tonnes a day for about 45 years. They are suitable for the manufacture of both Puzzolana and Portland cements. Pozzolana cement will be suitable as non-staining cement for laying tiles. An industry for the manufacture of asbestos cement can also be established to make use of this deposit in the area.

Salt Industry

As a number of salt springs occur in the state of Manipur, the spring water may be utilised for the manufacture of salt-cakes. Common salt may also be manufactured on large commercial scale.

Textile and Spinning Fibres

The asbestos found in Manipur has good flexibility, silkness and excellent spinnability with its good fibre length over 1.8 cm. Therefore, opening of textile industry manufacturing asbestos fibres can also be visualised in this state. Manipur Spinning Mill can use there asbestos fibres.

Ceramic Industry

Clay deposits are found in Tipan group of rocks of the area which can be utilised in pottery and glass industries. Cobalt which is associated with chromite deposits of the area will serve as pigment in such ceramic industries. Nickel is used in electroplating.

Chemical and Fertilizer Industries

Alkali and Bleaching Powder for water purification and sugar refining should be manufactured by utilising the sufficient reserves of limestones. Other chemicals such as chromates, bichromates of sodium and potassium, chromium pigments like chromic oxide and chromic acid, for use in chromium plating pigment in ceramic and glass industries, may be manufactured with the availability of chromite deposit in the area. The limestone can be further used for the production of caustic soda, soda-ash and in the manufacture of calcium ammonium nitrate fertilizer (nitrolime fertilizer).

Refractory Bricks

Chromite is associated with magnesia and alumina and it can be used as refractory bricks.

Hydroelectric Industry

The undulating terrain of Manipur and the turbulent streams flowing in the hilly districts of Manipur hold a good promise for hydro-potential. The feasibility study of a 934 m long 56 m high dam under Thoubal Project is under active study by Geological Survey of India. On completion, this is likely to generate 500 KW of hydroelectricity.

Khandsari Sugar Factory at Wangbal and Television Assembling Units at Imphal are the growing industries of Manipur. In the small scale sector there are 5,970 units with approximately 24,000 persons employed in it. Other minor enterprises comprise ivory, horn and bone work practised on small domestic scale. The tribal peoples of the hilly areas make beads of seeds, and from ivory, they make out designs such as bracelets and wristlets and other ornamental decorations are moulded. Bone is forged into several ornamental design. In addition to these there are rice-mills, motor workshops, furniture workshops, bakeries, printing press, repairs of motor vehicles, paper and soap making.

The Government of Manipur has set up a number of Industrial Cooperatives to promote weaving, carpentry, black smithy, ivory, and other small scale and cottage industries. Among other schemes for the promotion of the industries the government has taken several steps among which the following are worth mentioning: (i) Extension of assistance in carpentry, black smithy and sheet metal smithy (ii) Setting up of more black smithy units to cater to the production of agricultural tools, (iii) expansion of assistance in the pottery, Gur-making, soap and Candle making and hand-pounding, etc. (iv) making of moulded plastic articles.

To accelerate production rates, it has been decided to display exhibitions in the various parts of the state in different month of the year. During these exhibitions the local craft men are given national awards and certificates of merit for their artifacts. There are several factors which are coming in the way of proper and judicious exploitation and utilisation of minerals and other natural resources in Manipur State.

Lack of Pragmatic Planning

Owing to the state bureaucratic bottlenecks, the prospective researches are not encouraged and helped with necessary financial incentives to undertake geological investigations and prepare projects and advance plans which can eliminate many future operational problems.

Transport and Communication Problem

Mineral deposits are located in difficult terrains in the areas with little infrastructure regarding transport and communication. The transportation of minerals will be one of the major problems due to poor road conditions and prevailing landslide problems.

Water Supply Problem

Lack of sufficient water supply is a major constraint in introducing mining and mineral based industries.

Electricity and Power

The area suffers very much owing to the inadequate supply of electricity which again hampers the industrial prospects. The forest, water and agricultural resource base of Manipur is fairly rich. In the absence of basic minerals and coal, there should be concerted efforts to promote the small scale industries in the state. The Small Scale Industries generate more employment with low capital cost. It had been estimated that capital requirement for employing one person in Khadi and Village Industries was Rs. 1,000; for small industry Rs. 5,000; for heavy electrical goods Rs. 50,000 and for Iron and steel Industry Rs. 160,000. With the lapse of time and increase in prices of inputs, there figures might become double and triple.

The major thrust in the industrial development therefore should be on small scale industries in Manipur. Small scale and cottage industries can be established in the initial stage without separate building for factory, a large contingent of hired labour, and sophisticated high priced machinery. It is, therefore, ideal for unemployed youth to start small enterprises with small financial assistance for banks and government.

As stated at the outset in Manipur rearly 80 per cent of the total population lives in the rural areas and over 80 per cent of the workforce is engaged in agriculture. In such a situation development and expansion of the secondary sector of economy must be related to agriculture and allied activities. Thus, if the base of industrial sector is to be broadened, we should give more emphasis on expansion and modernisation of agriculture by encouraging use of manufacturing agricultural inputs, viz., chemical fertilizers, pesticides, improved implements and to develop small and middle size industrial units in the Eural and semi-urban areas.

In this context, priority should be given to processing of agriculture and local raw materials (forests and livestock). In addition, in certain centres adjacent to rural areas, some of the agricultural inputs (mixed fertilizers, repair workshop, etc.) and items required for everyday use (baskets, utensils, paper, rope, nails, etc.) are produced, it will benefit rural people and ensure substantial income to producers. In semi-urban and urban centres there are great potentialities for repairing shop, garage, furniture making, engineers tools, building materials, implements, plastic goods.

Although the Government of Manipur has been giving considerable attention and assistance to small scale industries by giving subsidies and concessions in the case of transport, purchase of raw materials, provision of credit from banks, the efforts have not yielded desired results.

Small Scale Industry Facing Problems

The most important problem facing small scale industries is the rocketing of their products. In the small sector a large number of commodities can be produced in widely separated parts of the state. But a small producers with his small quantity of surplus can not arrange even despatch of his products, not to speak of arranging sale on remunerative prices in the face of goods from large factories. Hence, it is necessary to have some organisation to collect surplus products from producer to store them near marketing centres and sell them quickly. Since an organisation can also insist on quality, guide to producers to produce the desired goods and train them to improve the existing policies of production, it will be difficult to have such a set up or organisation in each village; it will be better to have some production organisation for a group of industries. In selected centres within 15 to 20 villages, it may be advisable to start certain units by employing local artisans and craftsmen under the supervision of technicians. It will then be possible to improve quality and to sell the products easily. Assistance should also be rendered to artisans and craftsmen to procure raw materials, tools and implements; to introduce new designs and also guide them to adopt improved techniques of production. Such assistance should be rendered to household, cottage and small scale industries.

Where there is a scope to process or produce goods in small sector industries locally, the members or produce goods in small sector industries locally, the members should be encouraged and helped. For instance for setting up husking machines for paddy, small flour mills, printing presses, manufacture of tools, implements, utensils, furniture making, soap making, tailoring, book binding, production of office stationery and such other items will need some machinery, factory-shed, skilled labour and initial working capital. Capital needed for small purposed is not big and can be procured if financial institutions are sympathetic. The government and the commercial banks should come forward to assist small enterprises. Where there is scope, particularly in semi-urban and newly emerging towns, these enterprises should be encouraged and their products will have easy market.

So far as the technological aspect is concerned, improvement must be aim at production of goods of basic necessities at the lowest cost. Because of the increased number of unemployed and underemployed, it may not be possible to go in for capital intensive technology. But nevertheless there is scope for adoption of low valued simple machine to improve efficiency of production. Research is also necessary to evaluate market potentiality in the neighbourhood, within the state, in the country and abroad. To promote the trade of small scale industries products publicity, advertisement, exhibitions and display should be arranged.

Training facilities for persons engaged in cottage and small scale industries at various levels are also very necessary. The pace of setting up of small scale industries in Manipur, however, has not been very satisfactory.

In Manipur, the Small Scale and Cottage Industries have large potential for generating employment. Vigorous efforts have become necessary to develop and expand small scale and cottage industries. If it is not done now, the unemployment and underemployment will make the problem of poverty and hunger more acute. During the last three decades a large number of institutions have been established. A thorough review of work of these institutions is necessary to suggest more pragmatic approach and remedial measures to utilise in the small scale industries.

Business and Trade

Prior to the British advent big the end of the 19th century, barter played a dominant role in the local economy. The system was primitive and prevailed mainly among the neighbouring tribes. Its anomaly was that necessity and not value determined the price of a commodity. Merchandise comprising woven goods, yarn, cloth, livestock, foodgrains, agricultural implements, household furniture and household furniture were interchanged in a community.

Barter is still prevalent in the remote and isolated villages which have no regular means of communication with the towns and administrative centres. It is still conducted side by side with currency in the villages of the Manipur Valley. In the urban areas, regular trade in terms of currency and the present metric standards of weights and measures have replaced barter totally.

It was the Japanese invasion during the Second World War which brought another landmark in the trade history of Manipur. With the invasion by the great Japanese power, was gone an age-long splendid isolation of the territory of Manipur. The whole subcontinent became was shaken by the invasion of Japanese into the Valley of Brahmaputra. Troops from all over India and the other parts of the world poused in with the troops came the supplies, weapons and machines. It brought new tastes, new fashion, new style and new behaviour patterns quickly among the 'local people of Manipur. Meiteis and Naga dolls, toys, spears Daos, costumes easily found exit through the soldiers to the different parts of the world. Demand increased of the local building materials and manufactures.

Suppliers who amassed fortune during the war became noted businessmen. Even labourers got new ideas by coming into contact with the advanced technology. After the war electric power projects and piped water supplies were introduced in the valley of Manipur. Business became more brisk and trade was grew in proportions. These factors coupled with the multifarious developmental projects in agricultural, industrial, transport, building and other spheres have set about more patterns of economic activities. Almost all industrial activities are concentrated in Imphal and its suburbs.

The main articles and commodities of export from the state of Manipur are timber, bamboo, forest products, gum, lac, spices, sesamum (Til), ginger, mustard, cloths, shawls, bed-covers, bamboo-works, bags, honey, toys, dolls and articles of decoration.

Imports are much more varied which comprises of machinery, electric goods, foodstuffs, drugs, medicines, textile goods, utensils, furniture, salt, minerals, petroleum, Kerosene, chemicals, motor vehicles and electronic goods.

Village Economy

The people of the Manipur Valley have the typical forms of intensive subsistence agriculture. This intensive use of land produces relatively large yields per acre, but frequently little surplus occurs because of the vast food needs of the domestic population that is supported by agricultural system.

The introduction of high yielding varieties of seeds, modern irrigation practices, chemical fertilizers, insecticide and technology have enhanced the per unit production of the farmers of the Valley of Manipur. The standard of living of the intensive subsistent farmers in relatively high and one may observe a transformation in their agricultural and social landscapes.

The secondary and tertiary sectors in Manipur are weak, providing employment to only about 22 per cent of the total workforce. The underdevelopment of industries is a cause of concern as it is not absorbing more people from the primary sector.

Agriculture

Manipur is essentially an agrarian state and the population is mostly rural in character. Cultivation of crops is the dominant economic activity in Manipur. The agricultural sector employed more than 50 per cent of the total working population with agricultural labour constituting 8 per cent. Estimates of state domestic income reveal that 48 to 59 per cent of the state income was derived from the primary sector. The disparity between the size of employment in agriculture and its relatively smaller contribution to state income may also be observed.

Nearly 92 per cent of the total land area is hilly and covered with forests. Reserve forest area covers 1,377 sq km while the protected forests spread in 4,171 sq km. The state has made significant advancement in the field of agriculture. Per acre consumption of fertilizer has reached 56 kg. Coverage under High Yielding Varieties has reached 70 per cent of the cropped area. The agricultural systems of Manipur may be broadly classified into: (i) sedentary subsistence agriculture, (ii) shifting cultivation. The Manipur valley consisting of about only ten per cent of the total geographical area of the state is characterised by subsistence agriculture. The farmers grow two to three cereal crops from the same field. The development of irrigation facilities have helped in the intensification of agriculture. Rice is the dominant crop of the Valley of Manipur followed by maize, pulses, oilseeds, sugarcane, vegetables and potatoes. The agricultural techniques are primitive. The High yielding varieties of rice and maize have been diffused in the fertile valley areas of Manipur. The per unit production of rice is appreciably high in the alluvial tracts, especially around Imphal.

Shifting Cultivation

Shifting cultivation, locally known as Jhuming represents the first endeavour of people to control static resources, that is, the bounty of the land. Agriculture, more than any of the economic activities is largely influenced by the natural environment and technological innovations and application of capital and energy. Jhuming is called primitive because if manifests only rudimentary technical management of the land, and limited amounts of time, effort, and capital are devoted to this activity.

In shifting cultivation a rudimentary technology is applied for sowing and planting. Because Jhuming is practised in he hilly areas of the hot and humid climate, the cultivators are continually confronted with the problem of clearing land from either dense forests or overgrown grasses. Trees and undergrowth are hacked out by using Div (machetes), and the vegetation is burned. Sometimes farmers dispense with the cutting and let fire alone do the job of clearing. This primitive technique is also called Slash, burn agriculture. Methods of preparing the soil are equally primitive. By using a digging stick (dibble) or a hoe, farmers simply scratch the surface of the soil at the time of sowing and planting. No other attempts are made to prepare the soil beforehand. Ploughing of fields is unknown in shifting cultivation.

The mountainous topography, undulating slopes surrounding the Manipur Valley and wet weather for over seven months (April to October) provide conditions in which people are practising shifting cultivation. The people who are scattered over the mountains depend for their sustenance on shifting cultivation and food gathering from the forest. All the five hill districts of Manipur are most sparsely populated having a density of about 15 persons per sq km as against the density of 345 persons per sq km of the Central District. The hill man has to bear with steep slope, poor soils, mosquito infested and less invigorating climate, poor means of communication and a life of isolation and relative isolation. Under such an adverse physico-sociocultural environment his life is that of a desperate struggle for survival. Consequently, he is compelled to adopt a primitive mode of cultivation on the undulating slopes of the surrounding hills of Manipur.

In the hills and mountains, the land around the village within certain fixed bounds is usually the property of the village. In the midst of sharp relief gentle slopes, if any, are used for terracing, in the absence of which, the land is put to shifting cultivation. According to prevailing custom all land adjoining the village belongs to the community and exclusive right of an individual is not accepted. Those patches of forests which are rich in humus are best suited for shifting cultivation. The site for Jhuming is selected by the village headman in advance and individual families are allotted their share. In the months of November and December slashing of trees starts. Hundreds of trees are to be cut down to clear a hectare of land.

The felling of trees is done with Dao and axe. Unfortunately, trees of high timber value which would have fetched the cultivators many times more than what he can earn cultivating the plot are destroyed in Jhuming operations. The Jhumias (shifting cultivators) on the basis of their empirical experience reveal that it is easier to cut a bamboo jungle to that of a tree-jungle. After felling the forests, the wood and twigs are allowed to dry, so that it may be fired in the month of March when the weather is sunny and overcast skies are rare. If the failed jungle has large trees, reduced to ashes. The uncontrolled fire, in many cases spreads beyond the Jhum area and does great damage to the valuable virgin forests of the region. The soil for a depth of one inch or two gets completely burnt. The soil is, thereafter, scratched up with little hoe and in this process the soil and the ash get mixed up together. The land, thus, becomes ready for the reception of seeds.

The day of sowing is considered to be a ceremonial day for the whole village. It is interesting to observe that the male members of each family on reaching the Jhum field in the morning engage themselves in preparing the digging sticks. The seeds are sown either by broadcast or by dibbling. The dibbling and planting of seeds is an exclusive job of the female members of the village. The male members broadcast seeds of crops like millets and small millets, while crops like maize, pulses, cotton, sesamum and vegetables are dibbled by the females. While dibbling the seeds, the female walk over the field with a digging stick or bill-hook in hand, make a hole in the ground, sow a few seeds and cover it over with earth by pressing it down with her toe.

At the advent of rains, the seeds begin to sprout. Thus the soil is never ploughed and no artificial irrigation is made. After sowing the crop, farmer pays cursory attention to the crop and to remove weeds from the field. The crop is, however, protected from stray cattle and wild animals by fencing the fields with bamboo. Many of the shifting cultivators construct a hut in the field to look after the crop properly.

In the fields, at regular distance apart, they place the unconsumed trunks of trees which serve as Bunds to the water which comes down the face of the hill. Thus they try to reduce soil erosion. In the event of heavy downpour, as it is usual in these mountains, the soil is carried down with running water sometimes along with seeds of standing crops. Then there is the traditional problem of soil creep and landslide which is more frequent in Manipur north, Manipur West, and Manipur south districts. In the course of two to three years the land gets devoid of soil and becomes unfit for cultivation. If the jhum field happens to be near the village settlement, the cultivator can return in the evening after a full day's work; but if it is at a considerable distance, as it often is, he must either give up work early to get back to his home before it is dark, or if working late, remain in the field in his temporary shelter.

Cropping Pattern

So far as the cropping pattern is concerned, the Jhumias adopt mixed cropping. The mixture of crops varies from tribe to tribe and from region to region owing to the prevailing geo-ecological conditions. The Jhumias grow cereals, vegetables and cash-crops mixed with each other. In fact, the grower aims at growing in his Jhum land everything that he needs for his family consumption or use. In other words, the choice of crops to be grown is consumption oriented.

Among the foodgrains the coarse varieties of rice, followed by maize, millets, job's tears and small millets are the principal crops. The cotton, ginger, linseed, rape-seeds, sesamom, pineapple and jute are the important cash crops of Jhum fields of Manipur. Among the vegetables, soya beans, pumpkins, potato, cucumbers, yams, tapioca, chillies, beans, onion, arun are cultivated. Tobacco and indigo are also grown. By and large, the cash crops are sold in the neighbouring markets or to the middlemen by which the Jhumias get cash money or commodities for family consumption.

In the mixed cropping, soil exhausting crops, e.g. rice, maize, millets, cotton, etc., and soil enriching crops, e.g. legumes, are sown together. This practice has many direct and indirect advantages. These crops harvest at different periods, thereby providing the tribes with varied food for nearly six to eight nine months in a year. The same jhum land is cropped by the community for two or three years, thereafter, the land is abandoned to recuperate. Occasionally, some residual crops are collected from the abandoned fields.

The Jhumias are quite conscious of this arduous and wasteful method of cultivation for crops. But they are tradition-bound and have no alternative source of sustenance.

Terracing of gentle slopes is an alternative but a few terraced fields cannot supply food required for the whole year. In case the ilium jas are completely prevented from practising shifting cultivation, they may face starvation.

The patches of land for shifting cultivation are not selected or cleared in any given order or sequence. There is always a room for choice. The period of consecutive cropping and fallowing differs from region to region and from tribe to tribe. We do not know after what length of time, the primitive inventor of shifting cultivation had to come back to the same plot, because he had vast areas to move about. But at present, with the increase of population and being somewhat staked down to smaller areas, a shifting cultivator has not got much choice left to shift about. His world has become small, he has to content moving about in narrow circles and the circle is getting smaller and smaller. In brief, in the earlier decades, the period before which the Jhumias returned to cultivate the same plot was quite long. This was due partly to the limited population and partly owing to the better fertility to the soil which was rested for nearly thirty to forty years. With rising population this interval has shrunk and now Jhuming cycle varies between two to eight years in the various parts of Manipur Hills.

The abandoned Jhum land remains fallow far a period of three to eight years. During this period of following, grasses, reed, bamboo, pines and numerous trees and bushes grow on the slope. The decayed plants and animals during this period add to the fertility of the soil by providing humus. The period of Jhum cycle is reduced if the land and soils are poor in fertility.

Almost all the tribes living in the hills one involved in the shifting cultivation. It is, however, more prevalent in the case of Thado in the Manipur East District. The other dominant tribes actively busy in shifting cultivation are Purum, Koireng-Chothe in Tengnoupal district, Hmar Gangte, Ralte, Paite in Manipure north district; Chiru chothe, Hmar and kacha Naga in Manipur west district. The Kabuis of Manipur west district and Maring of Tengnoupal district do practice Jhuming with some modification in the same, that their villages are fixed and they Jhum the adjoining land year after year in set rotation. However, the Kabuis round the Khoupur valley have taken to plough cultivation in the alluvial plain. Jhuming has led to soil erosion, soil exhaustion, loss of productivity, loss of valuable forests and have created numerous and geo-ecological imbalances.

The practice of shifting cultivation has been severely attacked by the ecologists, environmentalists and planned as it disturbs the ecosystems coming great ecological imbalances. There are, however, some people who support the continuance of shifting cultivation with necessary and effective reforms. They are of the opinion that it does little damage to soil in the form of erosion as the high humidity and heavy rainfall in the hills of the state does not permit the soil to remain uncovered for long.

Some farm of vegetation immediately covers the top soil which contains it from further erosion. During the agricultural operations also, as no ploughing, hoeing and pulverisation of soil is done, the soil remains compact and gets eroded by water at a slow rate. Moreover, Jhum lands are generally steep slopes on which sedentary cultivation cannot be developed easily. In fact, Jhuming is a evolved as a reflex to the physiographical character of land under the special ecosystem. It is practised for livelihood and without the knowledge of its adverse effects. The system, in spite of planning efforts, therefore cannot be transformed easily.

The Jhum lands need to be changed into terraced fields and sedentary farms. Apart from terracing, other soil conservation measures like bunding, trenching, gully plugging, etc. should be adopted according to the need of the area. Equally important is the development of protective covers, like forests or fruit trees, suitable cash crops, grasses and leguminous crops, especially on steep slopes. In short land use planning and soil management practices should be based according to land capability and land suitability.

Terraced Cultivation

Terraced cultivation in Manipur is confined to the gender slopes on either banks of the river where the long profile of the river favours the diversion of water through channels. In Manipur east district water from big rivers like Iril, Thoubal and their tributaries is diverted to channels by erecting dams with stones and logs of woods with such skill that even the modern engineering will wonder at their ingenuity.

The task of terracing the hills is quite arduous. It has however, a decided advantage over the shifting cultivation, there are large villages like Mao, Maram on the National Highway No. 39, the people of which have carved out beautiful terraces. There terraced fields are magnificently irrigated with water brought from considerable distance in channels so well aligned that every advantage is taken of any slope encountered, and awkward corners avoided or turned with admirable ingenuity. By dint of hard labour they have converted large suitable tracts into narrow, flat fields where water may remain standing for long. It is to be noted that irrigation facility is a precondition for terrace cultivation," the terraces present the expenditure of vast amount of energy and fanning ability, as well as much practical engineering skill.

All the terraced fields are invariably put to rice cultivation. In case of large plots even plough is used in preparing the fields as in Khankhoi area about eight kilometres to the northeast of Ukhrul town. In very narrow terraces in which ploughing is not possible, the field is prepared with spade involving muscle power. In the terraced fields, rice is the dominant crop. Rice, however, demands adequate irrigation in the terraced fields. In all the villages of terraced fields, there are customary laws for the distribution of water for the fields. For crops other than rice the cultivator has to practise some sort of shifting cultivation. In the same fields is to be sown year after, application of manures are done to enhance the fertility of the land. In such cases the cultivators, generally, grow maize, vegetables, potato, sweet-potato, rootcrops, cotton, chillies and tobacco. Maize, potato, sweet-potato, mustard, cotton, gingers, tobacco and chillies are the cash crops. In the year of scanty rains the rice crop fails, and failure of rice crop means dependence on maize in the absence of which hill men have to support themselves on wild yams which is available in abundance throughout the mountainous regions of Manipur.

The crops grown, however, barely suffice the needs of the hill men. Consequently, their standard of living is very low as compared to that of the people of the alluvial tracts of the Manipur valley. Owing to the inadequate infrastructural facilities in the form of assured irrigation, power supply and efficient network of means of transportation and communications the entire state, especially the hilly areas are underdeveloped.

The poor standard of living of the shifting cultivators and hillmen, however, can be appreciably improved by adopting pragmatic planning at the grass-root level. There is still a strong resource base in Manipur in the form of forests and water. There are valuable species of trees, e.g., cinnamon and bay-leaves are in abundance in the hills of the state, there are lac bearing trees. Agar (Aquilaria Agalloclia) also fetches handsome amount to the people. Rubber trees are found in abundance in all the hills of the state.

There are large tracts of timber forests along the Manipur-Burma border. In addition there are bamboo and cane forests. All these could be judiciously utilised for the benefit of the hill man. There is immense scope of plantation crops like rubber, sandalwood and tea, etc. Fruit orchards of pine apple, and orange may be developed. If all these activities are promoted in a planned manner, there is no reason why dependence on Jhuming cannot be reduced or done away with altogether.

The problem of shifting cultivations needs to be tackled in a planned manner. In order to achieve this objective cadstreal survey, soil survey, land use survey and survey of forest resources are called for immediately.

The planning Department of Manipur has laid much emphasis on the control of shifting cultivation. The problem of soil erosion has been tackled on the priority basis. It is estimated that nearly 50 to 60 thousand hectares of land are Jhumed in Manipur every year. Almost the same acreage is abandoned by the Jhumias every year. The progress of soil conservation department has been reported to be not very satisfactory. Eradication of Jhuming calls for a comprehensive plan the Jhumias in the hills are too poor to take up large scale terracing programme. There are however, many small villages in Manipur in which terracing can be done for permanent and sedentary agriculture. The river water in such a case has to be diverted for irrigation purpose. The State Government is assisting the farmers and the two districts of the state of Manipur namely, Manipur east and Manipur south have been covered by Intensive Valley Development Programme (IVDP). It is a sort of regional approach to the problem. The target during the Seventh Plan was to terrace 10,000 hectares of land.

After terracing, all the land that cannot be brought under sedentary agriculture should be devoted to horticulture and forestry. At present pineapple and orange are the main horticultural crops. The various tropical, subtropical and temperate regions fruits have been planted on different locations on the experimental basis which are thriving well and showing encouraging results.

The slops of Manipur hills have been found appreciably suitable for the plantation of tea and coffee. Tea and coffee has been experimented and given a proper organisational structure. The plantation of such economic crops will generate employment to the Jhumias and people of the hilly areas. Considering the possibilities of development of the beverage crops. It is proposed to establish a Plantation Corporation in Manipur. The main task of this corporation would be to promote plantation crops in different parts of the hilly tracts. According to official statistics (1985), about 4.25 thousand hectare has been brought under plantation, out of which about 70 per cent is under coffee and about one thousand hectare is under rubber plantation.

Sericulture is an age old practice in Manipur. Silk yarn and silk products were used to be exported to Burma and China in the olden days. In the course of time this industry was adversely affected. The sericulture and silk industry are being revived. The state, in fact, has got a tremendous potential for the development of Tasar culture. Silk farms have been established at Tadubi, Kangpakpi, Chingarel, Boljang, Thangjae, etc. Jhum lands are being increasingly brought under sericulture.

Promotion of forest based industries may also reduce the pressure on Jhum land. The Loktak Hydroelectric Power Project when completed shall provide cheap electricity to silk industry. Based an local raw material, it will be possible to establish paper, pulp, furniture, timber factories and cement industry. Such schemes will divert a sizeable population away from agriculture and minimise Jhum cultivation.

The adverse effects of Jhuming may also be minimised if not eliminated altogether by adopting a few measures like controlled Jhuming, allowing natural forests in between Jhum lands, initiating resource survey, increasing the land under terraces, promoting horticulture, sericulture, plantation agriculture and a few forest based industries.

Future of Shifting Cultivation: As stated in the preceding paras much criticism has been levelled at the shifting cultivation. The physical constraints of this system of cultivation have been amply described above. Nontheless, it is obvious that rudimentary farms have been able to sustain themselves, albeit marginally, far millenia. In brief, shifting cultivation from the agricultural point of view is not considered objectionable as well as vegetation and the fertility of the soil are restored by nature. The opinion of those who regard it as a totally destructive agricultural system under all circumstance is largely unjustified.

In spite of the unjust criticism, a very serious problem does exist today. The extremely rapid growth of population in Manipur coupled with a slow movement away from a subsistence livelihood to a money economy, has placed incredible strains on land that possesses only limited productive capability. Shifting cultivation is an extensive economic system, wherein 90 per cent of a available land should be kept in fallow to make up for the low natural soil fertility. With the rapid growth of population in Manipur, the demand for food has increased concomitantly. To produce more food, the Jhumias cultivate plots that should be left fallow for many more years. The result is a continuing destruction of soil, a condition that perpetuates low land productivity, or in some extreme cases, accounts for densification of the land. On the brighter side, in some of the villages which one well connected by metalled roads with the markets, the Jhumias are doing plantation agriculture and fetching good amounts for their families. These Jhumias have a better standard of living.

A process of modernisation encouraged by the State Government has had an ambivalent effect. This process aims to improve the quality of life of the Jhumias with the knowledge that primitive activities provide only a very precarious livelihood. Modernisation has meant the introduction of new technologies, together with the requirement that primitive people undertake to apply them. Through extension service and persuasion some Jhumias have become permanently settled.

Irrigation and Power

Seven projects have so far been taken up under major and medium irrigation programme. These projects are:

- The Loktak Multi-purpose Project,
- Thoubal Multi-purpose Project,
- Khuga Multi-purpose Project,
- The Singda Multi-purpose Project,
- Khoupum Dam,
- Imphal Barrage, and
- Sekmai Barrage Project.

The Khoupam Dam has already been completed. The Loktak Lift Irrigation, Imphal Barrage and Sekmai Barrage Projects are also being completed shortly. These seven projects on completion, will give an ultimate annual irrigation benefit of 108,900 hectares, with water supply and power component of 19 mgd and MW respectively. Annual irrigation potential to the extent of 52,700 hectares has been created and utilisation is of the order of 42,362 hectares.

Loktak Multi-Purpose Project

The Loktal multi-purpose project was envisaged towards the later half of sixties for the Ministry of Irrigation and Power of the Central Government and work on the project commenced in 1971. In fact, it was the first Hydroelectric Power Project for the state of

Manipur. With the formation of National Hydroelectric Power Corporation (NHPC), the Project was transferred to the Corporation with effect from January 1st, 1977. The Project site is situated about 39 kilometres to the south of Imphal.

The project envisages the inter-basin transfer of water from Loktak Lake to Leimatack river by diverting 58.8 cusecs of water from the Loktak Lake. Of this 42 and 16.8 cusecs will be used for power generation and lift irrigation respectively. The major components of the project are:

- A barrage 10.7 metre high with 5×10 m waterways across the Manipur river at thai to provide adequate storage of water in the Loktak Lake.

- A trans-basin water conductor system 10.29 kilometres long comprising 2.32 kilometres of open channel, 1.07 kilometre of cut and cover section, 6.61 metres of head-race tunnel, and 0.273 kilometre of pipe tunnel and thereby utilising a gross head of 312 metres.

- A surge shaft 9.15 m dia. and 60 m high.

- Three sets of penstock pipes with an average length of 1,346 m and 2,286 m. diameter.

- A generating station on the bank of Leimatak river with three generating units of 35 MW each.

- Atail race channel from the power house to Leimatak river. The installed capacity of the project is 105 MW and it will be able to generate 70 MW of firm power of 60 per cent load factor. The electricity generated will be fed to Manipur and neighbouring states of Nagaland and Assam as the present need of the state is hardly 20 MW.

The life irrigation scheme which is part of the project will enable to irrigate 23000 hectares of land in the central plain. With assured supply of water multiple cropping will be possible. A number of transmission lines will help in the electrification of the rural areas, and abundant water shall be available for the existing and future industries. Thus the processes of industrialisation and urbanisation shall be accelerated.

The project, however, could not be completed within the stipulated time. The period of construction activity was replete with a number of technical problems and challenges, demanding at all times man's ingenuity and improvisation skill as mentioned below:

- The weak geological conditions of the entire area posed numerous unforeseen problems which came in the way of timely completion of the project.

- The penstock area situated at Leimatak also posed innumerable problems owing to heavy landslides.

- The explosion of methane gas inside the tunnel also hindered the progress of the work. In January, 1975 the methane gas explosion killed sixteen workers instantaneously.

Apart from huge amount of money spent and lost of precious lives, the completion of the project took very long period. Had the persons entrusted with the geological investigation undertaken a few bearings to ascertain the nature of the underneath strata, the methane gas could have been detected, the nature of loose rock determined and most of the construction problem averted.

Even after the completion of the project a major landslide occurred in July 1983 on Laktak-Leimatak Road as a result of which a crack developed in the tunnel and the power house was shut down.

One of the limitations of the project is that it is not certain whether adequate volume of water would be available far the power house and lift irrigation all the year round. In fact, Loktak Lake is a shallow swamp and the inbuilt capacity of the lake to supply water is very limited. Moreover, the project does not include a programme of dredging of the lake to increase its water holding capacity. It is rapidly being silted up due to silt and coarse sand brought down by numerous streams which discharge their waters in the lake. The streams which discharge their waters in the lake are rain-fed.

The Loktak project has immense value and may help in transforming the rural and urban scenario at a faster pace, but it is bound to disturb the geo-ecological balance of the region. Apart from the increasing extent of siltation its effect on the environment and the present life form including fauna and flora has to be investigated, and appropriate checks and balances have to be applied. In this area is the location of the Leibul Lamjao National Game Sanctuary, noted for brown antlered deer. It has to be seen that the Loktak project does not disturb the ecosystem beyond repair and recognition.

Animal Wealth

In the state of Manipur the principal domesticated animals are cattle, buffaloes, pigs and poultry. The undulating topography of the surrounding areas of the Valley of Manipur, the warm moist to cool-moist climate for outer greater part of the year, luxuriant growth of grasses and good market for the animal products provide ideal conditions where the cattle thrive. On the undulating slopes the abundance of nutritious grasses are conducive for the keeping of cattle and development of dairying industries.

The people of the Manipur valley generally keep cows and buffaloes as the milch animals, while in the tribal areas of the mountains pigs are attended with more care. The Nagas, Mizos and Kukis have more pigs than cattle and poultry. In some of the tribal groups milk and milk products are considered as a taboo, though they relish beef and mutton. The intensively cultivated valley has hardly any place in the farm of pastures. Consequently, cows and buffaloes are kept in the house enclosures. In the hills the Nepalis rear cattle in large numbers. In the slack agricultural seasons the cattle are let loose. Elsewhere a porch during the rainy season serves as a cow shed. There are about cattle pigs in the state.

Poultry keeping is a common practice in Manipur. The people, however, do not raise special pens for poultry birds but keep them inside the house. Herds of sheep have been observed grazing along the grasslands of the Kohima-Imphal National Highway Number 39. The sheep are, however, weak and less sturdy owing to the warm and moist climate of Manipur.

Good breeds of cows like Hereford, Friesians and Australian have been diffused in the valley by the State Government. Animal husbandry has been taken up in almost all the upgrading farms located in and around Imphal. Special fodder plants have been grown and steps have been taken to increase the daily dairying capacity. The state of Manipur has immense swipe for the development of cattle, pigs and poultry.

Forests

Total area under forest cover is 17,384 sq km of which 1,467 sq km fall under reserved forests while 4,171 sq km is protected forest and 11,746 sq km are unclassified forests. Siroy village in Ukhrul district, Manipur is the abode of *Shiroy Lily (Lilium Macklineae)*, the paradise flower which, is not found elsewhere in the world. The Dzuko valley is the only habitat of the endemic and the rarest species *Dzuko Lily (Lilium Chitrangadae).* The state is also the only home of the Brow-Antlered Deer *(Cervus-eldi-eldi)* locally known as *Sangai* surviving in its natural habitat, the Keibul Lamjao, the only floating National Park in the world.

9

Polity

Manipur enjoyed independence right up to the first two decades of the nineteenth century, except during the brief period of Burmese occupation between 1819 and 1826. In 1826, Raja Gambhir Singh liberated Manipur from the Burmese, but in the process he took help of the British, and Manipur had to pay the price of it, it now had to work under British suzerainty.

After the memorable uprising of 1891, it came under British paramountcy, and functioned as such as a princely state. Within this political paramountcy, the administrative, executive, policy-making and judicial functions were performed by a new institution known as the durbar from 1907 to 1947. For the first two years the Maharaja functioned as the President of the durbar but in 1916 the Raja vacated the post of the president in favour of an English ICS, though he continued to be responsible for the administration of the state assisted by the durbar. When democratic stirrings had been taking place in the princely states in different parts of the country, the states people's conference had been launched and Manipur could not remain unaffected for long. The Raja announced the formation of a Constitution-making body in December, 1946; this led to the Manipur State Constitution Act, 1947 and the Manipur Hill People (Administration) Regulation Act, 1947. The Maharaja inaugurated an Interim Council on August 14, 1947 with a Chief Minister (Younger brother of the Maharaja), four ministers from plains and two from the hills.

The state of Manipur merged with India on October 15, 1949. The Manipur State Legislative Assembly and the Council of Ministers were dissolved and Manipur became a Chief Commissioner's Province.

Under the Constitution of the Indian Republic (1950) Manipur was initially placed in category 'C' of states. An Advisory Council was formed in 1950 to advise the Administrator. Manipur was made an Union territory on November 1, 1956. In consequence thereof, the Advisory Council was replaced by a Territorial Council composed of thirty elected and two nominated members early in 1957. Later, under the Government of India Territorial Act, 1963, a Legislative Assembly consisting of thirty elected and three nominated members, was established. On December 19,1969 the status of the Administrator was raised from Chief Commissioner to that of Lieutenant Governor. Manipur became a full-fledged state on January 21, 1972 as a result of the Northeastern Areas (Regulation) Act, 1971. This inaugurated a new chapter in the political history of Manipur.

The state has unicameral Legislature; the Legislative Assembly consists of sixty members of which 19 are reserved for scheduled tribes. The state has two seats for the Lok Sabha of which one is reserved for scheduled tribes. It has one seat in the Rajya Sabha. The state has a common Governor with Nagaland and a common High Court with Assam. The state is divided into 9 districts for administrative convenience. It has a fairly developed Panchayat Raj system.

Politics and Political Parties

The dawn and growth of modern political consciousness was rather slow in Manipur. Bad communication and a number of allied factors were responsible for it, and yet from 1891 to 1946 far reaching developments took place which left deep impact on the political outlook of the people of Manipur.

The period 1946-49 was specially marked by a sustained movement for responsible government launched by the state Congress. The reforms, earlier referred to, introduced by the Maharaja did not satisfy the state Congress, the Socialist Party of India (which came into existence in the state in 1947) and the CPI. Slowly the demand for responsible government widened into a demand for replacement of monarchy and later into merger of the state with the Indian union. In this movement people both in the valley and hills (specially Ukhrul area) participated.

An upshot of this period was the division of the state Congress into two, the Tompok Congress and the Tomel Congress, and thus the germ of factionalism was laid inside the Congress, a phenomena which has bedevilled it. To meet the bellicosity of the state Congress towards himself the Maharaja, floated yet another political party, Manipur Praja Shanti Seva in November 1947. A non-political body to begin with, it consisted of anti-Congress elements. It soon became a party and was used as such by the Maharaja to beat the Congress in 1948 elections held on adult suffrage. The party was both anti-Congress and anti-Communist. It was the first regional political party in Manipur after independence. It went into decline after the merger of the state with the Indian Union.

During this period in 1948 another regional political party known as the Kuki National Assembly as a party of the Kukis of Manipur was formed. The party has displayed remarkable surviving power, in as much as it is the only regional political party which survives even today.

During the period the national political parties in the state were: (i) the Indian National Congress, (ii) The Socialist Party of India, and (iii) the C.P.I. Of them Indian National Congress was the most powerful, operating both in the hills and valley, but factionalism, defections, lack of discipline and inadequate tackling of the main problems, etc., limited its functioning. Yet another may be attributed to the fact that though the party was in power in the Union Territory from 1963 to 1971, except for a brief spell, it could not extract statehood for Manipur from its own ruling party at the Centre, though Nagaland attained statehood in 1963. And yet the late sixties were a period of great upheaval in Manipur for statehood.

During this period the Socialist Party, which had become the Samyukata Socialist Party, split in the state. One section of it formed the Nationalist Socialist Democratic Party on May 1, 1966. Another section formed a local party called Manipur National Organisation on the eve of the 1972 general election. In effect both these became local regional, political organisations.

Though at the popular level the merger of Manipur with the Indian Union was taken for granted, yet there were elements who based themselves on local nationalism emanating from a distinct culture and race and demanded 'independence' of Manipur. This demand was not always explicit; sometimes it was underground. Paradoxically enough there was also demand by some tribals to merge Naga areas of Manipur with Nagaland and Kuki-Lushai areas with Mizoram. During the second half of the sixties there were stirrings in both the Naga Kuki regions on this score.

Various groups and parties were advocates of independence and revivalism (both as a means of resistance to external influences, and for building a case for Manipuri sub-nationalism). Often the political concomitant to cultural revivalism tended to be an independent Manipur.

Among these groups and parties mention may be made of the following:

- Meitei Marup.
- The Manipur Cultural Association.
- The Pan-Manipur Youth League.
- The Manipur People's Convention.
- The Cultural Integration Conference.

Among the political groups mention may be made of the following:

- The Meitei State Committee.
- Revolutionary Nationalist Party.
- Pan-Mongoloid movement in the form of United National Liberation Front.

- The Naga Integrational Council.
- The Manipur National Party.
- The Manipur People's Party.
- Janata Party.
- Manipur Hill Union.
- People's Revolutionary Party of Kanglepak.
- The People's Liberation Army.
- The National Socialist Council of Nagaland.

Certain features of the parties are discernible. With the exception of the National Congress, no other party, national or regional, extends to whole of Manipur. They are confined either to the valley or to the Hills. The main opposition party, the Manipur People's Party - a party pertaining to valley, tried to extend its influence to the hills, but did not have any appreciable success. From this arises the politics of permutation and combination and resultant manipulation. For example, during and after elections in March 1972, a United Legislature Party was formed, and it succeeded in forming the Ministry. A similar United Democratic Party was formed in 1985 elections. Such combinations continue so long as chances of coming to power are there, but once this recedes they tend to join a ruling party, for which the present ULP is a case in point. Except the National Congress other national parties have only a limited following, they are national only insofar as they are branches of respective national parties.

Government and Administration

Monarchy was the form of government in early Manipur. The subjects considered their King as the regent of God. Thus early Manipur was a theocratic State. Law and religion were hardly distinguishable from each other. In those early days, the King administered his land by following a system called 'Lallup'. In this system, the entire Meitei population was divided into Pannas. The Pannas are like districts or subdivisions in a modern state. Each 'Panna' consisted of a number of families and tribes. The head of each family or tribe would select from his family or tribe the men who can render service (Lallup) to the King for and on behalf of the Panna to which they belonged.

Land revenue was a source of royal (public) income. The King also administered justice. The principles of criminal law were very severe. Cattle theft was punishable with mutilation of legs; burglary, with the mutilation of hands; giving false statement and false accusation were punishable with deprivation of the tongue; even indecency towards the Queens of King was an offence punishable with deprivation of the eyes. Before the integration of Manipur with the Indian Republic, there was a demand for the establishment of a responsible government in the state of Manipur.

Consequently, a Constitution-making body was set up. Two subcommittees were constituted. These two subcommittees drafted the Manipur State Constitution-making committee and sanctioned by the authority concerned including the Government of India.

The Manipur State Constitution Act, 1947 comprised 58 Sections. It laid down the constitutions, powers and functions of the three organs of government — Legislature, Executive and Judiciary. It also laid down the Fundamental Rights and Duties of the citizens. Under this Act, an Assembly comprising representatives returnable from general, hill and Muslim constituencies at the ratio of 30:18:3 with additional two seats for the representatives of education and commercial interests, freely elected by the people on an adult franchise and on the principle of joint electorate was established. There was a council of six Ministers who were elected by the State Assembly, but the Chief Minister was appointed by the Maharaja in consultation with the elected Ministers. But there could be no full-fledged democracy in the state of Manipur since the Chief Minister was the appointee of the Maharaja. The Manipur State Constitution Act, 1947 was never, repealed, and is supposed to remain in force.

Under the Manipur State Hill People's (Administration) Regulation, 1947, the responsibility for administration in the Hills was vested in the Maharaja in Council and exercised in accordance with the Constitution Act of the state and the provisions of this regulation. Subject to the provisions of this Regulation, the Minister of the State Council for the Hill Administration was responsible for the administration of the Hill Peoples under this Regulation. Subdivision officers, circle-officers, etc., were administrative officers on the spot; they were under the control and supervision of the Minister-in-change of Hill Administration.

The Regulation, in so far as it related to the Constitution and functions of village authorities and the administration of justice-both civil and criminal by court of village authorities was repealed by the Manipur (Village Authorities in Hill Areas) Act, 1956. The new act instals democratic elements into the constitution of the Village Authorities. The Village Authorities were earlier nominated, but they are now to be elected. The schedule to the Act lists the criminal offences triable by village court. They are petty offences under the Indian Penal Code and other enactments.

But the responsible Government established under the Manipur State Constitution Act, 1947 did not operate long. The Government constituted under this Act stood dissolved when Bodhachandra, Maharaja of Manipur signed at Shillong on 15th October, 1949, the Merger Agreement for the merger of the Manipur State with the then Indian Dominion. Article I of the Agreement of cedes the state of Manipur to the Dominion of Indian with effect from 15th October, 1949. Other articles deal with the resultant conditions. The merger of the state of Manipur to the Dominion of India is an 'Act of State'. It is more akin to a treaty entered into between two or more sovereign States. It cannot be questioned in the municipal courts.

When the Constitution of India, 1950 came into force, Manipur became a Part 'C' State and continued to be so until the state reorganisation Act 1956 was passed. The Act necessitated the amendment of the Constitution. Hence, the Constitution 7th Amendment Act, 1956 was passed and Manipur became a Union Territory, in 1963, the Government of India passed the Government of the Union Territories Act, 1963. Manipur continued to be a Union Territory till 21st January, 1972, the date on which Manipur became a State of the Indian Union under the Northeastern Areas (Reorganisation) Act, 1971.

The Governor, Shri Chintamani Panigrahi, aided and advised by the Council of Ministers is the head of the state. In the field of legislation, the state has now a 60 member Legislative Assembly. Regarding Judiciary, the Guwahati High Court is the State's High Court. Regarding the representatives in Parliament, it has two members in the Lok Sabha, and one in the Rajya Sabha. From the administrative point of view Manipur was reorganised into eight districts in 1983. The district headquarters bear the same name as the districts. The names of the districts are:

- Imphal,
- Bishanpur,
- Thoubal,
- Ukhrul,
- Senapati,
- Tamenglong,
- Churachandpur, and
- Chandel.

State Government

Imphal being the capital and the seat of the government, all the head offices of the various departments are located at Imphal. The following Heads of Departments have a vital role in the administration of the state.

- The Secretariat with the Chief Secretary to the Government of Nagaland.
- Commissioner of Taxes.
- Development Commissioner.
- Commissioner of Transport.
- Director of Education.
- Director of Agriculture.
- Director of Health Services.
- Director of Industries.

- Conservator of Forest.
- Director of Information and Publicity.
- Director of Veterinary and Animal Husbandry.
- Director of Supply.
- Chief Engineer PWD.
- The Chief Electoral Officer.
- Superintending Engineer, Electricity.
- The General Manager, Manipur State Transport.
- Registrar of Cooperative Societies.

At the Secretariat level the following Departments are mentioned with the nature of business assigned to them:

- *Home Department*
  - All matters relating to Law and Order, State Police including Police Battalions, from other States, Fire Service, Security Matters, Jail and Prisions, disciplinary cases, etc. Warrant of Precedence, Passport/Visa, Foreigners Press Law, Copyright, Prescription of Books and Journals, Awards, Honours and Distinctions, Arms and Ammunition/Explosives, Soldiers, Sailors and Airmen's Board, etc. Eastern Zonal Council Matters and Service Association, etc.
  - Civil Services, Governor's Establishment, Administrative Reforms, Service Rules of Executive Business and General Matters Relating to Local Self Government such as Tribal, Area and Range Councils including Town Committees and Municipalities, Scheduled Castes and Scheduled Tribes Commission, Land Requisition and Acquisition, Rehabilitation, Labour and Employment, Interstate migration, Regulation on Betting, Gambling and Lottery, etc.
  - Secretariat establishment including ACRS, etc. of Officers and Staff, Cash, Printing and Stationery, Publicity and Tourism, Motor Car and House Building Loans and Advances.
  - State Houses outside Nagaland excluding Nagaland house at Calcutta.
- *Finance and Revenue Department*
  - All matters relating to General Finance including Finance Establishment and Administration which covers Pension Cases of State Staff, Interpretation of Finance Rules and Codes, etc.
  - Budget and Expenditure Control, Treasury, Finance Accounts and Audit classification of Budget heads and delegation of Financial Powers, etc.

— Finance Revenue and Taxation, Land Records and settlements and Miscellaneous cases involving all Finance and Revenue Matters, Foreign Exchange, Registration and Stamps.

- *Planning, Coordination and Community Projects Department*

  — All matters relating to planning, Statistics, Evaluation and implementation.

  — Plan Projects, Coordination of all Departmental Plans, Man Power, and Town Planning.

  — Community Projects and Tribal Welfare including Audit and Accounts of C/D, T/D, Blocks.

  — Water Supply.

- *Law and Parliamentary Affairs*

  — All matters relating to judiciary, Assembly, Parliament, High Court, Appointment of Magistrates and Judges.

  — Drafting of Revision of Rules, Codes, Acts and Codes, Magisterial and Legal Matters, Registration and any matter connected with them, Arrangement of Business in Assembly.

- *Public Works and Electrical Department*

  — All matters relating to buildings, Roads and Bridges including National Highways, Housing Schemes.

  — Electricity including Hydel Power Projects.

- *Medical Public Health and Cooperative Department*

  — All matters relating to Medical, Public Health including Rural, Sanitation, Family Planning, Women and children case, etc.

  — Cooperation

  — Excise.

- *Industry, Commerce and Election Department*

  — On matters concerning Trade and Industry.

  — Weights and Measures.

  — Elections.

- *Agriculture, Animal Husbandry, Fisheries, and Forest Department*

  — All matters relating to Agriculture and Irrigation, Food Production, Horticulture and Pisciculture.

  — All matters relating to Veterinary, Animal Husbandry, Dairy and Poultry Development.

— All matters relating to Forestry, Botany including Forest based Industrial Services, Soil Conservation and Wildlife Preservation, Geology and Mining.

- *Education including Cultural Research, etc. Department*

    — All matters relating to General and Technical Education.

    — All matters relating to Cultural and Anthropological Research, etc. Museum, Sports, Games, Libraries, etc.

    — Social Welfare.

    — Border Affairs

- *Transport Department*

    — All matters relating to Transport, Registration of Motor Vehicles, etc., and Workshop organisation and Nagaland State Transport.

- *Supply and Transport Department*

    — All matters relating to supply, control and Administration of State House.

    — Relief.

- *Coordination of Matters Relating to the District Administration and Development of the Hill Districts.*

The Chief Secretary carries most of his function in the name of the Governor and enforces statutory orders and Cabinet decision and reports to the Cabinet on matters relating to law, order administration, finance and development. A brief note on the composition of the Directorates is given below:

> The Department of Agriculture is in the charge of a Director. At the Directorate level there are a Deputy Director, Agricultural Chemist, Plant Pathologist, Entomologist, Horticulture Officers, Agricultural Engineer, Soil Survey Officer, Research Assistant and Print Technological or Development officer. There is a District Agriculture officer in each District assisted by a subdivisional Agricultural officer and a team of technical officials.

The extension training centre is headed by a principal; a team of Instructors, Demonstrators, Village Level Workers, Mechanic-cum-Carpenters, Fishery Demonstrators, and overseers is also attached.

Various Departments

Forest Departments

The Director designated as chief conservator is in-charge. A Deputy Director is also appointed in each district. Each district is under the Divisional Forest Officer (now designated as Deputy Conservator) assisted Conservators at the divisional Headquarters.

Animal Husbandry and Veterinary Department

The Director is the in-charge of the Department of Animal Husbandry and Veterinary. A team is further constituted of a Deputy Director, a poultry development Officer, a Piggery Development officer, a Dairy Development Officer, a Disease Investigation Officer at the State Level. The District is in the charge of a District Veterinary Officer assisted by Veterinary Assistant -Surgeons, Farm Managers, Field Assistants and other officials distributed all over the veterinary centres.

Education Department

The in-charge of the Department of Education is an Education Director. The Deputy Director, an Assistant Director and a special officer are the other principal personnel, Textbook Production Branch being supervised by the latter. In addition, there are a Hindi Training School, a State Institute of Education Teachers training Institute and other institutions.

Health Department

Health Services Department is under the charge of a Director. A Deputy Director is also attached. A civil Surgeon is in-charge of a district assisted by Medical Superintendent and a team of hospital staff.

Information and Publicity Department

The Department of Information and Publicity is under the charge of the Director. The Deputy Director and Information Officer are attached. A District Publicity Officer is in-charge of the District.

Supply Department

The Department of Supply is under the supervision of a Director. He is assisted by a Deputy Director and Superintendent.

Soil Conservation Department

There is a separate Directorate for soil conservation. Earlier it was attached to the Director of Forest.

Police Department

The Inspector-General is assisted by an Assistant Inspector-General, the staff officer of the Inspector-General, the Superintendent of Police and the Deputy Superintendent of Police. At the district-level there are a Superintendent and Deputy Superintendent of Police. The Armed Police force is looked after by a Commandant, Deputy Commandants and Assistant Commandant. The Police Training School is under the charge of the Principal.

The Wireless (Telephone) Department and the Fire Service Organisation are attached to the Inspector- General of Police.

Local Government

Under the Manipur State Hill Peoples (Administration) Regulation, 1947 especial provisions have been made for the administration of the villages situated in the hilly tracts. The responsibility for the administration of the Hill people is vested in the Maharaja in council and shall be exercised in accordance with the Constitution Act of the State and the Provisions of this regulation as amended from time to time. Appointments to all executive posts in the Hill Administration shall be made in accordance with the rules for the Manipur State Appointment Board excepting where specific provisions shall be made for such appointment in this Regulation. For the purpose of administration all villages to which the Regulation of 1947 applies shall be grouped into circles and subdivisions as provided in the Regulation.

In each village of 20 tax-paying houses or over, there shall be constituted a village Authority which shall be nominated in accordance with the custom of the village and shah consist of chief or Khullakpa of the village with his council of elders, if any. The village authority so nominated shall formally recognised by the Subdivisional Officer who shall be final authority in all matters concerning the appointment and constitution of a Village Authority saving that an appeal shall lie to the Minister-in-charge of Hill Administration from the decision of the Subdivisional Officer in such matters.

In each circle, there is a circle authority which comprise the circle officer and a council of five members elected by the village authorities falling within the circle. The Subdivisional Officer exercise general executive control over the local authorities in the subdivision tinder the orders of the Minister-in-charge of Hill Administration. The circle authorities are responsible for the maintenance of law and order within the circle and they exercise this authority wherever such authority exist.

The ordinary duties of Police in respect of crime are to be discharged by the village authorities where such exist and by the circle authority where there is no village authority to maintain peace and order within their jurisdiction. When the Village Authority is unable to arrest an offender, they may apply to the circle officer or a Heal Lambu of assistance.

Legislature in State

With the enactment of the Manipur State Constitution Act, 1947, by the then Maharaja, His Highness Maharaja Kumar Bodh Chandra Singh, the election to the Manipur State Assembly was held in July 1948 on the basis of adult franchise, the first of its kind in India. In all, 52 members were elected for a period of three years. It was a unicameral legislature. The State Assembly was the law-making authority but in actual practice the framing of laws was subject to the approval of the Maharaja. Later, on 15 October, 1949, Manipur was merged with the then Dominion of India in the dissolution of the State Assembly and the Council of Ministers. On adoption of the Constitution of India on 26 January, 1950, Manipur became a Part C State.

The Union Territories (Laws) Act, 1950 came into force on 16 April, 1950 and the Chief Commissioner became the Administrator of the State. A Council of advisors with five members, three from the valley and two from the hill areas was constituted on 6 May, 1953 to assist the Administrator and it continued to function till the election to the Territorial Council in 1957. The same year, under the Union Territories Act, 1956, election of 30 members of the Territorial Council was held.

Manipur had a Legislative Assembly consisting of 30 elected members under the Government of the Union Territories Act, 1963. There was a Council of Ministers to aid and advise the Administrator. The Assembly had the power to make laws with respect to all subjects enumerated in the State List and the Concurrent List in the Seventh Schedule of the Constitution in so far as any such matters are applicable in relation to the Union Territories. With the declaration of statehood on 21 January, 1972, election to the Legislative Assembly of the full-fledged State of Manipur was held in February 1972.

The structure of the Legislature of Manipur State is unicameral. From 1972 onwards, when Manipur became a full-fledged state, there are 60 members in the Legislative Assembly. There is no nominated member and all the 60 members are elected on the basis of adult franchise.

Council of States

- *Amendment of Fourth Schedule to the Constitution:* On and from the appointed day, in the Fourth Schedule to the Constitution, in the Table:
  — for entries 19 to 22, the following shall be substituted namely:

"19	Manipur	1
20	Tripura	1
21	Meghalaya	1
22	Delhi	3
23	Pondicherry	1
24	Mizoram	1
25	Arunachal Pradesh	1"

  — for the figures "226" the figures "232" shall be substituted.

- *Allocation of Sitting Members Representing the Existing Union Territories of Manipur and Tripura:* On and from the appointed day, the sitting members of the Council of States representing the existing Union territories of Manipur and Tripura shall be deemed to have been duly elected under clause (4) of Article 80 to fill the seat allotted to each of the States of Manipur and Tripura respectively in that Council and the term of office of such sitting members shall remain unaltered.

- *Election to fill the Seats Allotted to the State of Meghalaya and the Union Territories of Mizoram and Arunachal Pradesh:* As soon as may be after the appointed day, steps shall be taken to fill the seats in the Council of States allotted to the state of Meghalaya and the Union Territories of Mizoram and Arunachal Pradesh.

- *Amendment of Section 27A of Act 43 of 1950:* On and from the appointed day, in section 27A of the Representation of the People Act, 1950:

  — in subsection (1), for the words "For the purpose of filling any seat" the words, brackets and figure "Subject to the provisions of subsection (5) for the purpose of filling any seat" shall be substituted;

  — in subsection (4), for the wards "The electoral college for each of the Union territories of Manipur, Tripura and Pondicherry", the words "The electoral college for the Union territory of Pondicherry" shall be substituted;

  — after subsection (4), the following subsection shall be inserted, namely:

- The seat allotted in the Council of States to each of the Union Territories of Mizoram and Arunachal Pradesh shall be filled by a person nominated by the President in this behalf."

House of People

Allocation of Seats in the Existing House of the People:

(1) On and from the appointed day and until the dissolution of the existing House of the People, the allocation of seats to the states of Assam, Manipur, Tripura and Meghalaya and the Union territories of Mizoram and Arunachal Pradesh in the House of the People and the number of seats, if any, to be reserved for the Scheduled Castes and for the Scheduled Tribes of each state and Union territory shall be as specified in the Table below and the First Schedule to the Representation of the People Act, 1950 (43 of 1950); shall be deemed to have been amended accordingly.

Number of seats in the existing House of the People

Name of the State/ Union Territory	Total	Reserved for the Scheduled Castes	Reserved for the Scheduled Tribes
I. States			
1. Assam	14	1	2
2. Manipur	2	-	1
3. Tripura	2	-	1
4. Meghalaya	2	-	2
II. Union Territories			
1. Mizoram	1	-	1
2. Arunachal Pradesh	1	-	1

- On and from the appointed day and until the dissolution of the existing House of the People, Part A of Schedule 11 to the Delimitation of Parliamentary and Assembly Constituencies Order, 1966 shall stand amended as directed in the first Schedule.

Parliamentary Constituencies of the States of Manipur and Tripura and Provision as to Sitting Members:

(1) On and from the appointed day and until the dissolution of the existing House of the People:

(a) the two parliamentary constituencies of the existing Union territory of Manipur shall be deemed to be the two parliamentary constituencies of the state of Manipur; and

(b) the two parliamentary constituencies of the existing Union territory of Tripura shall be deemed to be the two parliamentary constituencies of the state of Tripura; and the Delimitation of Parliamentary and Assembly Constituencies Order, 1966 shall be construed accordingly.

(2) Every sitting member of the House of the people representing parliamentary constituency which on the appointed day, by virtue of the provisions of subsection (1) becomes a parliamentary constituency of the state of Manipur or Tripura, as the case may be, shall, as from the day be deemed to have been elected under sub-clause (a) of clause (1) of Article 81 to the House of the People from that constituency.

Provision as to sitting members representing Cachar and Dhubri Parliamentary Constituencies in the House of the People and the Election of Representative from Diphu Parliamentary Constituency:

(1) The sitting member of the House of the People representing the Cachar parliamentary constituency which on the appointed day, by virtue of the provisions of subsection (2) of section 14, stands altered shall, as from that day, be deemed to have been elected under sub-clause (a) of clause (1) of Article 81 to the House of the People from the constituency as so altered.

(2) The sitting member of the House of the People representing the Dhubri parliamentary constituency which on the appointed day, by virtue of the provisions of subsection (2) of section 14, stands altered, shall, as from that day, be deemed to have been elected under sub-clause (a) of clause (1) of Article 81 to the House of the People from that constituency so altered.

(3) As soon as may be after the appointed day election shall be held to the House of People to elect a representative from the Diphu parliamentary constituency as if the seat of the member elected to the House of People from that constituency has become vacant and the provisions of section 149 of the Representation of the People Act, 1951 (43 of 1951), shall, so far as may be apply in relation to such election.

Parliamentary Constituencies of the state of Meghalaya and provision as to sitting member representing the Autonomous Districts Parliamentary Constituency in the House of the People and the election of Representative from Tura Parliamentary Constituency:

(1) There shall be two parliamentary constituencies in the state of Meghalaya to be called the Shillong Parliamentary constituency and the Tura Parliamentary constituency.

(2) The area falling within the Garo Hills District as it exists immediately before the appointed day shall form the Tura parliamentary constituency and the remaining area in the state of Meghalaya, shall form the Shillong parliamentary constituency and the said two parliamentary constituencies shall be deemed to have been delimited accordingly.

(3) The sitting member of the House of People representing immediately before the appointed day the Autonomous District parliamentary constituency shall as from that day, be deemed to have been elected under sub-clause (a) of clause (1) of Article 81 to the House of the People from the Shillong parliamentary constituency.

(4) As soon as may be after the appointed day election shall be held to the House of the people to elect a representative from the Tura Parliamentary constituency as if the seat of the member elected to the House of the People from that constituency has become vacant and the provisions of section 149 of the Representation of the People Act, 1951 (43 of 1951) shall, so far as may be, apply in relation to such election.

Parliamentary Constituency of the Union Territory of Mizoram: The whole of the Union territory of Mizoram shall form one parliamentary constituency to be called the Mizoram parliamentary constituency and as soon as may be after the appointed day election shall be held to the House of the People to elect a representative from that constituency, as if the seat of the member elected to the House of the People from that constituency has become vacant and the provisions of section 149 of the Representation of the People Act, 1951 (43 of 1951) shall, so far as may be, apply in relation to such election.

Provision as to the Member to represent Arunachal Pradesh in the House of the People: The sitting member nominated to fill the seat allotted in the House of the People to the Tribal Areas of Assam specified in Part B of the Table appended to paragraph 20 of the Sixth Schedule to the Constitution, known as the North-East Frontier Agency, shall on and from the appointed day, be deemed to have been nominated to fill the seat allotted to the Union Territory of Arunachal Pradesh in the House of the People.

Legislative Assembly

Allocation of Seats in the Legislative Assemblies:

(1) On and from the appointed day, the total number of seats in the Legislative Assembly of the state of Assam, to be filled by persons chosen by direct election from territorial constituencies, shall be reduced from one hundred and twenty-six to one hundred and fourteen; and every sitting member of Legislative Assembly representing a constituency which ceases to be a constituency in the state of Assam by virtue of the provisions of subsection (3) as from the appointed day, cease to be a member of that Legislative Assembly.

(2) The total number of seats in the Legislative Assembly of the state of Manipur, to be constituted at any time after the appointed day, to be filled by persons chosen by direct election from territorial constituencies shall be sixty, out of which one seat shall be reserved for the Scheduled Castes and nineteen seats shall be reserved for the Scheduled Tribes.

(3) The total number of seats in the Legislative Assembly of the state of Tripura, to be constituted at any time after the appointed day, to be filled by persons chosen by direct election from territorial constituencies shall be sixty, out of which six seats shall be reserved for the Scheduled Castes and nineteen seats shall be reserved for the Scheduled Tribes.

(4) The total number of seats in the Legislative Assembly of the state of Meghalaya, to be constituted at any time after the appointed day, to be filled by persons chosen by direct election from territorial constituencies shall be sixty, out of which fifty seats shall be reserved for the Scheduled Tribes.

(5) On and from the appointed day, Part B of Schedule II to the Delimitation of Parliamentary and Assembly Constituencies Order, 1966 shall stand amended as directed in the First Schedule.

Amendment of Second Schedule to Act 43 of 1950:

(1) In the Second Schedule to the Representation of the People Act, 1950:

(i) under the heading "I. STATES":

    (a) in item 2 relating to Assam, for the figures "126", the figures "114" shall be substituted;

    (b) after item 17 and entries relating thereto the following shall be inserted namely:

"18.	Manipur	60	1	19
19.	Tripura	60	6	19
20.	Meghalaya	60	-	50"

(ii) under the heading "II. UNION TERRITORIES" items 3 and 5 and the entries relating thereto shall be omitted.

(2) The amendment made by clause (i) (a) of subsection (1) shall have effect on and after the appointed day in relation to the Legislative Assembly of the state of Assam and the amendments made by clause (i) (b) and clause (ii) of subsection (1) shall have effect in relation to the Legislative Assemblies of the state of Manipur, Tripura and Meghalaya to be constituted at any time after the appointed day.

Delimitation of Constituencies:

(1) The Election Commission shall, in the manner herein provided, distribute, whether before or after the appointed day, the seats assigned to the Legislative Assemblies of the states of Manipur, Tripura and Meghalaya under section 20 to single member territorial constituencies and delimit them on the basis of the latest census figures having regard to the provisions of the Constitution and to the following provisions:

    (a) all constituencies shall, so far as practicable be geographically compact areas and in delimiting them, regard shall be had to physical features, existing boundaries of administrative units, facilities of communication and public convenience;

    (b) every assembly constituency shall be so delimited as to fall only within one parliamentary constituency;

    (c) constituencies in which seats are reserved for the Scheduled Castes shall be distributed in different parts of the states and located, as far as practicable, in those areas where the proportion of their population to the total population is comparatively large; and

    (d) constituencies in which seats are reserved for the Scheduled Tribes shall, as far as practicable, be located in those areas where the proportion of their population to the total population is the largest.

Explanation: In this section "latest census figures" mean the census figures with respect to the state concerned ascertainable from the latest census of which the finally published figures are available.

(2) For the purpose of assisting in the performance of its functions under subsection (1) the Election Commission shall associate with itself as associate members:

   (a) in respect of the state of Manipur, all the sitting members of the House of the People representing the Union Territory of Manipur or, as the case may be the state of Manipur under subsection (2) of section 15, and such six persons who were members of the Legislative Assembly of the Union Territory of Manipur immediately before its dissolution by order of the President published in the Gazette of India, dated 16th October, 1969 with notification No. S.P. 4223, dated 16th October, 1969 of the Government of India in the Ministry of Home Affairs, as the President may, by order, nominate;

   (b) in respect of the state of Tripura, all the sitting members of the House of the People representing the Union territory of Tripura or, as the case may be, the state of Tripura under subsection (2) of section 15, and such six persons, being members of the Legislative Assembly of the Union Territory of Tripura as it functioned immediately before the 1st November, 1971, as the President may, by order, nominate;

   (c) in respect of the state of Meghalaya, the member of the House of the People representing the Autonomous districts parliamentary constituency or, as the case may be, the Meghalaya parliamentary constituency under section 17, and such of the six members of the Legislative Assembly of the Autonomous State of Meghalaya constituted under section 62 of the Assam Reorganisation (Meghalaya) Act, 1969 (55 of 1969) or, as the case may be, of the Provisional Legislative Assembly of the state of Meghalaya referred to in section 27, as the President may, by order, nominate.

   Provided that none of the associate members shall have a right to vote or to sign any decision of the Election Commission.

(3) If owing to death or resignation, the office of an associate member falls vacant, it shall be filled, if practicable, in accordance with the provisions of subsection (2).

(4) A member of any Legislative Assembly nominated under clause (b) or clause (c) shall continue to be an associate member notwithstanding that he ceases to be a member of such Legislative Assembly, otherwise than consequent on the incurring of any disqualification.

(5) The Election Commission shall:

   (a) publish is proposals for the delimitation of constituencies, together with the dissenting proposals, if any, of any associate member who desires publication thereof, in the Official Gazette and in such other manner as the Commission may consider fit, together with a notice inviting objections and suggestions in relation to the proposals and specifying a date on or after which the proposals will be further considered by it;

(b) consider all objections and suggestions which may have been received by it before the date so specified;

(c) after considering all objections and suggestions which may have been received by it before the date so specified determine by one or more orders the delimitation of constituencies and cause such order or orders to be published in the Official Gazette; and upon such publication, the order or orders shall have the full force of law and shall not be called in question in any court.

(6) As soon as may be after such publication, every such order shall be laid before the Legislative Assembly of the concerned State.

Power of the Election Commission to maintain Delimitation Orders Up-to-date:

(1) The Election Commission may, from time to time, by Notification in the Official Gazette:

(a) correct any printing mistake in order made under section 22 or any error arising therein from inadvertent slip or omission;

(b) where the boundaries or name of any territorial division mentioned in any such order or orders are or is altered, make such amendment as appear to it to be necessary or expedient for bringing such order up-to-date.

(2) Every notification under this section shall be laid, as soon as may be after it is issued, before the Legislative Assembly of the concerned State.

Validation of Acts done previous to the Commencement of the Act: All things done, and all steps taken, before the commencement of this Act with a view to delimiting the territorial constituencies of the states of Manipur, Tripura and Meghalaya for the purpose of elections to the Legislative Assemblies of those States shall, insofar as they are in conformity with the provisions of sections 22 and 23, be deemed to have been done or taken under those sections as if those sections were in force at the time such things were done or such steps were taken.

Amendment of Scheduled Castes Orders:

(1) On and from the appointed day, the Constitution (Scheduled Castes) Order, 1950 shall stand amended as directed in the Second Schedule.

(2) On and from the appointed day, the Constitution (Scheduled Castes) (Union Territories) Order, 1951 shall stand amended as directed in the Third Schedule.

Amendment of Scheduled Tribes Orders:

(1) On and from the appointed day, the Constitution (Scheduled Tribes) Order, 1950 shall stand amended as directed in the Fourth Schedule.

(2) On and from the appointed day, the Constitution (Scheduled Tribes) (Union Territories) Order, 1951 shall stand amended as directed in the Fifth Schedule.

Provisions as to Provisional Legislative Assembly of the State of Meghalaya and as to Rules of Procedure and Conduct of Business of the Legislative Assemblies of the States of Meghalaya, Manipur and Tripura:

(1) On and from the appointed day and until the Legislative Assembly of the state of Meghalaya has been duly constituted and summoned to meet for the first session under the provisions of the Constitution, the Provisional Legislative Assembly of the Autonomous State of Meghalaya, excluding the members nominated thereto, constituted under section 62 of the Assam Reorganisation (Meghalaya) Act, 1969 (55 of 1969), and functioning immediately before the appointed day shall be the Provisional Legislative Assembly of the state of Meghalaya and that Assembly shall exercise all the powers and perform all the duties conferred by the provisions of the Constitution on the legislative Assembly of the State. Provided that for the purposes of this subsection, the member representing the Autonomous District of United Khasi-Jaintia Hills in the said Provisional Legislative Assembly of the autonomous State of Meghalaya shall be deemed also to represent the territories specified in clause (b) of section 5.

(2) The term of office of the members of the Provisional Legislative Assembly of the state of Meghalaya shall, unless the said Legislative Assembly is sooner dissolved, expire immediately before the first meeting of the Legislative Assembly of the state of Meghalaya.

(3) The persons who, immediately before the appointed day, are the Speaker and the Deputy Speaker of the Provisional Legislative Assembly of the autonomous State of Meghalaya shall be the Speaker and the Deputy Speaker respectively of the Provisional Legislative Assembly of the state of Meghalaya.

(4) The Rules of Procedure and Conduct of Business of the Provisional Legislative Assembly of the autonomous State of Meghalaya, as in force immediately before the appointed day, shall until rules are made under clause (1) of Article 208, be the Rules of Procedure and Conduct of Business of the Provisional Legislative Assembly of the state of Meghalaya, and of the Legislative Assembly of the state of Meghalaya duly constituted under the provisions of the Constitution, subject to such adaptations as may be made therein by the Speaker of the Legislative Assembly concerned.

(5) The Rules of Procedure and Conduct of Business of the Legislative Assembly of the Union territory of Manipur, as in force immediately before its dissolution by order of the President published in the Gazette of India, dated the 16th October, 1969 with notification No. S.O. 4223, dated the 16th October, 1969 of the Government of India in the Ministry of Home Affairs, shall until rules are made under clause (1) of Article 208, be the Rules of Procedure and Conduct of Business of the Legislative Assembly of the state of Manipur, subject to such modifications and adaptations as may be made therein by the Governor of that State.

(6) The Rules of Procedure and Conduct of Business of the Legislative Assembly of the Union territory of Tripura as in force immediately before the 1st November, 1971, shall, until rules are made under clause (1) of Article 208, be the Rules of Procedure and Conduct of Business of the Legislative Assembly of the state of Tripura subject to such modifications and adaptations as may be made therein by the Governor of that State.

Significant Courts

Under the Regulation, 1947, Criminal justice shall be administered by the court of the Village Authority, the Court of Circle Authority, the Hill Bench at Imphal and the Chief Court of the Manipur State as Constituted for the trial of Hill cases under the Manipur State Court Act, 1947. In any area for which there is no Village Authority, Original Criminal Powers shall be exercised by the Circle Bench of that area provided always that the Chief or Elders of any village may try any case which it is customary for them to try and may pass such sentence as it is customary. The Court of a Village is empowered to the persons or person accused is or are resident within their jurisdiction.

(a) Theft including theft in a building.

(b) Mischief not being mischief by fire or any explosive substance.

(c) Cattle theft and illegal slaughter of cattle.

(d) Simple hurt.

(e) Assault or using criminal forces.

The Circle Bench exercises the powers of a Magistrate of the first-class as defined in the Criminal procedure Code and shall comprise the circle officer and any two members of the circle council.

Cases Regarding Land and Village Settlement: Where any dispute arises regarding the ownership of land or the right of cultivation over land, the village authority shall, where the land in dispute falls within their jurisdiction and where both the parties to the dispute reside within their jurisdiction, take all steps necessary to effect a compromise between the parties. If compromise proves impossible or if the parties to the dispute reside within the jurisdiction of two or more Village Authorities, the dispute shall be placed before the circle Bench who shall decide the care. The Hill Bench may call for the proceedings of any subordinate Court and may amend any decision of that court if in the opinion of the Hill Bench gross injustice has been done.

The Budget of the Hill Administration shall be dealt with according to the rule provided that in no financial year shall the total expenditure on Hill Administration under all heads fall below a figure equal to 171/2 per cent of the average real revenue of the state for the immediately preceding three years.

Taxation System

With an ex-officio Commissioner of Taxes assisted by The Assistant Commissioner.

Planning for Towns

The Town Planner undertakes preparation of Town Planning Schemes, there is also an Assistant Town Planner.

Election System

The Chief Electoral Officer is assisted by the Assistant Chief Electoral Officer and District Election Officer. Government's Secretariat is in the charge of a Secretary to the Governor. Advocate General and Government Advocate Officer on Special Duty: engaged in matters relating to appeals and cases with High Court. Excise is under an ex-officio Superintendent of Excise. A regular Superintendent is being proposed with headquarters at Imphal.

Revenue: A Revenue Officer at the Headquarters is assisted by one Sub Deputy Collector.

Jails: Each Jail is under the Supervision of a Superintendent Known as Jailer.

Information and Publicity: A useful work is being done on educational propaganda among the masses of the people by the distribution of audiovisual sets, production of posters and display of documentary films relating to various subject matters. Community receiving sets have also been distributed. A team of language translators has been appointed to cope with the preparation of publicity literatures in different languages.

Social Welfare: The Social Welfare Board has been instituted with an object of promoting Social Welfare Works amongst children and women. A few selected officials under the scheme are being deputed elsewhere for training in Social Service Administration.

10

Tourism

- -

Manipur is a mountainous land locked state with hills and dales forest-clad slopes, mountain brooks of crystal clear water, waterfalls, rapids and gorges. It is known as the 'Switzerland of the East, and a paradise for the lovers of scenic beauty, photographers, artists and landscape painters. In the central part of the state is a high level plain at an elevation of about 815 metres closed on all sides by mountain ranges. It is dotted with hills and mounds and there are a number of lakes and swamps. Loktak lake in the southern part of the plain is the largest fresh water lake in North-East India. During the rainy season the water of the lake covers about 150 square kilometres of area. The central plain, viewed from a vantage point looks exceptionally beautiful and is in fact, a unique craftsmanship of nature.

Nature Tourism

The Keibul Lamjao National Park is one of its major tourist attractions. Located near the capital city of Imphal, this is a must visit tourist spot of Manipur. The sight of rare animals and birds is a delight for the nature lovers. Spread over forty square kilometres of wetland, the Keibul Lamjao National Park is debatably the world's only floating sanctuary. Apart from the foliage and topography the park consists of the Loktak Lake, which is the biggest freshwater lake in India. The star appeal, of the park is the browantlered deer. This is a breed of the Thamin deer. Because of its fragile way of walking it is also affectionately called Manipur's dancing deer. Other species of deer seen here comprise the hog deer, sambar and muntjac. Various birds such as the Waterfowl, the Hooded Crane, the Black Eagle and the Shaheen Falcon are found here. The major fresh water lake of Manipur is the Loktak Lake which is also well known by the name of 'Floating Lake' as it one of the exceptional lakes in the world which have the Phundies or floating islands on it. Tourists visiting the lake can also go for the nearby attraction which is the ancient temple of the pre-Hindu deity, Lord Thangjing, located in the Moirang. The Zoological gardens in Manipur is a prime attraction of the place. Flocks of vacationers stopover in the Zoological Gardens to see the diverse species of animals and birds that are kept there. The Zoological Gardens in Manipur is a well-maintained garden that is located at a distance of about six kilometres from Imphal in Manipur in India. A trip to the Zoological Gardens is actually a pleasant expedition for family and friends. The Khonghampat Orchidarium in Manipur is a nature lover's delight. The comforting fragrance of the flowers and wide-ranging colours refreshes the mind and spirit of the tourists. More than hundred and ten varieties of orchids, including quite a few rare species, are grown here.

Leisure Tourism

The Shahid minar in Manipur is a must see tourist location. The monument is an emblem of the bravery of the valiant soldiers who laid down their lives for their nation. The war cemetery in Manipur is also a popular destination. This place is toured by large numbers of visitors every year. The Manipur War Cemetery is an emblematic memorial raise as a reference for the supreme human sacrifices made by the officers and men of the associated forces during the Second World War. Ukhrul is the highest hill station of the state of Manipur. Siroi hills and Khang Khui lime caves are striking excursion destinations in this place. The Khayang peak is the highest peak of the region and the tourists from here can have exquisite views around the place. The Khangkhui Cave is an outstanding natural lime stone cave in Ukhrul and is a popular visiting site for the tourists. Langthabal in Manipur is a small hill situated about eight kilometres from Imphal. The place houses an old significant palace and efficiently planned temples. The different structures found here are marvellously placed between pine and jackfruit trees. Langthabal offers an impressive sight of the well-known Manipur University. This picturesque place is a must see location of Manipur. The Manipur State Museum focuses on tribal costumes, jewellery and weapons along with geological, archaeological and natural history displays. A visit to this museum will give the visitors an idea of the culture and heritage of the people of Manipur.

Pilgrimage Tourism

Temples in Manipur are remarkable pilgrimage sites which makes the trip to this state more captivating. Almost all the temples of Manipur are created on Brahmanical rules of Vastu Shastra and have the Mandapas. The architectural style of the temples in Manipur resembles the Bengal temple architecture. The Vishnu temple of Bishanpur town in Manipur is the oldest temple of the state. This temple is a significant religious structure of Manipur and is an important pilgrimage site. The temple is a eminent pilgrimage sight of the Hindus. Shri Govindaji temple in Manipur is one of the most visited religious centres of the state. It is a popular Hindu temple and the deities worshipped here are the Hindu gods, Radha and Krishna Govinda. Located in an easily accessible place in the capital of the state, Imphal, the temple is visited by large numbers of pilgrims every year. The tourists also have a high regard for the temple structure. Built of red bricks, the temple features a rectangular medieval style of architecture.

Tourist Points

Imphal

The capital city and cultural centre of Manipur state has a cosmopolitan look. Situated on the National Highway No. 39 in the central, plains of Manipur, Imphal is a historical, administrative and educational seat of the state. Among the places worth visiting in Imphal and its environs are the Golden Temple of Shri Govindaji in Rajbaree or the Palace of the Maharaja, War cemetery, Mahabali, Manipur Museum, Jawaharlal Nehru Manipuri Dance Academy and Imphal Zoo, etc. The Khwairamband Bazar, in the centre of the town in the biggest shopping centre for artistic hand-looms and handicraft products.

In the Khwairamband Bazar the shop keeping and business activities are looked after by womenfolk. There are numerous temples, religious places and cultural centres in Manipur. In these cultural centres many aspects of life are given expression through the medium of dance. On religious and social occasions functions are held followed by dance performance. Manipur is rich in festivals, dance and music. The Naga dances are too many as each tribe has its own dance, some of which are night long performances accompanied by beat of drums. Among the Manipur dances may be mentioned Rasalila, Laiharoba, Maibee dance, etc. It is a memorable experience for the tourists to witness such performances.

A tourist may pay a visit to the ancient temple of Bishanpur by the side of Tiddem Road, on way to Moirang. This is the historical 'Temple of Vishnu' built during the reign of King Kyamba in 1467 AD. Bishanpur is also famous for stoneware industry. A few kilometres south is the ancient village of Moirang on the shores of Loktak Lake. There is the temple of Thangjing where dresses of the tenth century are said to have been kept preserved and are displayed on ceremonial occasions. In Moirang is situated the INA Memorial with a life-size bronze statue of Netaji Subhash Chandra Bose. There is a library attached to the Memorial. Loktak is 48 kilometres from the city of Imphal and is the most enjoyable place in Manipur. The vast expanse of water offers scope for shooting, fishing and boating. The small hills in the Lake Sendra, Thanga, Karang Ithing, etc. serve as observation posts to view the picturesque scenery of nature reflected on the water of the lake. During the moonlit nights the scene is beyond description. In the southern end of the lake there is the floating reed forest, the habitat of the brown antlered deer, a threatened species. The Government of Manipur has declared the reed forest as a game sanctuary. It is a beautiful place worth visiting.

The town of Churachandpur on Tiddin is the Headquarters of the south district of Manipur. It is situated at the foothill, at the junction of the hills and the central plains.

Churachandpur reflects the culture of hill people of this region. It has three colleges, many High Schools, Churches, libraries and playgrounds. It is the most developed town of the hilly regions. The Loktak Multi-purpose Project, nearing completion is going to be a great attraction in the near future. A traveller coming from Dimapur to Imphal enters Manipur at Mao. This place is the highest point along the road with an elevation of about 2,000 metres. Being fairly high in altitude, this place remains pleasantly cool even during the months of summer season. Mao is an important health resort. It is also a place of historical importance. The Mao and its surrounding areas are inhabited by Mao-Naga-Tribe.

Tengnoupal, the Headquarters of the district of the same name is about seventy kilometres from Imphal. This is the highest point at the Indo-Burma Road. Tengnoupal has a cool climate. From some vantage point one can have a full view of the central plain of Manipur. A few kilometres downhill towards east one can also have a view of the modern town. The landscape of the area is enchanting. Moreh, about 107 kilometres from Imphal is the border customs outpost between India and Burma. On the Burmese side across the river the town is called *Tamu*. A substantial business is transacted between the two towns and one comes across cross cultural short distance apart across the international boundary. There is regular bus service from Imphal to Moreh.

Towards north, overlooking the central plain, there is a mountain peak called *Koubru*. Its elevation is 2,562 metres above the sea level. Koubru is a place of scenic beauty. It is a sacred place believed to be the abode of gods. It attracts a large number of pilgrimage every year. Towards the top one comes across flat surface and a big lake. There are surface evidences of the last glacial episode on way to obliteration. Around this peak short thorny bamboo grows in abundance. The climate is cool and invigorating. It is a worthwhile experience to be at the top even for a few hours.

To the east of the plain of Manipur is the Baruni hill. It is a place of great aesthetic attraction, scenic beauty and also considered as an abode of God. An annual fair takes place on this Hill. The altitude of the peak is about 1,585 metres. From a vantage point one can have a good view of the Central Valley of Manipur. At the top of the peak there is a temple which is surrounded by alpine-meadows. The other place of tourist attraction in the hills is Tamenglong in the Manipur west district. There is a regular bus service from Imphal to Tamenglong. A few kilometres from Tamenglong is the famous Tharon cave. The cave is quite gigantic in size. In the vicinity of Tamenglong one can visit the waterfall on Barak, the largest river of the state of Manipur.

Nungba is a small township midway between Jiribam and Imphal, on the new Cachar road. A few kilometres from Nungba, to the south, is the beautiful Khoupum valley. This valley is a miniature of the central plain, at an elevation of about 685 metres. The Old Cachar Road passes through this valley. It is a fertile alluvial plain surrounded by high mountains. People belonging to Kabuid Tribe inhabit in this valley. The importance of the Khoupum valley has been enhanced owing to the construction of the Khoupum Dam. The stream draining this valley joins the Irang river. This stream has a number of rapids, cataracts, and waterfalls. The Manipur east district has many natural sites as special attraction for the tourists. Ukhrul, the Headquarters of the district is at a distance of about 70 kilometres to the northeast of Imphal. The town is situated on a ridge which also serves as a water-divide. It is inhabited by the tall, sharp-nosed colourful Tangkul Naga Tribe. About ten kilometres to the southeast of Ukhrul is the Hundung limestone region famous for Khankhoi caves. There are a number of caves and tunnels with chambers, stalactites, stalagmites and associated features. About ten kilometres to the east of Ukhrul there is the Sirohi village, which is accessible by a jeepable road.

From here one has to follow the footpath leading to Sirohi peak. The Sirohi peak is 2,568 metres high above the sea level. It is an area of volcanic topography where traces of the last glaciation are still evident, though rohi peak is 2,568 metres high above the sea level. It is an area of volcanic topography where traces of the last glaciation are still evident, though greatly modified. Here one comes across the famous Sirohi lily which grows on the lofty mountains. This plant is a threatened species, on way to extinction. The Sirohi lily's plant is about one and a half metres in height. Its flowering period is in July and August. This wonder flower has a combination of seven colours and looks brown in the sunlight. Its colour changes automatically when taken to shade. The Sirohi lily attracts a large number of tourists annually in this region.

Tourist Attractions

The tourist attractions of the state include breath taking lakes, beautiful landscapes, historic monuments and display of arts and ethnic traditions. Some major tourist centres are:

War Cemetery

This cemetery for the British and the Indian Army who sacrificed their lives during the World War II is serene and well maintained with little markers and bronze plaques recording brief accounts of their sacrifice. These graves are maintained by the Commonwealth War Graves Commission.

Loktak lake, Sendra Island and Keibul Lamjao National Park

Loktak lake is the largest fresh water lake in the North-East Region with the only floating National Park of its kind. The lake is located at the distance of 45 km from Imphal and the National Park is on an island inside the lake. Sendra is an island hillock and visitors can get a complete view of the unique lake and floating masses of water hyacinth. The fisherman and their families who live in small huts on its surroundings make full use of the aquatic environment. The National Park is the only floating park in the world and this is the last habitat of the marsh — friendly brow antlered deer of Manipur.

INA Memorial at Moirang

It is a place where India's tri-coloured flag was hoisted by Netaji during World War II. There is a Netaji Memorial Museum in this complex displaying letters, photographs, badges of ranks and other memorabilia reminding the noble sacrifices made by the INA under the leadership of Netaji Subhash Chandra Bose.

Other Tourist Centres

Shri Shri Govindaji Temple, Shahid Minar, Manipur State Museum, Langthabal, Khonghampat Orchidarium, Manipur Zoological Garden in Imphal district. Khongjom War Memorial Complex at Khongjom, Waithou, Kaina in Thoubal district, Red Hill (India Peace Memorial, Loukoi Pat, Phubala at Bishenpur district, Moreh, Tengnoupal in Chandel, Ukhrul, Tamenglong and Mao are other attractive tourist centres of the state.

Bibliography

Abraham, N.: *The Religion of Manipur*, Oxford, London, 1913.

Allen, B. C.: *Gazetteer of Naga Hills and Manipur*, Mittal Publications, New Delhi, 1905.

Anand, B.: *Investigation of Nickle and Copper Mineralization in Moreh Area, Manipur State, Manipur Gazetteer*, Govt. Pub., Imphal, 1968.

Ansari, S.A.: *Economic Geography of Manipur*, Educational Pub., Imphal, 1976.

Anthony, Brett: *Imphal*, MacMillan, London, 1986.

Archer, W.G.: *The Hill of Flutes: Life, Love and Poetry in Tribal India: A Portrait of the Santals*, University of Pittsburgh Press, Pittsburgh, 1974.

Atombaur, S.: *The Brief Description of Manipur*, Greenland, New York, 1978.

Au, A.: *Notes on Early History of Manipur*, Koli Pub., Calcutta, 1923.

Austin, Granville: *The Indian Constitution: Cornerstone of a Nation*, Oxford, New York, 1966.

Averd,: *Meitei Villages: Imphal East Block-Manipur*, Rural Development Plan, New Delhi, 1975.

Bahadur, M.: *Manipur Artki Wan Shin*, Educational Pub., Imphal, 1975.

Barua, Hem: *The Red River & The Blue Hill*, Laywer's Book Stall, Guwahati, 1954.

Barua, K.L.: *Studies in the Early History of Manipur*, M. Jorhet, Manipur, 1973.

Basu, Pradip Kumar: *The Communist Movement in Tripura*, Progressive Publishers, Calcutta, 1996.

Bhagabati, K. Abani and Kar, K. Bimal: *Survey of Research in Geography on North-East India 1970-1990*, Regency Publication, New Delhi, 1999.

Bhatia, B.: *Census Handbook of Manipur*, Bhat Pub., Calcutta, 1964.

Bhaumik, Subir: *Insurgent Cross Fire: North-East India*, Lancer Publishers, New Delhi, 1996.

Bhola Nath Ghosh: *Women in Governance in Tripura*, Concept, 2008.

Bhuyan, B. C.: *Political Development of the North East,* Omsons Publications, New Delhi, 1989.

Bodding, P.O.: *Santal Riddles and Witchcraft among the Santals,* A.W. Brøggers, Oslo, 1940.

Bompas, Cecil Henry and Bodding, P.O.: *Folklore of the Santal Parganas,* D. Nutt, London, 1909.

Brajamani, S.: *Economic Growth in Manipur: An Emperical Analysis,* S. Romesh Singh, Manipur, 2003.

Brown, R.: *Statistical Account of the Native State of Manipur and the Hill Territory under its Rule,* Govt. Printing, Kolkata, 1873.

Chakrabarti, Dr. Byomkes: *A Comparative Study of Santali and Bengali,* KP Bagchi, Calcutta, 1994.

Chaliha, D.: *Origin and Growth of Manipuri Language and Literature,* Safder Pub., Jorhat, 1949.

Chandrika Basu Majumder and Paramita Saha: *Ageing in North East India,* Tripura Perspective, Akansha, 2008.

Chaube, S. K.: *Hill Politics in Northeast India,* Orient Longman Limited, Patna, 1973.

Chaudhuri, A.B.: *State Formation among Tribals: A Quest for Santal Identity,* Gyan Pub. House, New Delhi, 1993.

Chaudhury, Jagadis: *Manipur: The Land and its People,* MacMillan, New Delhi, 1979.

Chaudhury, N.R.: *Manipur Through the Agas,* Koli Pub., Calcutta, 1977.

Chauley, G.C.: *Art Treasures of Unakoti,* Agam Kala Prakashan, Tripura, 2007.

Clarke, C.B.: *On the Plants of Kohima and Manipur,* Oxford, London, 1889.

Constantine, R.: *Manipur: Maid of the Mountains,* Lancers Publishers, New Delhi, 1981.

Cosh, J.: *Topography of Manipur,* Bengal Military Orphan Press, Kolkata, 1937.

Culloch, E.: *An Account of the Valley of Manipur and Hill Tribes,* Bengal Printing Company, Calcutta, 1859.

Culshaw, W.J.: *Tribal Heritage: a Study of the Santals,* Lutterworth Press, London, 1949.

Das, Gurudas and Purkayastha, R. K.: *Border Trade: North-East India and Neighbouring Countries,* Akansha Publishing House, New Delhi, 2000.

Das, N.C.: *Ferns and Fern-Allies of Tripura: North East India,* International Book Distributors, 2007.

Datta, P.S.: *North East and the Indian State: Paradoxes of a Periphery,* Vikas Publishing House, New Delhi, 1995.

Deb, Dasarath: *Mukti Parishader Itikatha*, National Book Agency, Kolkata, 1999.

Debendra Bijoy Deb: *The Flora of Tripura State: 1981-1983,* 1990.

Deepa, D. Nair, Gupta, A.K. Himangshu Bikash Das and Atanu Chakraborti: *Medicinal Plants of Tripura*, A Photo Descriptive Field Manual, Concept, 2009.

Dena, Lal: *History of Modern Manipur 1826-1949,* Orbit Publishers-Distributors, New Delhi, 1991.

Deva, Naoroibam: *Urban Settlement System of Manipur*, R. K. Sachirani, Imphal, 1998.

Devashish Kar: *Fundamentals of Limnology and Aquaculture Biotechnology: A Treatise on the Limnology and Fisheries of the Water Bodies in Southern Assam*, Mizoram and Tripura, Daya, 2007.

Devender Kumar Sikri: *Census of India 2001: Tripura Administrative Atlas*, Controller of Publication, 2006.

Dipannita Chakraborty: *Land Question in Tripura*, Akansha Pub, 2004.

Dun, E.W.: *Gazatteer of Manipur*, Superintendent of Govt. Printing, Kolkata, 1886.

Dutta, Arup Kumar: *The Brahmaputra*, National Book Trust, New Delhi, 2001.

Edward Duyker Tribal Guerrillas: *The Santals of West Bengal and the Naxalite Movement*, Oxford University Press, New Delhi, 1987.

Elwin, V.: *The Nagas in the 19th Century*, Popular Prakashan, Bombay, 1969.

Endle, S.: *The Kacharis*, Low Price Publications, New Delhi, 1990.

Esqr, Asok Bose: *Geological Survey of Hill Tippera 1909-10,* Tripura State Tribal Cultural Research Institute & Museum, Tripura, 1995.

Gassah, L. S.: *Survey of Research in Political Science on North-East India 1970-1990,* Regency Publication, New Delhi, 1999.

Gautam Kumar Bera, Birinchi K. Medhi, Athparia, R.P. and Jose K. SVD: *Tribal Development in Tripura*, EBH Pub an imprint of Eastern Book House, 2009.

Gimson. C.: *Notes on Maring Nagas of Manipur*, Oxford, London, 1926.

Gopalkrishnan, R.: *Insurgent North-Eastern Region of India*, Vikas Publishing House, New Delhi, 1995.

Goswami, P.C.: *The Economic Development in Manipur,* Popular Prakashan, Bombay, 1963.

Gourahari, S.: *Manipur and the Second World War*, Imphal, 1983.

Guha, Amalendu: *Freedom Struggle and Electoral Politics in Manipur, 1826-1947,* Sumit Pub., New Delhi, 1977.

Gunindro, P.: *Coins of Manipur*, Reproduction of the Silver Coins, Imphal, 1892.

Hembrom, T.: *The Santals: Anthropological-Theological Reflections on Santali and Biblical Creation Traditions*, Punthi Pustak, Calcutta, 1996.

Hudson, T. C.: *The Meitheis*, Low Price Publications, New Delhi, 1908.

————: *The Naga Tribes of Manipur*, Low Price Publications, New Delhi, 1911.

Hunter, W.W.: *Statistical Account of Manipur*, Trubner & Co., London, 1879.

Ibungohal, L.: *Introduction to Manipur*, Imphal, 1969.

Jagadis Gan-Chaudhuri: *A Cultural History of Tripura*, Basudeb Pal, 2006.

Jagadish Ganchaudhuri, S. Sailo and Datta, M.S.: *People of India*, Tripura, Seagull Books, 1996.

Johnstone, James: *Manipur and the Naga Hills*, Gyan Publishing House, New Delhi, 2002.

Joshi, L.M. Printworld, D.K.: *Lalita-Sahasranama: Roman Transliteration*, Critical Explanation of Each Name, Reprint, 2006.

Kakati, B.K.: *Manipur: its Formation and Development*, Rakesh Pub., Gauhati, 1938.

Khanna, S.K.: *Encyclopaedia of North-East India: Arunachal Pradesh, Assam, Manipur, Meghalaya, Tripura, Sikkim, Mizoram and Nagaland Tripura Sikkim*, Indian Pub, India, 1999.

Kiran Sankar Chakraborty: *Entrepreneurship and Small Business Development: With Special Reference to Tripura*, Mittal, 2006.

Krishna Nath: *Status and Empowerment of Tribal Women in Tripura*, Kalpaz, 2005.

Kulabidhu, H.: *Manipur Dances*, MacMillan London, 1964.

Maitra, S.R.: *Ethnographic Study of the Chakma of Tripura*, Anthropological Survey of India, India, 2002.

Majumder, Benimadhab: *The Legislative Opposition in Tripura*, Tripura State Tribal Cultural Research Institute & Museum, Agartala, 1997.

Malabika Das Gupta: *Economic Impact of Raids on the Shifting Cultivators of Tripura*, The Asiatic Society, 2008.

Manas Paul: *The Eyewitness: Tales From Tripura's Ethnic Conflict*, Lancer, 2009.

Neufville, Capt.: *On the Geography and Population of Manipur*, Asiatic Researches, Imphal, 1995.

Orans, Martin: *The Santal a Tribe in Search of a Great Tradition*, Wayne State University Press, Chicago, 1965.

Owen, J.: *Notes on the Naga Tribes in Communication with Manipur*, W.H. Carey & Co., Kolkata, 1844.

Pemberton, R.B.: *Memoirs and Journals of Survey in Manipur*, Rohi Pub., Kolkata, 1827.

Prasad, Onkar: *Santal Music: A Study in Pattern and Process of Cultural Persistence,* Tribal Studies of India Series, New Delhi, 1985.

Projit Kumar Palit: *History of Religion in Tripura,* Kaveri, 2004.

Rahman, S.A.: *The Beautiful India,* Reference Press, Tripura, 2006.

Rajkumar, Manisana: *Customs of Manipuri Hindus,* Smt Usha Devi, Manipur, 2001.

Ramnika Jalali and Rajni Mankotia: *A Glimpse of Kalachuris of Tripurari,* Vinod Pub, New York, 2003.

Ranjit Kumar De: *Socio-Political Movements in India,* A Historical Study of Tripura, Mittal, 1998.

Roy Chaudhury: *Indu: Folk Tales of the Santals,* Sterling Publishers, New Delhi, 1973.

Roy, Amitesh: *Manipur, Dynamics of Change,* Pearl Publishers, Calcutta, 1982.

Roy, J.: *History of Manipur,* Eastlight Book House, Calcutta, 1958.

Sana, O.B.: *Sanamahi Laikhan in Manipur,* LDT, Imphal, 1972.

Sanjaboo, N.: *Manipur Past and Present,* Mittal Pub. House, Delhi, 1988.

Sankrityayan, Kamla: *Manipur and Tripura,* Vikas Pub., New Delhi, 1973.

Shakespear, J.: *History of the Manipur,* MacMillan and Co., London, 1929.

Sharma, R.K.: *Manipur Tribal Scene,* Inter India Publication, New Delhi, 1985.

Shri Tripura-Rahasyam: *Jnana-Khanda: Discourse on Wisdom,* Eastern Book Linkers, Tripura, 2003.

Singh, B.: *Politics of Alienation in Manipur,* Ajanta Pub., New Delhi, 1984.

Singh, O.K.: *Archaeological Research-Manipur in Eastern Himalayas,* Cosmos Pub., Delhi, 1980.

Singh, Rajkumar Manisana: *A Short Constitutional History of Manipur 1891-1971,* Smt Usha Devi, Imphal, 2000.

————: *Customs of Manipuri Hindus,* Smt Usha Devi, Manipur, 2001.

Sipra Sen: *Tribes of Tripura: Description,* Ethnology and Bibliography, 1993.

State Fauna Series: Fauna of Tripura, Part II. Insects, Zoological Survey of India, 2000.

Sukhendu Debbarma: *Origin and Growth of Christianity in Tripura: With Special Reference to the New Zealand Baptist Missionary Society 1938-1988,* Indus, 1996.

Suren Deb Barman: *Rabindranath Tagore and Tripura,* Minerva, 2006.

Syamal Kumar Ray: *India's North-East and the Travails of Tripura,* Minerva, 2003.

Trivady, A.N.: *A Note on the Finding of Vertebrate Fauna in the Surma Series of Tripura and its Bearing on the Stratigraphy of the Area*, 1966.

Troisi, J.: *The Santals: A Classified and Annotated Bibliography*, Manohar Book Service, New Delhi, 1976.

—————: *Tribal Religion: Religious Beliefs and Practices among the Santals*, Manohar, New Delhi, 2000.

Ward, K.: *Plant Hunter in Manipur*, MacMillan, London, 1952.

Woodthrope, R.G.: *Report of the Survey Operations in the Manipur*, Secretariat Press, Shillong, 1876.

Yumjao. W.: *An Early History of Manipur*, Imphal, 1967.

Zehol, Lucy: *Ethnicity in Manipur: Experience, Issues and Perspectives*, Regency Publications, New Delhi, 1998.

Zudaic, T.C.: *The Naga Tribes of Manipur*, MacMillan, London, 1911.

Index

Chingai, 71, 76.

Chiru, 93, 95, 205.

Chothe, 93, 205.

Christianity, 10, 21, 58, 82, 86, 113.

Churachandpur, 7, 30, 33, 69, 70, 74, 152, 154, 155, 218, 237, 238.

Climate, 5, 79, 91, 202, 203, 211, 212, 238.

College, 15, 22, 23, 54, 90, 121, 125, 127, 152, 153, 163, 190, 225.

Community Information Centres, 23.

Council for the Indian School Certificate Examinat, 154.

Custom, 44, 59, 60, 87, 88, 89, 100, 106, 108, 203, 223.

D

District Institutes of Educational Training, 163.

E

Early Period, 2, 110, 172, 173, 181, 182, 183, 184.

Economy, 10, 11, 27, 28, 40, 41, 77, 84, 158, 162, 193, 199, 200, 201, 208.

Education, 10, 21, 22, 23, 62, 85, 86, 131, 135, 151, 152, 153, 154, 155, 156, 157, 158, 159, 160, 161, 162, 163, 164, 165, 166, 167, 168, 169, 174, 177, 185, 217, 218, 221, 222.

Education Department, 21, 151, 168, 222.

Education System, 152, 155, 156, 157, 158, 165, 166, 169.

Election, 14, 15, 55, 62, 64, 85, 215, 220, 223, 224, 225, 226, 227, 228, 229, 230, 231, 234.

Elementary Education, 152.

Erang, 73, 74.

Ethnic Groups, 1, 14, 15, 39, 82, 85, 86, 90, 91, 174.

F

Flora and Fauna, 5.

Food, 4, 8, 9, 10, 25, 27, 60, 87, 96, 97, 108, 141, 162, 193, 201, 203, 204, 205, 209, 220.

Forest Departments, 221.

Forestry, 78, 208, 221.

Forests, 4, 5, 7, 11, 72, 77, 78, 79, 199, 202, 203, 205, 206, 207, 208, 212.

G

Gang-Ngai, 25, 29.

Gangte, 82, 93, 94, 205.

Gouralila, 147.

Government, 1, 2, 11, 12, 13, 14, 15, 20, 21, 22, 23, 27, 42, 43, 44, 46, 47, 48, 49, 50, 51, 53, 54, 55, 56, 57, 58, 61, 62, 63, 65, 90, 121, 127, 130, 136, 140, 150, 151, 152, 153, 154, 156, 157, 158, 162, 163, 164, 165, 166, 167, 168, 169, 172, 174, 179, 190, 194, 197, 198, 199, 200, 207, 209, 212, 214, 216, 217, 218, 219, 223, 224, 230, 233, 234, 237.

Governor, 19, 43, 44, 45, 47, 48, 54, 55, 56, 59, 66, 122, 214, 218, 221, 233, 234.

H

Handicraft, 117, 237.

Handloom, 11, 12, 16, 27, 117, 127, 161, 194.

❑❑❑

www.ingramcontent.com/pod-product-compliance
Lightning Source LLC
Chambersburg PA
CBHW061830260326
41914CB00005B/946